DATE DUE

MY 8 97			
JY 30 98			

Disaster and After

Social Work in the Aftermath of Disaster

of related interest

Social Work in the Wake of Disaster
David Tumelty
ISBN 1 85302 060 5

Post Traumatic Stress Disorder and Dramatherapy
Treatment and Risk Reduction
Linda Winn
ISBN 1 85302 183 0

Handbook of Theory for Practice Teachers in Social Work
Edited by Joyce Lishman
ISBN 1 85302 098 2

Introducing Network Analysis in Social Work
Philip Seed
ISBN 1 85302 106 7 pb

Disaster and After
Social Work in the Aftermath of Disaster

Tim Newburn

Jessica Kingsley Publishers
London and Philadelphia

First published in the United Kingdom in 1993 by
Jessica Kingsley Publishers Ltd
116 Pentonville Road
London N1 9JB

Copyright © 1993 Tim Newburn

British Library Cataloguing in Publication Data
Newburn, Tim
Disaster and After: Social Work in the
Aftermath of Disaster
I. Title
361.3

ISBN 1-85302-170-9

Printed and Bound in Great Britain by
Cromwell Press Ltd, Melksham, Wiltshire

Contents

Acknowledgements

A very large number of people have helped me during the course of this research. First and foremost I am grateful to all the people who so generously gave their time to talk about Hillsborough and the effect of the disaster on their lives.

Most fundamentally my thanks must go to the families, survivors, other relatives and carers who participated in this research, and who were promised anonymity. I am also grateful to the following for their help, support or encouragement: David Alexander, Anna Anderson, Paul Barnard, Mick Bond, Liz Capewell, David Crosbie, Roy Cunliffe, Sarah Darcy, Annette Dempsey, Rory Duff, Peter Dutton, Anne Eyre, Gerry Flanagan, the Football Supporters' Association, Peter Garrett, Sheila Gough, Sue Green, Terry Gilvin, Eleanor Grundy, Jane Harper, Norah Hart, Ken Head, *Hillsborough Interlink*, Martin Hinks, Pam James, Janet Lewis, Tricia Longhorn, the Reverend Kevin McGarahan, Don MacLeod, Steve Martin, David Mason, Christine Mead, Margaret Mitchell, Mike Morrisey, John Mullen, Ed Murphy, Jan Pahl, Howard Parker, Bill Pemberton, John Pilling, Eric Sainsbury, Sharon Sankey, Betsy Stanko, Rogan Taylor, Aileen Walker-Smith and Bev Wilkinson.

The research was supported by a grant from the Joseph Rowntree Foundation, and I am very grateful to them both for that and for their interest in this work. Many of the interviews that form the basis for Chapters 4 and 5 were undertaken with great skill and sensitivity by Social and Community Planning Research. My thanks to Tracey Higgins, Gill Keegan, Kit Ward and Jane Ritchie.

Through this work I met many people for whom I have the highest admiration. I feel particularly fortunate to have benefited from the sound advice, professional insight and friendship of Bernard Walker and David Whitham. During the course of this research project I was frequently away from home – though I was usually visiting my 'spiritual home' – and Huw Griffith and Alison Heaton were the kindest of hosts. To them my continuing gratitude. For two years I received much support and friendship from the Director and staff of the National Institute for Social Work, especially from the members of PADE: Lynette Domoney, Nancy Dunlop, Barbara Hearn, Nnennaya Onyekwere, Gerry Smale, and Ann Vandersypen. The Director of PADE, Gerry Smale, not only showed trust and faith in me from the beginning, but never failed to convey the impression that the work was important and interesting.

My love and my thanks to those with whom I live: Mary, Gavin and Robin, and my continuing thanks to Mary for her wise counsel. The impact of this research on me personally was huge. It brought home to me the importance of many things and the essential unimportance of many others. Most particularly, the joyful arrival of Lewis in our family in August 1991 underlined for me the enormity of the tragedy that occured on 15 April 1989. Even distant contact with a disaster increases one's sense of mortality. Sadly, given the way families and survivors were treated at offical inquiries and inquests, it is impossible to say that knowledge of what occurs in the aftermath of disaster increases one's faith in the system of justice.

Tim Newburn

Part 1

Organising the Service Response to Hillsborough

CHAPTER 1

Social Services and Disasters

Our recent history is littered with large-scale disasters and catastrophes. Indeed, there have been so many in recent years that a number of commentators have linked them together in what appears as a decade of disasters (Taylor 1989). The names of these recent tragedies – or, more accurately in most cases, the names of their locations – will, like others before them, continue to conjure up terrifying images of death and destruction. Part of the reason for the immediacy of these memories, and one of the factors which distinguishes some of these disasters from those of previous eras, has been the proximity of the mass media to the events as they unfolded. In most cases television cameras were at the scene within a very short space of time – the Bradford fire and Hillsborough disasters occurred at sporting events where outside broadcast cameras were recording – and the daily newspapers have been filled with all too graphic photographs of the dead, the injured and the suffering of witnesses and survivors.

Whilst little of a positive nature can be expected to emerge from such tragic events, one consequence of the frequency with which disasters occurred during the 1980s, and the high media profile that resulted, was an increasing realisation of the impact that they had upon those bereaved as a result of them, and those who survived them. With increasing knowledge about the impact and effects came a more structured response to helping those affected. Central to such responses – particularly the long-term responses – in recent years have been social services departments, together with a host of other caring organisations and individuals.

It is now generally accepted that the aftermath of the 1985 Bradford fire marked a watershed in welfare responses to disasters in Britain (Tumelty 1991). Although social workers have always been involved in offering comfort and support to those affected by disasters, whether large or small, it is only in the last few years that social services departments have provided an organised and 'long-term' response to major incidents. The work of social services after the Herald of Free Enterprise sinking, after Hungerford, Enniskillen, Kings Cross, Piper Alpha,

Clapham, Lockerbie, Hillsborough and others was in many ways shaped by the model adopted by Bradford Social Services.

The fire broke out underneath one of the stands at Valley Parade, Bradford City's football ground, on 11 May 1985. Within minutes of the fire being noticed the stand was all but engulfed in flames, injuring hundreds and killing fifty five (Harrison 1987a, Verity 1989). In the following days and weeks the Social Services Department organised and set in place a system of care and support for the 'victims' of the disaster (Harrison 1987a). It is the nuts and bolts of that system that have been so influential in this country in the responses to succeeding disasters. This system had a number of important characteristics, a brief consideration of which will help put the analysis of the response to the Hillsborough disaster that follows in context.

After Bradford, there was a recognition that the response needed to be *immediate*, and that any delay might have adverse consequences for the likely success of the service. Second, there was also recognition of the potential *breadth* of the impact of the disaster on the city, and the implications this had for service provision. Thus, in addition to those who were bereaved and those who were injured, it was felt that:

> ... the Bradford City fire presents unusual challenges for those dealing with its aftermath. Over 12,000 spectators were at the match. Many more Bradford residents were listening to live coverage on local radio, many knowing family and friends were at the match. Millions saw the horrifying television pictures. Amongst this huge number of people touched to varying degrees by the tragedy will be those who will face social, emotional and practical problems... they are unable to cope with. (Harrison 1987a p.3)

Support after the disaster was therefore targeted at a variety of groups: the bereaved, the injured and their families, workers involved in the disaster (emergency services, St John's Ambulance Service, staff of the Football Club), and workers providing continuing support to victims (GPs, social workers, voluntary counsellors etc).

The experience of working in the aftermath of the Bradford fire brought home the message that a considerable amount of proactive work needed to be undertaken if those affected were to overcome their basic resistance or fear of 'asking for help', and their particular reservations about the profession of social work (Jordan 1979, Stewart 1989c). Thus, Bradford Social Services made a policy decision that through its area offices it would not wait for the next of kin of those who died to come forward, but would make direct contact with them (Harrison 1987b). This approach has found widespread acceptance and has since had an enormous influence on post-disaster work. The influence of this approach on the organisation of the response to Hillsborough is detailed in Chapters 2 and 3, and the impact of the service and client views of it are analysed in Chapters 4 and 5.

It is accepted therefore that it is important to set up services that are sensitive to the difficulties people have in asking for help. Several implications stem from this. First, as has been suggested, as far as some of the 'primary' victims are concerned, it is necessary to provide a 'proactive' service in which help is *offered*. Second, the often justifiable suspicions that are held about the statutory agencies need to be recognised, and services presented accordingly. In addition, it has become increasingly clear that the problems that people experience after disaster may not surface until some considerable time has passed and that, even in cases where the problems are experienced fairly early on, reticence about asking for help and a suspicion of social services may mean that requests for help are not made until long after the disaster. Consequently, post-disaster services – channels through which help can be requested and provided – need to be kept in place long after public interest and curiosity in the disaster have abated. The Bradford fire co-ordinator, writing some 20 months after the disaster, said 'although the main thrust of the social services' response is now drawing to a close, a number of new referrals remind us that there are still people in the community who have not yet begun to come to terms with the events of 11th May' (Harrison 1987b p.8), and the Department of Health-sponsored Disasters Working Party (1991 p.13) has reinforced this message by recommending that social and psychological support services should be maintained '*for at least two years* following a disaster, albeit in a changing and reducing form' (emphasis in original).

The response to Hillsborough in this regard is an instructive one. Immediately after the disaster each of the social services departments involved in the main response – of which there were nine in all – began either to organise teams or a number of individual social workers to take on the long-term response to Hillsborough. Although there was considerable co-operation between the authorities, especially in the immediate aftermath, their views about the need for a long-term service and their commitment to keeping their teams in operation varied, with some staying in existence considerably longer than others. The explanations for this are explored in Chapter 3, the effects on the service provided are considered in Chapter 5, and the impact on the staff affected by such decisions are analysed in Chapters 6 and 7.

The planning of recent post-disaster services has been influenced by the increasing amount of contemporary academic research on disasters – undertaken mostly in Australia and the United States – which consistently pointed to groups further away from the epicentre of the disaster than the bereaved and the injured (Dudasik 1980, Taylor and Frazer,

1981), who were themselves at considerable risk from the reverberations of the tragedy (*inter alia* McFarlane and Raphael 1984, Taylor and Frazer 1982). One of the significant consequences of taking such research on board is that organising support and, where necessary, counselling for the staff who themselves are providing care for the 'primary victims' of the disaster (Taylor and Frazer 1987) is explicitly recognised as a vital component of the response. For social services, this means placing 'staff care' high on the agenda and giving it a profile that it perhaps usually lacks in the day-to-day priorities of such organisations (King 1991). In Bradford, the extremely distressing nature of the work that was often undertaken by social workers led their employers to set up support groups for some staff (Harrison 1987a) and to attempt to provide specialist support and training where possible.

Although Bradford Social Services felt they had not been entirely successful in their staff care initiatives (Harrison 1987a), the very fact that they explicitly recognised such 'need' made staff care issues impossible to ignore in subsequent disaster work. Thus, for example, one ex-Bradford social worker, writing of the response to the Piper Alpha disaster, suggested that the training of their 'outreach team' was 'unique, primarily because it happened, but also because it included a serious attempt, encouraged and supported by senior staff, to build into the programme vital elements of personal support for team members' (Stewart 1989a p.21). Although they were sometimes rather hastily put together, similar initiatives were organised after Hungerford (Fawcett 1987), Kings Cross (Walker-Smith 1990), the Herald disaster (Lunn 1988, Thomason and Hodgkinson 1987), Lockerbie (Dumfries and Galloway 1989), and the Kegworth/M1 aircrash (Whitham and Newburn 1991).

Indeed, staff care, supervision and support has been continually confirmed to be a vital part of the process of disaster planning and response. The report of the British Psychological Society on 'psychological aspects of disaster', for example, recommended that 'support for those offering assistance is an essential prerequisite for offering a service. Support structures including supervision must be in place' (British Psychological Society 1990 p.7), and the influential, government-funded Disasters Working Party report recommended that 'Directors of Social Services or Social Work offer to organise the provision of skilled psychological debriefing for all disaster workers, including those in the emergency services, after their work in all major disasters' (Disasters Working Party 1991 p.13).

Perhaps the most significant experiment in post-disaster staff care within social services in this country in recent years has been that undertaken in relation to Hillsborough (Newburn 1992). The initiative, known as 'Staffline' and set up under the auspices of the British Association of Social Workers (BASW), was originally conceived as a helpline for support staff. An evaluation of the work of Staffline, together with a more general assessment of staff care 'needs' and issues is contained in Chapters 6 and 7.

The Staffline initiative changed in a variety of ways during the two years in which it was in existence. Most important, perhaps, it moved from its original form as a 'helpline' to a more *proactive, outreach* service. In doing so, it built on a crucial lesson that had been learnt from the experience of providing support for the 'victims' of previous disasters. During the last decade it has become accepted (in relation to disasters) that if services are to reach those who are most likely to need them, then much of the *responsibility* for making contact will have to be taken by the caring agencies. This is based on the very simple observation that we live in a society in which it is unusual for people voluntarily to look for help with emotional or psychological problems (Raphael 1983). As Hodgkinson and Stewart (1991) suggest:

> The reasons for this are largely cultural – people are brought up to believe that only very vulnerable individuals have 'breakdowns' and that 'being in need' is a sign of failure. This is true of all segments of society and not just the affluent. The working-class survivors of the Hillsborough Disaster were just as cautious of helping professionals as Dorset business commuters following the Clapham rail crash. (p.104)

There are three other general areas of the work undertaken in Bradford that have become standard elements of disaster response work in this country. The first and most straightforward is the production of a 'disaster leaflet'. The leaflet, entitled 'Coping with a Major Personal Crisis', was designed in Australia after the Ash Wednesday bush fires, and was merely altered so that the front cover would say 'to help people affected by the Bradford City Fire Disaster'. So successful has the pamphlet been judged to be that it has been used (with the front page changed) after almost every disaster since (*inter alia* Tumelty 1990, Hodgkinson and Stewart 1991), including Hillsborough (Whitham and Newburn 1991).

Equally central to all disaster responses has been the 'helpline'. In Bradford, a special line was set up almost immediately after the disaster. Staffed by social workers, it acted both as a focal point for those seeking help and those offering help (Harrison 1987b), and was kept in operation for over a year. Its primary functions, in common with all helplines, are listening, providing information, advice and, where appropriate and practical, counselling (Haynes 1991). The assumption is that the helpline may well be the first point of contact between those affected by a disaster and the helping agencies, and the offer of an anonymous listening ear may be less threatening and more acceptable than more formalised offers of help. The Hillsborough Helpline was set up within one day of the disaster, and was kept in operation 24 hours a day for over two years. Little is known about the operation of helplines in the aftermath of disasters (Lindy and Green 1981) and therefore Hillsborough provides a particularly good opportunity to study not only the work of such a service, but also – given the eventual location of the helpline – the interface between the voluntary and statutory sectors in the aftermath of disaster. The history of the Hillsborough Helpline is discussed in Chapters 2 and 3, user's views of it are covered in Chapter 4, and the experience of those who staffed it in Chapter 6.

Finally, and again since Bradford, there is what has also become a ubiquitous facet of post-disaster work: the newsletter. *City Link*, although set up and funded by Social Services, was independent of them and was edited by bereaved and survivors from the fire. It served a variety of purposes from sharing information, thoughts and feelings, to acting as a forum in which issues which were of continuing importance to those affected by the disaster could be pursued. From the social workers point of view it was 'useful as a means of working with survivors in a non-obtrusive way, while at the same time keeping the door to help open should they feel like taking it up at any future date' (Hodgkinson and Stewart 1991). *City Link* has been followed by *Herald Link*, *Piperline* and for a period of two-and-a-half years, *Hillsborough Interlink*.

What follows, then, are the results of the only large-scale research project that has specifically focused on the work of social services and other carers in the aftermath of disaster. Concentrating on the response to the Hillsborough Stadium disaster, its central aims are threefold: to describe the ways in which services were provided for those affected by the disaster; to evaluate from the user's perspective the effectiveness of the services provided; and to consider the experience of providing a service in the aftermath of disaster, focusing on the impact on workers and the implications for training and staff care that arise as a result.

Part 1 of the book looks at the organisational context of the 'welfare' response to Hillsborough. As was suggested above, it is only since Bradford that thought has been given in this country to the question of how support work in the aftermath of disaster might be organised. With the experience gained after the Bradford fire and then in the aftermaths of the many other large-scale tragedies that occurred in the late 1980s, there was an increasing body of knowledge available to social services departments. By 1989, when Hillsborough occurred, much of this information was being openly discussed and debated and, as I have argued, some of the most crucial lessons appeared to be taken on board by those tasked with organising their departments' responses to Hillsborough.

Chapter 2, therefore, looks at the nature of the disaster, and the way in which the 'consortium' of local authorities responded to it. In particular it looks at the dynamics of inter-agency co-operation, the role of social services directors and of local politicians – all crucial to the success or otherwise of a disaster response. Chapter 3 considers the nuts and bolts of the response; the setting up and work of the helpline (including its transfer to the voluntary sector), the setting up of specialist social work teams across the North-West and in Sheffield and Nottingham, the work of voluntary groups the Church and others.

Part 2 considers the service response to the disaster from the user's perspective. It begins, in Chapter 4, by providing an account of the nature of the problems experienced by individuals as a result of Hillsborough. Many suffered severe psychological trauma, others a variety of emotional difficulties, as well as a range of financial and practical problems. Chapter 5 looks at the sources and nature of the help, if any, that people received. It looks at who and where people turn for help after tragedies such as Hillsborough and considers their evaluation of the 'formal' services that were provided. Crucially, it asks if social workers can help in such circumstances, and whether or not they do help?

Finally, Part 3 examines the experience of 'doing disaster work'. A quick scan of the disasters literature shows that there is a growing recognition of the potential effects of such events on those organisations which respond early on to the emergency (Raphael *et al.* 1984, Taylor and Frazer 1982). What we know less about is the effect of disaster on those 'entry' (Dudasik 1980) or 'third-level' (Taylor and Frazer 1981) victims of disaster whose involvement is often longer-term: social workers and other carers. Chapter 6 looks at the reality of providing support both in the short-term and the longer-term after disaster. It considers the sources of the stresses and strains inherent in the work, and the impact of the work on the lives of the social workers and other carers involved. Chapter 7 looks at the issue of staff care. Much was made early on after Hillsborough of the need to care for the staff who were undertaking the counselling and support work. This chapter looks at the needs of the Hillsborough workers, and evaluates the major staff care initiative that was set up in the aftermath of the disaster.

The conclusions attempt to address two basic tasks. First, what lessons can be drawn from the Hillsborough experience for future work in response to disasters? What are the implications for the management and organisation of the work, for the delivery of the services that are set up, and for the care of the staff who are tasked with delivering them? Second, what lessons can we learn from the Hillsborough experience for social work more generally? In this regard the conclusions focus on the public presentation and perception of social work, the management of workers – and, in particular, 'specialists' – lessons for social work education and training, as well as considering the issues of stress, burnout and staff care in mainstream social work.

CHAPTER 2

Managing the Response to a Disaster

> On 15 April 1989 a football match to decide a semi-final round of the FA Cup competition was to be played between the Liverpool and Nottingham Clubs. The neutral venue chosen was Hillsborough Football Stadium, Sheffield Wednesday's ground. Only six minutes into the game, play was stopped when it was realised that spectators on the terraces behind the Liverpool goal had been severely crushed. In the result, 95 died and over 400 received hospital treatment. (Home Office 1989 p.1)

These stark words are the Rt Hon Lord Justice Taylor's description of the tragedy that unfolded on that Saturday afternoon in South Yorkshire. Not surprisingly this tells only part of the story. In addition to those who died and were injured – many more, incidentally, than were estimated using hospital records – many thousands suffered considerable emotional trauma as a result of the disaster.[1] Part of the reason for such a widespread impact lies in the presence of the mass media, especially television, at the event. The unfolding disaster at Hillsborough, like that at Valley Parade four years earlier, became a live outside broadcast on BBC television. Relatives and friends of the thousands of Liverpool supporters who had travelled to Sheffield watched as the tragedy unfolded and the reality of what was happening slowly became clear. Many, of course, never saw their loved ones alive again. The power of those scenes behind the goal at the Leppings Lane end of the ground, and the images of Liverpool supporters tearing down advertising hoardings in a desperate attempt to save the lives of fellow fans whilst many in authority stood apparently paralysed by what they witnessed, has surely left few people in this country untouched by the Hillsborough disaster.

Hillsborough: A brief history

The build-up to the disaster

Approximately a month before they were due to be played, the Football Association began to make arrangements for the semi-finals of its cup competition. Their desire was that one of the ties should be played in the Midlands at Aston Villa's football ground, the other at Hillsborough in Sheffield. This 'Wembley of the North'[2] (Taylor 1989) was frequently used as one of the FA Cup semi-final venues and, indeed, in 1988 it had been host to the self-same teams that were to contest the 1989 match: Liverpool and Nottingham Forest.

Whilst the decision to use the same ground was largely uncontentious, the decision to use the same ticketing arrangements was widely criticised. The major problems lay in the numbers of tickets that were allocated to each club and to which sections of the ground they allowed entry. Following what had become standard practice for organising and controlling football supporters, ticket allocation was decided 'so as to achieve efficient segregation of Liverpool and Nottingham Forest fans' (Home Office 1989 p.5). Consequently, tickets for the north and west parts of the ground were allotted to Liverpool, and tickets for the south and east to Nottingham Forest. One result of this was that Liverpool, despite having a far higher average home League attendance were allocated only approximately 24,000 tickets compared with nearly 30,000 for Nottingham Forest. Liverpool Football Club immediately sought to have this decision overturned, but the police refused. Although Lord Justice Taylor in his Interim Report commented in relation to both the choice of ground and the allocation of tickets that 'no doubt in future the FA will be more sensitive and responsive to reasonable representations' (Home Office 1989 p.48, see also Home Office 1990) he rejected the suggestion that either were 'causative of the disaster'. In view of what happened on 15 April 1989 it is perhaps not surprising that there are few Liverpool supporters who would agree with that part of his judgment.

The descriptions and television pictures of the early build up to the match are not unusual and were largely typical of what one would expect prior to a Cup semi-final. The scene was one of a gradually increasing number of happy and expectant fans sometimes behaving exuberantly, but rarely in a way that was the cause of much offence. As is typical, however, there were relatively few supporters who made their way into the ground early. As kick-off approached the numbers outside the ground had increased enormously, whereupon the architecture and design of the ground took on a new significance.

The Liverpool supporters seeking access to the terracing and stand behind the goal at the west end of the ground, and those seeking access to the north stand were *all* required to enter the ground via the Leppings Lane turnstiles. Not only is Leppings Lane a route which is narrow and easily congested, but there were a mere 23 turnstiles available to admit the 24,256 spectators who were expected. By contrast, there were almost three times as many turnstiles to accommodate the Nottingham Forest supporters at the other end of the ground (60 turnstiles to admit 29,800 supporters). By 2.30/2.40pm (the kick-off was planned for 3.00pm) Taylor reports that there were over 5000 Liverpool supporters outside trying to gain entry (Home Office 1989 p.33).

Eventually, when it became clear to the police outside the ground that the situation was perilous, a request was made to open one of the main exit gates to allow entry into the ground. Fans were thereby enabled to enter in large numbers in a short space of time:

> In the five minutes it (exit gate C) was open about 2000 fans passed through it steadily at a fast walk. Some may have had tickets for the stands. No doubt some had no tickets at all. The majority had tickets for the terraces. Of these, some found their way either right to pens 1 and 2 or left through the dividing wall to 6 and 7. But a large proportion headed straight for the tunnel in front of them. (Home Office 1989 p.12)

They went via the tunnel down an incline into pens 3 and 4 which were by this stage already overfull. Taylor reports what happened there in the following way:

> At 3.04pm, Beardsley for Liverpool struck the crossbar at the Kop end. There was a roar from the Liverpool fans and at the same time a powerful surge forwards in pen 3. The several surges which occurred after the influx from gate C carried the pressure down the pens towards the pitch. The force became such as to twist and break two spans of a crush barrier towards the front of pen 3... When the barrier broke those whom it had supported were projected towards the perimeter fence. Many fell and the involuntary rush of those behind pressed them down. The crushing force was transmitted and dispersed so that all along the front of pen 3 fans were pressed hard up against the low wall and the wire mesh of the fence above it. (Home Office 1989 p.13)

Ninety-five people died, most of them in pen 3, although a few of the fatalities occurred in pen 4. The bulk of the deaths occurred towards the front of the pens, with a few thought to have happened further back (Home Office 1989 p.13).

Claims and counter-claims about causation

Before moving on to some brief details of the aftermath of the tragedy, it is important to consider the etiology of this disaster and, in particular, to consider the accounts given by the police (and certain sections of the media) about the causes of the tragedy. The reason for doing so is that Hillsborough is almost alone amongst disasters (certainly in the UK in the last decade) in having had the behaviour – indeed the 'innocence' – of its victims called into question. This issue and its impact on those affected by the disaster will be considered in more detail in the following chapters, and discussion here is confined to the most serious claims and counter-claims that were made about causation.

At the core of police accounts of the course of events, both immediately afterwards and much later on, were a series of assertions about the 'misbehaviour' of Liverpool supporters. These included such factors as the perceived late arrival of the fans, together with alleged drunkenness and unruly behaviour on the part of a large number. A key part of South Yorkshire Police's position was summarised by Lord Justice Taylor as follows:

> The case made for the police was that large numbers of Liverpool supporters arrived late; a high proportion of them were drunk and unco-operative; a high proportion had no tickets; all of them were hell-bent on getting in on time. They say this was unforeseeable and explains why they lost control. (Home Office 1989 p.33)

In the immediate aftermath of the disaster these claims made by the police were given some credence by the tabloid press that was, as ever, on the look out for 'good stories'.[3] The bulk of the allegations, however, were given short shrift in the Interim Taylor Report. Taking the issues in the quote above in order, Taylor (Home Office 1989 p.34) suggested that 'the likeliest explanations for the sparse Liverpool attendance in the ground before 2.30pm were four-fold – the warm weather, drinking, disinclination to enter the ground early and prolong the standing, and a tendency of Liverpool supporters to cut it fine'. Most importantly with regard to the general allegations, the clear implication in the report was that the behaviour of the fans was neither *unexpected* nor *unreasonable*.

It is drinking, however, that has been the central plank upon which allegations of misbehaviour have been based and which has seemingly had the most lasting impact upon public perceptions of the events of 15 April 1989.[4] Lord Justice Taylor, on the other hand, reported that he was:

> … satisfied on the evidence, however, that the great majority were not drunk nor even the worse for drink… In my view some (police) officers, seeking to rationalise their loss of control, overestimated the drunken element in the crowd. (Home Office 1989 p.34)

The next two related suggestions considered by Taylor concerned the suggestion that many of the fans who were trying to get in had arrived without tickets. The first implication drawn by the police was that they could not possibly have anticipated what happened outside the ground in the half hour or so before kick-off – and therefore made contingency arrangements – because of the large number of ticketless fans. More sinisterly, it was argued that the 'late' arrival of large numbers of fans was an organised attempt by those without tickets 'to buck the system' and force the police to admit them to the ground. Once again, however, Taylor was unequivocal:

> ... the figures do suggest that there was not a very significant body of ticketless fans in the crowd which built up. (Home Office 1989 p.35)

and

> I am satisfied that the large concentration at Leppings Lane from 2.30pm to 2.50pm did not arrive as a result of any concerted plan. (Home Office 1989 p.36)

Finally, in relation to specific allegations of misbehaviour, there was the claim from the officer in charge of the policing of the semi-final, Chief Superintendent Duckenfield, that the large inrush of fans to the ground just before kick-off had been due to one of the exit gates being forced open by the crowd, as opposed to being opened on his orders. As Lord Justice Taylor commented:

> This was not only untruthful. It set off a widely reported allegation against the supporters which caused grave offence and distress. It revived against football fans, and especially those from Liverpool, accusations of hooliganism which caused reaction not only nationwide but from Europe too[5]... The likeliest explanation of Mr Duckenfield's conduct is that he simply could not face the enormity of the decision to open the gates and all that flowed therefrom. (Home Office 1989 p.50)

The issue of football hooliganism permeated not only police accounts of the causes of the disaster, but was identified by Taylor as being their primary preoccupation in making arrangements for the policing of the semi-final. The central concern here is the extent to which considerations of public safety played a part in the planning of the policing operation and to what extent concerns about public order were allowed to predominate. Academic commentators have only just begun to open up what may well become an uncomfortable debate about the long-standing 'problem' of masculinity and violence in relation to the events that occurred at Hillsborough (Coleman *et al.* 1990, Taylor 1991).

In addition to the choice of ends, and therefore the numbers of tickets allocated to each club, the spectre of football hooliganism would appear to have played an important part in a number of other crucial policing decisions (or, perhaps more accurately in some cases, police indecision). First, and as a general point, there was the tone set by the police Operational Order which together with their tactics on the day:

> failed to provide for controlling a concentrated arrival of large numbers should they occur in a short period. That it might so occur was foreseeable and it did. (Home Office 1989 p.47)

and that furthermore in the Operational Order:

> the emphasis was upon prevention of disorder and in particular prevention of access to the field of play. There was no express requirement that officers on the perimeter track or in the west stand should keep watch for any possible overcrowding on the terraces. Indeed, the view was expressed in evidence that packing fans close together on the terraces assisted in controlling the unruly since the less room they had the less scope there was for misbehaviour. (Home Office 1989 p.32)

Perhaps the most crucial decision of the afternoon was the opening of gate C and the failure to ensure that the tunnel directly in front of the gate that led to pens 3 and 4 was shut off, which would have forced spectators to make their way to the far from crowded wing pens. The entry of the fans through this gate was not properly monitored whereas when another gate (gate A) was briefly opened a little later:

> Mr Duckenfield did order serials to go to that part of the concourse to monitor the influx towards the north stand. He did this because he feared that if fans went to the north stand without tickets, they would not get seats and, there being no perimeter fences at the north side, they might invade the pitch. This illustrates again the preoccupation with avoiding pitch invasion as against safety and the risks of overcrowding. (Home Office 1989 p.40)

Preoccupation with disorderliness and pitch invasion also underpinned what appeared to many to be the extremely slow recognition by the police that something had gone terribly wrong in the two pens behind the Leppings Lane goal. Some of the fans who managed to lever themselves over the fencing and on to the perimeter track and the pitch to escape the crushing were forced back towards the pens. One of the senior officers present, Superintendent Greenwood, climbed on the wall below the fence penning in the fans and attempted to signal to those at the back that they should make space for those at the front. Both this and the related decisions to keep the gates to the pitch closed were undoubtedly prompted by a desire to ensure that no fans should be allowed to encroach upon the pitch. The officers in the control room in the ground appear to have been completely preoccupied with the possibility of a pitch invasion, and even at 3.06pm the Chief Superintendent in control was still thinking in terms of a public order problem (Home Office 1989 p.16).

The picture of the policing of this major sporting event that is presented in the Interim Report by Lord Justice Taylor is, then, a sorry one. The overall impression presented is of a police force that failed to plan properly for a number of important contingencies; that was so preoccupied with the maintenance of public order that it failed to ensure public safety; that was dangerously slow to realise not only the potential for but the reality of catastrophe; and that was represented by senior officers who compounded all this by insensitivity and dissimulation in the aftermath:

> It is a matter of regret that at the hearing, and in their submissions, the South Yorkshire Police were not prepared to concede they were in any respect at fault in what occurred. Mr Duckenfield, under pressure of cross-examination, apologised for blaming the Liverpool fans for causing the deaths. But, that apart, the police argued that the fatal crush was not caused by the influx through gate C but was due to barrier 124a being defective. Such an unrealistic approach gives cause for anxiety as to whether lessons have been learnt. It would have been more seemly and encouraging for the future if responsibility had been faced. (Home Office 1989 p.50)

I have highlighted here the role of the police for two main reasons. First, there have been and continue to be so many inaccuracies talked and written about Hillsborough that it would be negligent to let this opportunity pass without reiterating the clear and unambiguous findings of the Official Inquiry conducted by Lord Justice Taylor into this matter. Second, and very importantly for this study, much of what those who were affected by the disaster have to say about their lives and their feelings since Hillsborough have been significantly affected by their perceptions of how the police behaved on that day and have behaved since. When seeking out something against which the opinions of the bereaved, the survivors and witnesses can be compared, the information contained in the Taylor Report comes closest to being an *objective* measure.

To reiterate, the purpose of the preceding discussion has not been to mount an attack upon the police, but rather to make clear the quite specific criticisms contained in the Report of the Inquiry of the senior officers who were responsible for the policing operation at the football ground. It is certainly not the intention to mask the often courageous work done by individual officers in their attempts at rescue and resuscitation, or to draw attention away from others who were criticised by Taylor. For example, although the Football Association were absolved of any responsibility in relation to the specific causes of the disaster, their decision to choose Hillsborough as one of the two semi-final venues was described as 'ill-considered' (Home Office 1989 p.48). The performance of the City Council was found to have been 'inefficient and dilatory' in regard to the Safety Certificate, and their failure to amend the certificate was felt to have been 'a serious breach of duty' (Home Office 1989 p.51). Finally, the unsatisfactory nature of the Leppings Lane end of the ground, the failure to liaise properly with the police, the 'misguided' removal of a barrier from the Leppings Lane terrace, together with breaches of the Green Guide[6] and poor signposting led Taylor to argue that Sheffield Wednesday Football Club also 'contributed to this disaster' (Home Office 1989 p.52).

The immediate aftermath in Sheffield

Those who watched the television coverage of the disaster as it unfolded will remember the scenes of large numbers of Liverpool supporters who attempted to save the lives of their fellow fans, whilst others, dazed and distressed, attempted to find those they had come with but were now separated from. For the majority of those who survived and were not seriously injured what remained was a long and often difficult journey home. Although they have barely been mentioned so far, it should not be forgotten that this was also true for the thousands of Nottingham Forest supporters that had made their way to Sheffield. Many stayed behind to look for missing friends and relatives and it was to the gymnasium at the ground, the Hammerton Road Boys Club, the Medico-Legal Centre and the Royal Hallamshire and Northern General hospitals that they went.

The immediate questions for those responsible for coping with the emergency was where to locate the bodies of those who had died, and where and how identification should take place. None of these decisions or their consequences have been unproblematic (Coleman *et al.* 1990). The gymnasium at the football ground was to be used as an emergency area in the event of a major incident, and in the aftermath of Hillsborough it was decided that it should be used as a temporary mortuary until all the bodies had been identified.[7]

In addition to the gymnasium, a local Boys Club was opened up and used as a focal point for relatives and friends making enquiries. Situated on Hammerton Road near to the closest police station to the ground, the Boys Club was quickly filled by relatives and by a large group of clergy, social workers and volunteers. The scene at the Club has been described by observers as 'chaotic'[8] and 'like bedlam'.[9] One of the major sources of confusion was the lack of clarity about where the identification of the bodies was to take place. It was not until mid-evening that a decision was made to use the gymnasium and relatives were transported back to the football ground so that the process could begin. It was few people's idea of appropriate accommodation for such a task.

The gymnasium was divided into three – the bodies were kept in one third, identification took place in the second area, and counselling and support work in the third. Relatives were brought back to Hillsborough by coach and then, often after considerable delay, brought to the gymnasium. Each body had been photographed and the photographs pinned up on a board in the gymnasium. If relatives recognised the person they were looking for among the photographs, the body was brought in on a trolley – still in a body bag – for formal identification.

Once formal identification had been made, a statement was taken by South Yorkshire Police and the body was transferred to the 'Medico-Legal Centre' in Sheffield.

During the afternoon and evening of the 15 April a call for help had been broadcast in Sheffield and large numbers of volunteers from social services, the medical profession, voluntary agencies, the clergy and so on came forward to offer help and support both at the football ground itself and at the other venues that were being used around Sheffield. A group of social workers and clergy were in attendance throughout the process of identification at the temporary mortuary, and in most cases relatives were accompanied by representatives from both groups until identification had been completed. Not all the bodies were identified at the football ground and, consequently, for some relatives the process had to occur at the Medico-Legal Centre – where the City Mortuary was located – where the post-mortems were to be undertaken.

In addition to these three major sites, further activity centred around the City's two major hospitals: the Northern General (NGH) and the Royal Hallamshire (RHH). Both hospitals were put on standby at approximately 3.10pm and the first casualties arrived at the NGH at around 3.25pm and at the RHH around 3.40pm. The casualties received at the two hospitals have been summarised as follows:[10]

Table 2.1: Summary of Hillsborough casualties taken to the Northern General and the Royal Hallamshire hospitals

	Northern General	Royal Hallamshire	Total
Casualties brought to A & E	88	71	159
Dead on arrival or died in A & E	11	1	12
Treated and discharged	31	46	77
Admitted	56	24	80
Admitted to ITUs (intensive care)	15	7	22

With relatively large numbers of people being taken to hospital it is not surprising that the two sites became a focus for many of those who were searching for missing friends and relatives. The situation was exacerbated by the lack of clear information being provided – particularly at Hammerton Road – and many people, not unreasonably, simply went from one place to another in an attempt to locate the person they were looking for. Once again, therefore, there was potentially a very important role for social services and the voluntary organisations to undertake in relation to the provision of information, food and drink and basic and comfort for those in distress. The canteen at the Northern General, for example, was set aside as a relatives' area, and a substantial number of social workers, members of the clergy and representatives from the Salvation Army and League of Friends attempted to co-ordinate the care and support work at the two hospitals.

The response to the disaster outside Sheffield

Although what happened that afternoon constituted the largest disaster at a sporting event in Britain it was, sadly, only one in what was a long line of disasters scattered through the middle and later years of the 1980s: the Bradford fire, the Manchester air crash, the Herald sinking, the Hungerford shooting, the Enniskillen bombing, the Kings Cross fire, the Piper Alpha fire, the Clapham rail crash, the Lockerbie bombing, the M1 air crash and then Hillsborough. One of the effects of this all too long list was to focus attention on the parlous state of many of our public services and on what often appeared to be the indifference of those in 'authority' – be it the government, the police, multinational corporations or others – to the issue of public safety. Such was the apparently overriding concern for public order, rather than public safety, by those responsible for policing football spectatorship, it came as little surprise to those who regularly stood on the terraces that a major tragedy had occurred not only at one of our major football grounds, but at what was intended to be one of the season's great spectacles. Thus, in addition to the shock and the sadness, there was a sense among football supporters that something like Hillsborough was almost inevitable.

One of the other consequences of this terrible catalogue of events was an increased awareness of the long-term consequences of disasters. Despite the fact that media interest in successive disasters, although intensive, was very short-lived, the enduring impact of such events received increasing attention. This was partly due to increased academic interest, especially amongst the medical profession, in this issue and the growing body of knowledge that developed as a result. After the First World War, and especially since Hiroshima (Lifton 1967) and later the Vietnam war (Keane *et al.* 1985, Fairbank and Nicholson 1987), there was a much increased emphasis on the study of the etiology and consequences of traumatic stress. One of the central lessons from such work was that the psychological consequences of traumatic incidents may well be recurrent and persistent.

Increased attention on the long-term was also partly a consequence of the campaigning work that many of those who have been affected by disaster have engaged in. The willingness or desire of such people to devote their time, often at the expense of their jobs, to campaigns to improve safety records and controls, to improve access to information, for compensation and legal redress, made public their long-standing and continuing anger, suffering and distress. Here were people who were not willing to keep quiet, were not just 'going to get on with their lives', but wanted to make sure that what had happened to them, and in many cases what was continuing to happen, remained in the public domain.

The role of the emergency services in the aftermath of disaster, including medical services, has long been established, and it is only recently that social services have entered the frame. With growing knowledge of the impact of disaster came an increasing realisation on the part of 'caring agencies' that they had a role to play in the process of recovery (Cohen 1991). This had much to do with the developing awareness of the potential scale of the effects of disaster, and the fact that it was whole communities that were threatened. As the social services report on the aftermath of the Bradford Fire stated: 'apart from the bereaved and the injured there were many other people vulnerable as a result of the disaster, for there was *not a local family untouched* by what happened' (Harrison 1987a p.3 emphasis added).

As was suggested above, when the disaster occurred at the Hillsborough stadium therefore, social services and related organisations followed the examples of previous tragedies and set about the task of setting up a service for those likely to be affected. The majority of those who died and those who were injured came from Merseyside and it was, consequently, the social services departments in that region who carried the greatest social work burden as a result of the disaster. However, both the Family and Community Services Department in Sheffield and the Social Services Department in Nottinghamshire also became quite heavily involved in the 'care' response, and a number of individual social workers and other carers and counsellors from around the country took on work as a result of Hillsborough.

Aside from the televised pictures of the disaster itself, perhaps the most powerful images of Hillsborough were of the public grieving at Anfield (Liverpool FC's ground) and at Liverpool's two cathedrals in the weeks following. From the evening of the 15 April the Shankly Gates at the entrance to Anfield, and thereafter the Kop end of the ground itself, became a shrine at which fans, friends, relatives and anyone touched by the disaster came to pay their respects to those who had died in Sheffield. The ground was open for a week during which time it is estimated that upwards of a million people passed through. Huge numbers of floral tributes, scarves and other personal mementos were left, the pitch being covered almost to the half-way line by the end of the period. This most moving display of ritualised mourning – referred to elsewhere as a 'pilgrimage' (Davie 1992) – illustrated the extent to which Hillsborough was a disaster which reached nationwide, but which was also rooted in the traditions and history of one of our most distinctive cities. For, as Tony Walter (1991 p.621) suggested:

> With Hillsborough... it was as though the very soul of the city had been attacked. And indeed it had, for football is Liverpool's soul. This was what brought the entire city, including all those who do not follow football, into mourning: the city of Liverpool, in the form of its totem, had died.

The formal rituals followed close on the heels of the informal with the City Council declaring a week of mourning, the Great George Bell at the Anglican Cathedral being rung 94 times[11] and a Requiem Mass held at the Metropolitan Cathedral on Sunday 16th where the 4000 or so inside were at least matched by the numbers outside. Solidarity, so rarely evident in such Thatcherite times, was visible for all to see in Merseyside (not just Liverpool) in the week(s) following Hillsborough. Such an 'explicit, conscious and collective acknowledgement of death' (Davie 1992 p.27) was, to say the least, unusual in modern British culture. It was against this background that social services and other organisations began to organise the 'care' response to the disaster.

The Director of Social Services in Liverpool at the time of Hillsborough first became aware of what was happening in Sheffield at about 3.20pm that afternoon. He was telephoned by a social worker from his Department inquiring about what social services were going to do in response. After several hours on the telephone making initial plans, he and the then Leader of Liverpool City Council set off to Sheffield to see for themselves what was happening. A short time later a small team of social workers from Liverpool also left for Sheffield.

Arriving about midnight, the Director's view at the time was that there was probably little that they could do, but that anything that they could offer would be of benefit. They visited the temporary mortuary at the gymnasium and the Hammerton Road Boys Club and made contact with their colleagues in Sheffield and with the police before returning to Liverpool in the early hours of the morning. On the journey back the Council Leader and Social Services Director discussed how best to respond to what they had seen unfolding in Sheffield. They were agreed that whatever was set up couldn't be run as a City Council service in the normal sense – going through all the normal channels for setting up an initiative – but rather would have to be put in place almost immediately. That so much was eventually put in train without undue delay is in no small part due to the 'charismatic leadership'[12] from Liverpool's Director of Social Services in the first week after Hillsborough and the enormous support he received from his Council Leader.

Inter-agency co-operation.

The information that was available to them at that time – early on the Sunday morning – suggested that in terms of casualties, Liverpool was no more significant than the other local authorities in the area. Consequently, a regional response was going to be required. Arrangements were made for a mid-Sunday morning meeting of the five Mersey authorities: Liverpool, Sefton, Knowsley, Wirral and St Helens. This was the beginning of what became known as the Inter-Agency Group (IAG), consisting of representatives of those authorities, joined early in the week by Lancashire and Cheshire and later by Sheffield and Nottinghamshire, Merseyside Probation Service, Mersey Regional Health Authority, and the Emergency Planning Unit of the Merseyside Fire and Civil Defence Authority.

The first task was to set up a national 24-hour helpline 'to enable those affected by the tragedy to make contact with trained and experienced counsellors able to listen and help'.[13] The Group able to get a helpline in operation in the Liverpool Social Services headquarters by the Sunday afternoon – within 24 hours of the disaster. One director described the process in the following terms:

> The Information Technology people were there. We had the plugs pulled on a few lines, redirected them, cleared an office, photocopied some referral forms, issued a press release and off!

As was suggested above, the group decided fairly early on that their aim should be to co-ordinate a region-wide response to the disaster. What they wanted to avoid were the dangers of authorities working autonomously and setting up overlapping services which would merely replicate what others were doing. As an example, although a helpline was set up at the headquarters of Liverpool Social Services, and this was designed to be the central contact point for anyone who either wished information about Hillsborough, wanted help or wanted to offer help, there were for a short period of time a number of other helplines in operation, and this resulted in some quite unnecessary confusion. It was the avoidance of such difficulties that was, perhaps, the primary purpose of an inter-agency committee.

The authority representatives then returned to their departments to make local arrangements for responding to the needs of those affected in their region. Under the federal umbrella of the IAG, authorities set in motion initiatives in their own regions. By and large this involved the setting up in each area of a team of social workers under the management of a team leader or co-ordinator, with the sole or major task of responding to the needs of the victims of the disaster. These initiatives are described in greater detail in the following chapter. In Liverpool, for example, the search began for a suitable site for a drop-in centre, and negotiations were opened with Merseyside Youth Association with a view to using a sports centre located near Anfield. In addition, a drop-in facility was briefly operated on the Wirral at Tranmere Rovers' football ground, and Lancashire Social Services also attempted open evenings at the library at Skelmersdale, though the latter were reportedly largely unsuccessful.

Support for staff

Again based on the experience of others, it was recognised early on that the workers who joined any of the specialist teams that were being set up – or, indeed, became involved in other capacities – would themselves be put in a position of considerable stress and might require access to sources of help and support beyond that offered by normal supervision. Initially, the British Association of Social Workers (BASW) offered to act as a co-ordinating body for all agencies offering staff counselling – of which there were several. From the 26 April, an office in Liverpool run by BASW was operating as the centre of this operation and a staff helpline (Staffline) had been set up. A co-ordinator was appointed in June, and she worked on a part-time basis as a staff counsellor for Hillsborough workers in the two years the initiative was in operation.

Training

It was the view of the IAG that training needed to be provided for staff who would be likely to come into closest contact with those affected by the tragedy. A series of presentations for front-line social workers, other social service staff, health authority staff, teaching staff and voluntary sector organisations were organised fairly quickly. The training was provided by Michael Stewart and his associates from a private organisation called the 'Centre for Crisis Psychology'. Stewart had been a social worker in Bradford at the time of the fire at the football ground in 1985. As a result of his experiences there, he set up the consultancy to provide advice, support and training in the aftermath of traumatic events. He did an initial briefing for all those who turned up at Liverpool Social Services Department headquarters on the Monday, and then further training for middle managers, senior members, elected members and front-line workers in the following few weeks.

Information

In addition to the setting up of the helpline, and the opening of drop-in centres, the other 'standard' course of action that was followed on Merseyside which had been learnt from previous disasters was the production and distribution of a 'disaster' leaflet. Entitled 'Coping after Hillsborough' it was based on the leaflets used in previous British disasters which themselves were based on a crisis leaflet originally produced for use in Australia (Hodgkinson and Stewart 1991). The North West Association of Social Service Authorities (NWASSA) offered to print the leaflet free of charge and the first run of 35,000 copies were ready by 21 April. A version for younger people was also produced entitled 'Were you at the match'?. The IAG was also the major conduit through which information about the disaster could flow, and one of the first tasks it was able to undertake was to notify social services departments around the country about people in their area who might require support or other help. The passing on of such information was fairly straightforward to achieve in cases where the next of kin was identified as living in that area, but the passing on of information about more distantly related members of the bereaved families was extremely difficult, and the identification of survivors all but impossible. The issue of support for those living outside Merseyside is returned to in Chapters 4 and 5.

The Trust Fund

With donations pouring in soon after the event, a Trust Fund to deal with the money was soon set up. Four independent trustees were appointed by 19 April. By 21 April, £660,000 had been received and a further £500,000 had been promised by the government, and £25,000 each from the cities of Liverpool, Sheffield and Nottingham. In the weeks after Hillsborough the Trust Fund became the channel for the enormous public sympathy around the country for those affected by the disaster. Immediate payments to relieve hardship were made by social services early on after the disaster to the bereaved and some survivors and the trustees of the fund agreed to take responsibility for these and to continue to meet immediate payments. In particular, they agreed to pay, where requested, all funeral expenses. A commitment to pay for such expenses had also been made publicly during the first weekend by the Leader of Liverpool City Council.

The voluntary sector

Parallel to the co-ordinating body established for the statutory agencies, and in close co-operation with them, was the establishment of a voluntary sector co-ordinating committee (VSCC). Its development also parallelled that of the IAG in many ways. The Chief Executive of Liverpool Council of Voluntary Service (LCVS) was one of the people that the Director of Liverpool Social Services had telephoned during the Saturday afternoon, with a view to mobilising the voluntary sector. On the Monday afternoon approximately 120 representatives from different organisations met with the Leader of the City Council and agreed to set up a committee to co-ordinate their work. It was chaired by the Chief

Executive of LCVS who liaised with the IAG via the Director of Sefton Social Services.

The immediate tasks for the VSCC were to mobilise local counselling resources and to link them into the work being organised by the IAG, to mobilise the social work resources of the voluntary social welfare agencies, to organise systems of practical support (transport for relatives visiting Sheffield, advice about benefits, funeral arrangements and legal information and advice), as well as trying to locate sources of money to pay for all this work.

In many respects Liverpool was well placed to respond in such a way. It has what is probably the oldest, strongest and richest voluntary sector in the UK as well as the oldest, strongest and richest CVS in the UK. Furthermore, the relationship between the two was very positive and very strong – as illustrated by the role of the CVS's Chief Executive in the aftermath. Finally, the voluntary sector in Liverpool has a very positive record of co-operative working with the local authority, and there were well established lines of communication between the two which were quickly utilised during that first weekend. Derek Nuttall, the then Director of CRUSE-Bereavement Care, visited Merseyside over that weekend and gave some advice about potential pitfalls for voluntary organisations, especially with regard to issues of ownership and rivalry. The Chief Executive was very clear in his mind – and conveyed this to the VSCC – that the role to be played by voluntary organisations was a subsidiary one to Social Services. It had been established that the Chair of the IAG would take the lead in organisational matters and that the VSCC would respond to any requests that the IAG might make. Thus, the chief organisational role was to mobilise resources as and when they were needed. Transport has already been mentioned as one of the major activities and counselling, support and advice work in the early weeks was, perhaps, the other. The Churches were centrally involved in much of this work, as were Victim Support who, quite coincidentally, had just completed the training of their counsellors for the 'families of murder victims' project (Brown *et al.* 1990).

The key long-term role that the voluntary sector played however, was in relation to the helpline. Although in the very early days after the disaster, staffing the helpline was largely unproblematic – though organising the shifts of workers was a major task – as time passed it became progressively more difficult to keep the rotas going. Social workers were starting to show signs of fatigue as a result of the demands of the helpline alongside their normal duties and, where colleagues were covering for them, there were reports of tensions arising as a result of the redistribution of workloads.

Any local authority (or group of authorities), however well resourced it is, will find very quickly that it simply cannot take on complete responsibility for the care response to a disaster. Consequently, the IAG began to look at alternative means of staffing and running the service, and it was to the voluntary sector that they turned. A number of possible solutions were floated including trying to keep the rota system going but having it staffed mainly by the voluntary sector or, alternatively, trying to place the service with one voluntary agency. In the event it was the latter model that was adopted.

Regional Assistance Unit

Within the first week a working party was set up to consider the possibility of establishing a 'regional support unit' in Liverpool which would form the focus for the inter-agency partnership that the response to Hillsborough was intended to be. The Working Party, was drawn from the statutory and voluntary agencies in the region and its precise aim was 'to consider the feasibility, including costings, of establishing a regional unit in order to marshal and organise the allocation of a variety of resources so that help can be made available in the right place at the right time to the people affected by the Hillsborough disaster'.[14] The Working Party recommended the establishment of a co-ordinating body for a minimum of two years, which would ensure that resources were used effectively, that staff were trained and supported, that effective channels of communication and partnerships between authorities were established and that services were monitored and evaluated. Under this plan the helpline would have been sited at the regional unit, as would the disaster database that had been set up with the help of Kent Social Services using the 'Herald Information System'. Finally, it was hoped that the BASW staff care service that was being set up at this time (and which became Staffline), as well as a training officer would also be located in the Regional Assistance Unit as it was to have been known. Costs were estimated at around £350,000 *per annum* for two years.

The report was discussed by elected members on 29 April and support was given to the idea of a regional unit. There were already signs, however, that the hoped-for mutual support and co-operation between authorities was not going to be sustained by all the politicians. No agreement for funding was forthcoming from this meeting, and the IAG took forward plans to seek financial backing for the unit from the government and from the EEC. As time passed, however, the cracks in the unified approach were beginning to show, with the politicians in some authorities beginning to appear reluctant to continue to fund their local initiatives, let alone provide monies for a regional unit based in Liverpool. However, a revised proposal was put to politicians in September, with projected costs reduced to about £200,000 *per annum*. An in-principle commitment was given by leading members, although several authorities still seemed reluctant to commit resources to the project. There followed considerable delay before any posts in the unit were advertised. When they finally appeared in March 1990 – almost a year after the disaster – they produced a very poor response.

In April, a week before the first anniversary, Wirral Social Services Committee withdrew its promised contribution to the regional unit. The IAG asked for advice from the team leaders of the Hillsborough support teams that had been set up around the region, and their view was that there was no longer any need for a unit manager and that the money would be better spent on outreach workers who would attempt to meet the needs of people not living on Merseyside. Without the support of all the Local Authorities involved, lacking the support of the specialist teams already in existence, and with a paucity of suitable job applicants, the plan for a regional assistance unit had run its course.

The regional assistance unit was important not only for the promise that it held, but for what it symbolised. Although no doubt there were a variety of motivations for wanting such a resource, there can be little doubt that it was, in part, prompted by a genuine desire to promote inter-agency, pan-Merseyside co-operation. Trying to persuade such a varied group of authorities to work together would have put most people off from the beginning, especially when set against the backdrop of the convoluted politics of local government in the region. That they got as far as setting up and sustaining the Inter-Agency Group (it lasted for over two years) is a major achievement in itself. Sadly, as will become clear in the following chapter, the IAG was unable to achieve any sort of directive or real organisational role in relation to the initiatives that were established in each of the authorities. The teams that were set up were, for example, staffed in different ways and were funded for differing lengths of time, for, although the senior social services representatives met regularly to discuss strategy and future development, many of their political masters continued to act entirely independently and without reference to what was happening elsewhere in the region.

Conclusion

- Hillsborough, as is inevitably the case with disasters, came without warning. Social services departments were thrown into crisis by having to respond to something that they had few plans, prior arrangements or agreed methods for dealing with. It is vital, given this and the copious other examples from the 1980s, that social services put into place some plan of action for local disaster response.

- After a disaster such as Hillsborough, regional inter-agency co-operation is vital. It is, however, difficult to organise and even more difficult to maintain. Despite the difficulties, this must continue to be the aim of any senior managers involved in disaster repsonse work.

- Any local authority (or group of authorities), however well resourced it is, will find very quickly that it simply cannot take on complete responsibility for the care response to a disaster. Close co-operative links need to be established with the voluntary sector, with a view to involving voluntary groups in the response as quickly and thoroughly as possible. As one example, albeit the major long-term one, the Hillsborough Helpline was run very effectively for a period of 18 months by the voluntary sector in Liverpool. It would have been enormously burdensome for social services to have attempted to maintain the organisation and staffing of the helpline.

Notes

1. See Coleman *et al.* (1990), and the many and varied personal recollections and testimonies contained in *Hillsborough Interlink* nos.1–9.

2. No doubt this description was intended as a compliment, a tribute to the size and importance of the ground. For those football supporters who have spent much time at Wembley, however, such a description would not necessarily be interpreted entirely positively and therefore, after Hillsborough, might be viewed as being even more fitting.

3. This is not the place for a full description and discussion of the reporting of Hillsborough. A lot of material, however, can be found in Coleman *et al.* (1990), Chapter 4.

4. On the evening prior to writing this section of the book (almost three years after Hillsborough) I attended a public lecture where one of the subjects discussed was disaster. At the end of the talk I asked the speaker a question and illustrated the point I was trying to make with an example from Hillsborough. When the meeting broke up I was approached by a member of the audience (a criminal justice professional) who asked me 'when someone was going to let the public know that it was the drunken fans who were at fault'? This was by no means a one-off experience for me and illustrates, despite all the evidence to the contrary, the continuing currency of the 'drunken hooligans' thesis.

5. The President of UEFA, Jacques Georges, speaking after Hillsborough said in a French radio interview: 'This region (Merseyside) seems to have a particularly aggressive mentality. One can talk of people's frenzy to enter the stadium come what may, whatever the risk to the lives of others. One had the impression they were beasts who wanted to charge into the

arena'. *Daily Mail* 18 April 1989. His critics included Douglas Hurd, the Home Secretary.

6. The Home Office *Guide to Safety at Sports Grounds* is also known as the 'Green Guide'.

7. Such a necessarily simplistic presentation hides what appears, however, to have been a scene of considerable confusion, poor decision-making and a lack of overall control. See for example the description contained in Coleman *et al.*, (1990) Chapter 5.

8. *Community Care* 27 April 1989 p.6

9. Social Services Manager. Research interview, November 1990.

10. The data are taken from *Hillsborough: the Lessons for Health Care. Recommendations of a joint symposium held by Trent Health and Mersey Regional Health Authority*. Published by Trent Regional Health Authority (undated).

11. The ninety fifth death as a result of Hillsborough did not occur until later in the week.

12. Weber, M. (1966) *The Theory of Economic and Social Organisation*. New York: Free Press. I am grateful to Howard Parker for making this connection. This example points to the importance of effective leadership during crisis. Without such leadership, many opportunities – especially for inter-agency co-operation – would be missed.

13. 'Hillsborough Tragedy'. Unpublished briefing document for Social Services staff produced by the IAG, approximately 26.4.89.

14. After Hillsborough: A Report and Recommendations for Co-ordinating and Delivering Helping Services of the Directors of Social Services of the areas affected. Unpublished. April 1989.

15. All would do well to implement as many of the recommendations of the Disasters Working Party Report as possible.

CHAPTER 3

The Longer-Term Response

Having outlined some of the contours of the immediate response to Hillsborough, the primary aim of this chapter is to provide a broader, more detailed account of the structure and nature of the response in the three years since the disaster. The model of setting up a team dedicated to working with the bereaved and survivors rather than dispersing the work throughout a Department had been taken from a number of other disasters. Indeed, Tumelty (1990 p.13) suggests that 'moving from operating a helpline to establishing a longer term disaster team is the next *obvious* step' (my emphasis). Given that not all the authorities on Merseyside believed this to be the case and, consequently, not all did so, provides a good opportunity to examine the *obviousness* of this strategy.

The Teams

Teams of various types were set up in Knowsley, Sefton, Liverpool, Wirral, Sheffield, St. Helens and Lancashire and Nottinghamshire. Slightly different arrangements were made in Cheshire. The teams were not all set up at the same time, they did not operate for the same lengths of time, they were not selected and staffed in the same ways, and their methods of working varied. Several, however, were put into place within a week of the disaster.

The *Knowsley* team, for example, was set up on 17 April and consisted initially of a co-ordinator and six social workers. No fixed time period was put on the life of the team and after the initial crisis period was over, there were several changes of personnel. The team was eventually closed – after discussions with team members – towards the end of October 1990. The team took approximately 272 referrals in all, of which 168 (62%) were taken during the first two weeks after the disaster. The referrals can be further broken down as follows:

Table 3.1: Hillsborough referrals – Knowsley support team

Category	Number
Survivor	95
Injured	40
Relation of survivor	21
Relation of injured	2
Friend of survivor	4
Bereaved parent	25
Bereaved sibling	25
Bereaved partner	6
Bereaved child	5
Bereaved relation	12
Bereaved friend	4
Other	30
Non-Hillsborough	3
Total	**272**

The Knowsley experience was that the majority of survivors were referred within the first month of the aftermath and that there were a much smaller number thereafter. However, two particular events afterwards triggered a temporary increase (in referrals and in distress) – the playing of the Sheffield Wednesday v Liverpool match at Hillsborough later in the year (November 29) and the broadcasting of a documentary programme on the disaster (*First Tuesday*) on television on 2 February 1990.

The Wirral team was also set up in the week following the disaster (Green 1991). Late in the week the group of social workers – initially a team leader and five social workers – were brought together. This team, which remained in existence until Christmas 1990, took a total of 202 referrals broken down as follows:

Table 3.2: Hillsborough referrals – Wirral support team

Category	Number
Bereaved	26
Injured	26
Survivor	130
Relative	25
Total	**207**[1]

Again, like Knowsley, the bulk of referrals came within the first four to six weeks after the disaster. However, after this period the referrals appeared to dry up completely. The Wirral team requested a two-year life-span from the outset, but the original arrangement was that they would be guaranteed six months and that this would be reviewed. In October 1989 they were told they could continue for a further six months, and in March 1990 they were informed that they would have to close by the end of the month. The low community charge rate set by the council led to cuts in services, with the Hillsborough support team due to be among them.

The announcement of the decision less than a month before the first anniversary of the disaster led to the establishment of a campaign by service users who lobbied the council, campaigned in the press and eventually (with intervention from NALGO as well) earned a reprieve for the team who were told that they could continue until 25 June. On 18 May the team were approached by John Moores – Chairman of the locally-based Littlewoods Group and a supporter of a variety of local initiatives (the Moores family being long-standing major shareholders in both Everton and Liverpool football clubs) who offered to help the team keep going for up to another year. After fairly tricky negotiations a solution was found and on 10 September the team in consultation with social services management decided to continue until Christmas 1990.

The Sefton team, four social workers and a co-ordinator, were brought together during the first week after the disaster, and were established and *in situ* in premises by Friday 21. During the first week staff from Sefton SSD (some future team members, some not) had made contact with the local bereaved families, and the team continued the work with them from that point onwards. All the teams stressed the chaotic and overwhelming nature of the first week or possibly fortnight. The following brief description by the team leader of the activities of team members on Wednesday 19 gives some indication of what was happening during this crisis period:

> Visits to Sefton families are focused on practical matters. It is quite clear that, at this stage, with wider family rallying round, the social services role should be practical and/or facilitating in nature, and conscious efforts are made not to intrude uninvited on families' grief. There are many people trying to offer 'something' to families, with the danger that their privacy will be invaded. It has already become clear that the Press have erred grievously in this regard. Contact with Sefton survivors and other people variously affected by the disaster has stretched to the limit the time resources of the core team and it is not possible to respond to all referrals, which are therefore prioritised and those that appear less urgent are added to a waiting list for contact. Much tele-

phone counselling takes place, conversations lasting in excess of two hours in extreme cases.[2]

In all, the Sefton team took a total of 407 referrals and they can be broken down as follows:

Table 3.3: Hillsborough referrals – Sefton support team

Category		Number
Bereaved		34
Injured (m)		56
(f)		1
Survivors/Traumatised (m)		218
(f)		98
Total		**407**

A decision was taken to disband the Sefton team – with the agreement of the team members – at the end of April 1990, one year after Hillsborough. They were not receiving any new referrals and felt that it was hard to justify their continued existence. Their view, however, was not widely shared by colleagues in the other support teams.

Although Liverpool SSD was, at least in the early days, at the epicentre of post-disaster activity, the Liverpool Hillsborough support team was formed several months later than most of the other teams. It was established in July 1989 with an original complement of twelve social workers and two senior social workers/team leaders. In August 1989 the team moved into a refurbished lodge – which became known as the Hillsborough Centre – on the corner of Stanley Park near Anfield. (At the time of writing this team is still operating, although there are plans to close it down after the fourth anniversary of the disaster.)

Because of its central location and relatively high profile referrals came from far and wide to the Hillsborough Centre. It received a lot of media attention and general publicity. Thus, for example, between July 1989 and May 1990 it received 359 referrals. They may be broken down as shown in Table 3.4.

In addition to the social workers from Liverpool SSD at the centre there was also a further post funded by the Children's Society, which had as its focus the needs of children and young people. This work has included some contact on an individual basis with youngsters identified as giving cause for some concern, to the establishment of a Young People's Group at the Centre, and family/community work such as the organisation of day trips and other events.

Table 3.4: Hillsborough referrals – Liverpool support team

Category	Number
Bereaved parent	24
Bereaved partner	10
Bereaved sibling	4
Bereaved friend	8
Other relative	33
Survivor	194
Survivors' parent	14
Survivors' partner	18
Survivors' sibling	0
Survivors' friend	4
Other relative	2
Professional	2
Not known	11
Other (inc non-Hillsborough)	35
Total	**359**

As was the case in Sheffield, much work was also undertaken in Merseyside by hospital social workers – though this was in many ways less visible than the work done by the core teams. In Liverpool, two hospitals – Fazackerly and Walton – undertook the bulk of the work in relation to the disaster. At Walton, for example, between the 15 and 22 April there were 101 attendances at casualty directly related to Hillsborough. Of these, the social workers saw 62 – in effect everyone presenting at casualty during the hours the social workers were present, with the exception of anyone who refused to see them. In addition they had a further five patients who were transferred from Sheffield, and six who were admitted but not via casualty.

As in the other authorities, a large number of social workers in Cheshire responded to the immediate crisis after Hillsborough on a purely voluntary basis, staffing the helpline and drop-in centre. In addition in Cheshire, contact with families and with some survivors was also made by social workers who were continuing their normal jobs alongside this new and pressing demand. In June 1989, the Social Services Committee agreed that a number of posts should be established to cover the Hillsborough work. Unlike other areas, however, these did not form the basis of a core team but rather worked largely independently of each other. They received over 100 referrals county-wide.

One of the interesting features that distinguished one of the districts from the others and, indeed, from all the other teams, was the fact that it (Halton) had a joint Social Service/Health Authority response. This was largely unplanned, but occurred because a local community psychiatric nurse (CPN) made contact with families very early on after the disaster to offer help and support. There were four bereaved families in that district and the work was divided between the CPN and the local social workers.

Indeed, it might be more accurate to view the work undertaken in Halton as truly multi-agency or multi-disciplinary. Cheshire, like Liverpool, was quite heavily involved in youth work. Once again, this was largely because of the efforts of someone locally who took such work on board as a self-generating exercise. The bulk of the work was based at a youth centre in Runcorn (which is in Halton) and considerable links were made with the other workers involved with people affected by Hillsborough.

The county of Lancashire had, in many respects, only a peripheral involvement in Hillsborough support work. There were, for example, only two bereaved families from the Lancashire area, and the team only took 42 referrals in all. The team was set up on April 17, and eventually comprised a team leader and six social workers. Unlike most of the other teams, however, these workers, although given the Hillsborough brief, were not excused other duties. Indeed, almost without exception caseloads were not even reduced. Because the team operated in this rather unofficial or informal manner it never officially closed down, but slowly ceased operating as a Hillsborough team as the amount of work declined, and as workers moved on to other jobs. In addition to the team, which was based in Skelmersdale, a number of workers in other parts of the county took on cases as and when they were presented. There were relatively few of these cases, however, and the workers were themselves isolated from the wider response.

The workers in St. Helens also felt very much on the periphery of the Hillsborough response. There were relatively few St. Helens people at the match, though one was killed and one seriously injured. The team, which comprised three social workers, took up their posts on Monday 17 and relinquished their previous caseloads for a period of a few weeks. Like Lancashire, they took a small number of referrals early on and made contact with everyone referred either by letter, telephone or visit. Things started to tail off fairly soon and this prompted a management decision to close the team after four weeks.

The immediate response on the day of the disaster in Sheffield has already been described. However, in addition to the work that was done at the football ground, the hospitals, Hammerton Road Boys Club and at the Medico-Legal Centre, longer term plans were put in hand. As was happening over in Merseyside, representatives of social services met on the morning of Sunday 16 to discuss setting up what they were to call the 'task team'.

As on Merseyside, one of the first tasks was to get a report before elected members in order to convince them that there was going to be a long-term impact which would require the resourcing of a semi-permanent response. The task was set out as supporting what was happening on Merseyside whilst at the same time trying to address the needs of the people of Sheffield. Once that was agreed by the Council, social services were able to go ahead and advertise the posts for what was to become the 'permanent' task team.

The team was recruited during June and July (at the same time as the core team in Liverpool) and was in place by the end of July. They were based in the public library in Hillsborough Park and continued in existence for approximately nine months, being officially disbanded on the Friday after the April inquests had been held in the city. In all the team took 131 referrals which can be broken down as follows:

Table 3.5: Hillsborough referrals – Sheffield task team

Category	Number
Bereaved	36
Survivor	50
Helper	7
Injured	10
Friend	7
Resident	2
Steward	16
Other	3
Total	**131**

When, six months later, the full inquests were held (November 1990 onwards) the Department approached the workers with a view to reconstituting the team. Although individually they were keen that there should be cover for the inquests, there was a reluctance to re-form. In the event, a social work service was provided with present (including ex-team members) and past members (on a voluntary basis) of the Department attending on a rota basis during the five months that the inquests ran.

Although the vast majority of the Nottingham Forest supporters were located at the Kop end of the ground, opposite the Leppings Lane end, the experience for many Forest fans was profoundly shocking. There were also, of course, Liverpool supporters at Hillsborough who lived in Nottinghamshire. Because of events just a few months previously, the Social Services Department realised that something needed to be put in place quite quickly.

On January 8 1989, just three months prior to Hillsborough, British Midland Flight BD 092, a Boeing 737–400 *en route* from Heathrow to Belfast crash-landed on the M1 motorway, close to the East Midlands Airport and to the cities of Derby, Leicester and Nottingham. Many of the most serious casualties were taken to hospital in Nottingham, where the Social Work Department in tandem with the hospital chaplaincy set up services for the relatives of the injured. That experience, and the lessons learnt from it, influenced Nottinghamshire's response to Hillsborough.[3]

A drop-in and helpline was set up at the football ground and contact was made with over 700 people during the time the service was in operation. Contact was re-established with a voluntary counselling network that had been established after the M1 disaster, and anyone for whom it was appropriate and who agreed could be referred on for further counselling to one of the agencies involved. Within a week or so the service at the football ground was transferred to County Hall, and once it became clear that few were going to come forward to use the service there, the workers withdrew. The helpline was kept in operation for a few further weeks but took few calls. Nottinghamshire officials quickly made contact with colleagues in Merseyside and joined the IAG. Although in some senses their community may be said to have been less seriously affected by Hillsborough than many in the North-West, Nottinghamshire continued to participate in and support the work of the IAG right up until its close some two years after Hillsborough.

The voluntary sector

The Hillsborough Helpline

Apparently, the social services departments had never intended to keep on the helpline indefinitely and began fairly early on to look for a group in the voluntary sector that could take over responsibility for its day to day running. There is an important lesson here for post-disaster services and, particularly, for the role of social services within such a response. Although Hillsborough provoked an enormous reaction from social services departments around the country, which allowed a 24-hour helpline to be set up and staffed almost immediately and at minimal cost, there was a problem in sustaining this situation. First, it was difficult for those departments that were geographically distant from the location of the helpline to continue to justify the expense and the logistical problems incurred as a result of allowing staff to volunteer their services. Second, the authorities that were centrally involved in the disaster tended to concentrate their resources in establishing and maintaining a support team. Third, in the early days, when a large number of organisations that were geographically dispersed were involved in providing staff for the helpline, organising and arranging rotas and schedules was extremely difficult and time-consuming. Under such circumstances, it is perhaps not surprising that the IAG began to look to offload the responsibility of the helpline, and it was the voluntary sector that it turned to.

Whilst all this seems straightforward, the willingness to use the voluntary sector is nevertheless deserving of comment. A number of reports (cf *inter alia* Walker-Smith 1990) have noted the existence of professional rivalries and jealousies in the aftermath of disaster. Frequently such rivalries occur between the statutory and voluntary agencies – the focus often being the 'professional's' unwillingness to recognise the skills of the volunteer. Such conflicts may occur on both an individual and an organisational level, and Hillsborough was no exception in this regard. However, the IAG – made up largely of representatives of social services – did recognise that the local authorities were unlikely to be able to staff and run the helpline indefinitely, and further recognised that the skills and abilities existed within the voluntary sector to take over the work. Nevertheless, this represented a new departure for social services for, as the Advisor to the helpline described it:

> They [the statutory and voluntary sectors] had worked together before insofar as the voluntaries had been given money to go away and do a job, but never before had they shared responsibility.

As has already been noted, the voluntary sector in Liverpool is quite highly developed and many organisations contributed volunteers to the shifts at the helpline in the first weeks after the disaster. One of these was 'Walton Hospital Relative Support Group' (RSG).[4] RSG had originally become involved in the helpline via contacts with Catholic Social Services in Liverpool, and early on had been asked to provide volunteer counsellors for a memorial service that was being held on the Royal Iris ferry on the Mersey. It was eventually agreed that they should take over the running of the helpline, and it was moved on 1 October 1989 to accommodation at Walton Hospital in Liverpool. It had a full-time co-ordinator and part-time advisor and was staffed by volunteers from RSG and a small number of other local organisations.

The management – particularly the financial management – of the helpline was assumed by the Chief Executive of Liverpool CVS who, as was suggested above, had been instrumental in organising the voluntary sector response from the very early days onward. The relationship between the statutory and voluntary sectors was generally positive, although elements of 'rivalry' remained. The helpline co-ordinator commented for example:

> … it was nevertheless a long time before they [social services] realised that we weren't a threat and their jobs weren't in jeopardy.

The helpline was a 24-hour 7-day a week telephone service, designed to provide a confidential response to anyone affected by Hillsborough. By March 1990 well in excess of 3000 calls had been made to the helpline, though only a small proportion of these were made by people seeking help. Counselling and advice was generally done over the phone where appropriate, though some callers' names and addresses or telephone numbers were passed on to the relevant social work team in other cases. The numbers of calls diminished quite sharply from about three months onwards, and the helpline was officially closed in the July after the second anniversary of the tragedy.

In the eighteen months from 1 October 1989 to the end of March 1991, a total of 3942 calls were made to the helpline. Of these, 392 (10%) were Hillsborough-related calls for help. A further 1299 (33%) were offers of help or for information related to the disaster. The rest were largely made up of calls of an administrative nature (37.5%), and unsuccessful, wrong number or nuisance calls (16.5%). During this period the helpline took a further 34 calls that were from people who had suffered some personal tragedy that was unrelated to Hillsborough.

The pattern of calls to the helpline was fairly predictable, with a very high number being made in the first few days after the disaster (offering and well as requesting help), followed by a steady but slowly declining flow of calls after that. There were occasional peaks around the times of the anniversaries when there was a short-lived but significant increase in the number of calls, and there was an even larger increase after the broadcast of the 'First Tuesday' programme in February 1990 (in the week of the programme there was an increase of 68% in the number of calls for help compared with the previous week). The programme, which used some of the video material of the disaster that had been recorded by the police, was undoubtedly very distressing for many people to watch. The helpline number was broadcast at the end of the programme and the impact was immediate. Although all the authorities and the helpline were well briefed about the contents and potential impact of the broadcast, the power of the reaction nevertheless took

them by surprise. The helpline co-ordinator, who was at home watching
the programme, described the evening as follows:

> At 9.30ish when diverting the night line to [one of the volunteers] I
> mentioned the programme and told [her] if she had a lot of calls to
> phone me and I would take the line off her... I had the second line... set
> to my home... As the programme finished and the helpline number
> appeared on the screen my telephone rang. Because I assumed it was
> a personal call I did not answer with the usual 'helpline' and was
> unprepared for a helpline call, which it was. This meant [the volunteer
> who had the other line] must already have had a call... As soon as my
> call finished the phone immediately rang again. This then was the
> pattern, with no time to fill out referrals.

In addition to the telephone service the volunteers involved with the
helpline also took on a variety of other tasks. The most onerous of these
duties was providing support at the inquests that were held in Sheffield.
In all, three helpline staff provided 34 full days of cover at the Town Hall
in Sheffield, illustrating again the skills available in the voluntary sector
and the potential for collaboration between the statutory and voluntary
agencies.

Victim Support

The response from the voluntary sector was a fluid one. Organisations
became involved and then withdrew at different points depending upon
the needs and the priorities at the time, and their particular capabilities
and organisational priorities. Victim Support (VS), for example, were
very heavily involved in the first few weeks after Hillsborough, but
subsequently withdrew and had a relatively low-key role in the longer-
term.

The organisation (formerly the National Association of Victim Support Schemes) has been in existence about eighteen years, and its main
aim is:

> ... to provide the best possible services to those members of the com-
> munity who have suffered injury, loss fear or distress as a result of
> crime. The aim is to minimise the bad effects of crime and to help people
> through the uninvited crisis as fully and as quickly as may be possible.
> (Reeves 1984)

Generally speaking, individual victim support schemes have a full- or
part-time paid co-ordinator and are then staffed by volunteers who
undertake the outreach work with victims of crime.

One of the great strengths of VS is the breadth of its operation. It is a
national organisation, and at the time of Hillsborough had long-estab-
lished schemes in all three major cities affected by the tragedy. Consequently, VS was able to become directly involved in the response as it

unfolded in Sheffield (there were VS volunteers at the football ground
and the Boys Club), Nottingham and, of course, on Merseyside. The
organisation was one of the many voluntary groups represented at the
meeting of the voluntary sector in Merseyside on Sunday 16, and local
co-ordinators and volunteers quickly became engaged in work at Anfield, at the drop-ins at the Vernon Sangster Sports Centre and at Prenton
Park (home of Tranmere Rovers in Birkenhead) (cf Hart and James 1990a
and 1990b).

As one, albeit small, example of inter-agency co-operation, the VS
work on Merseyside was co-ordinated by the Chairman of the Merseyside Federation of Victim Support Schemes, a senior probation officer
who was given time off work by Merseyside Probation Service to see
through this task. A meeting of local co-ordinators and Federation
officers was called and they agreed to adhere to social services' request
that the lead role should be taken by the statutory sector, with the
voluntaries taking a subsidiary role. By and large the pattern at Anfield
was similar to that arranged by social services and clergy at Hillsborough, with a social worker being assigned to each of the families
together, on this occasion, with a VS volunteer. In addition to the
counsellor that was assigned to each family, there were also footballers
and their wives present, and they were also assigned to families. Indeed,
many of the Liverpool team were heavily involved in the support work
that took place in the weeks and months after Hillsborough. There were
players in attendance at all the funerals and at the ground every day in
the period it was open, in addition to visiting hospitals, peoples' homes
and so on. The role of the football club generally, and some of its staff in
particular, is returned to in Chapter 5 but, for the time being, Dave Hill's
(1989 p.191) insightful comments on the club, the game and disaster will
suffice:

> Propriety was finally provided by the club's supporters, the people of
> the city of Liverpool and the men who play for the team and their
> wives. It was an alliance of compassion whose components were
> symbolic... For all the media flannel about Liverpool the 'family club',
> the compassion was real because, for once in modern football, no-one
> was trying to sell anything to anyone else.

One of the major reasons that VS was well geared up to respond to
Hillsborough was the then recent completion of what was known as the
'Families of Murder Victims Project' (Brown *et al.* 1990). This was a
project that examined the needs of the families of murder victims, and
assessed the role that VS, in concert with other agencies, could play in
providing advice and support. The project, which was run on a pilot
basis for two years from January 1988, was based in four areas, two of
which coincidentally were Sheffield and Merseyside. As a result these

two areas had a large number of workers who were both specifically trained and experienced in providing support for families who had been bereaved unexpectedly and tragically. The following description of the work undertaken in connection with the 'murder project' provides a good illustration of the relevance of the work to working in the aftermath of disaster (Brown *et al.* 1990 p.30):

> In most cases volunteers were introduced to families within the first forty-eight hours following the murder... The nature of their interventions concerned both emotional and practical issues... Simply sitting and listening was a first step... Volunteers coped with deeply emotional and painful feelings expressed by families. They acted as intermediaries with the police, mortuary officials, Coroners, funeral practitioners, DSS and numerous other agencies... The volunteers sometimes found it difficult to retain sufficient distance from the family in order to prevent themselves from being overwhelmed by their grief. However, where good supervision took place, the volunteers were able to manage this tension and intervene appropriately.

This description could easily pass for a general overview of much of the social work that is undertaken after disasters, and it is these skills, together with the everyday 'good neighbour' approach of VS that were called upon during the aftermath of Hillsborough.

The Church

For obvious reasons it is all but impossible to catalogue the role played by the Church in the aftermath of a disaster in an overview such as this. However, from the first evening at Hillsborough itself and at the Boys Club, to the present day support of individual family members, the work of members of the clergy and of more formal Church groups has been wide-ranging and in some cases long-lasting. There is some instructive material on the role of the Church in the immediate aftermath of the disaster which is summarised below, and some of the personal experiences of those who received support from clergy are described in Chapter 5.

Large numbers of clergy were present at Hillsborough during the immediate aftermath of the disaster. As with the social workers, many had responded to the general call for help that was broadcast on the Saturday afternoon. The work of the clergy at Hillsborough on April 15 was co-ordinated by the Archdeacon of Sheffield (Lowe 1989). As soon as he heard the news of what was happening, he contacted any rural deans, hospital chaplains and other clergy who were at home and arranged to meet them near the football ground. The clergy were largely divided between the Boys Club and the temporary mortuary at the football ground. At the gymnasium, where formal identification took place, the Archdeacon and the Assistant Director of Social Services collaboratively organised their staff:

> When we arrived, the police wanted us to attach our support *after* the identification had taken place. This was clearly unacceptable and the police quickly learned that we were most helpful if there was an established relationship *before* the identification process began... We tried to attach a social worker and clergyman to each inquiring group or small group. (Lowe 1989)

Meanwhile, arrangements were being made for there to be cover at the Medico-Legal Centre from that evening onwards for the whole of the following week until the bodies were removed. By contrast with these venues, the work at the two hospitals seems to have been somewhat less well organised. Social workers attempted to take charge at the Hallamshire, but the situation at the Northern General appears to have been fairly chaotic. The situation at the Boys Club was, if anything, even worse. Bagshaw (1991 p.4) quotes a senior Anglican priest as saying:

> We also faced a massive problem of the Boys Club being a) unsuitable to do any work; b) being overwhelmed by too many people coming, both clergy and social workers; and c) not being able adequately to distinguish who was what and what they were doing and so on.

Clergy reported that there was some rivalry between social services and themselves (Cranwell 1989) but that the situation improved as time went on as those involved got to know each other and to know what each other's skills were, and to trust each other. Such rivalry appears to be almost endemic in the aftermath of such tragedies, and it will only be through joint working and planning that such problems will be avoided in the future (Bagshaw 1991).

On Merseyside the role of the Church was most clearly illustrated by the power of the memorial services that were held at the two cathedrals. Tony Walter's (1991 p.616) description of the 6.00pm mass conveys some of its power:

> At a big do in Liverpool's RC cathedral, if it is half full twenty minutes before the start, the cathedral authorities know the place will be comfortably full. On this occasion, it was full to its 4000 capacity fifty minutes before, with thousands still on their way. The authorities at that point decided to hold a makeshift mass on the plaza outside while the main service was being held inside. Inside the cathedral, a large red Liverpool FC banner – made the night before by a nun on the cathedral staff – hung by the altar. Before the mass began, one lad haltingly darted to the front and laid an item of football regalia at the altar...

Not only was another service taking place outside the cathedral, but the 'official' service was broadcast live on local radio. Churches opened their doors around the city, and the tone of memorial services very much reflected the ritualised grieving that took place around the region, and that was particularly evident at Anfield. Certainly in the very early days after the disaster, it was the religious leaders rather than the local politicians who were able to articulate the pain of the city.

Much of what happened in Liverpool was ecumenical in character. Many of the funerals were ecumenical, as were local services and, entirely expectedly, the two Bishops once again worked in tandem (Bishop's Council 1990). In addition, the Church was involved or represented in a wide variety of other activities. For example, the Diocesan Board for Social Responsibility and Catholic Social Services put forward people for the helpline; a team of clergy offered back-up help at the Vernon Sangster Sports Centre and the Church was strongly represented among the membership of Walton Hospital RSG.

Conclusion

- The majority of authorities' core teams were set up in the immediate aftermath of the disaster, although Liverpool and Sheffield made somewhat different arrangements in the first few months. The core teams were kept in existence for differing lengths of time (e.g. Sefton for a year, Wirral and Knowsley approximately eighteen months, with the Liverpool team still in existence at the time of writing).

- The 'Hillsborough model' – a 'federal' response from a region, with individual teams placed in each of the authorities – worked well in many important respects, but had certain shortcomings. First, all the authorities pulled together only during the 'honeymoon' period just after the disaster. After that, a few started going their own ways, with the consequence that services were not maintained for comparable periods across the region. Although, in a region like Merseyside, there would have been some logic in slowly closing down teams as demand decreased, whilst directing any future referrals to those teams that remained, this was not the basis upon which the decisions were taken.

- The maintenance of the response over an extended period of time is one of the most crucial objectives, yet one of the hardest to achieve. The good intentions expressed by senior managers caught up in the emotion of the tragedy, that are visible at the outset, either soon disappear or are undermined by changes in the local political climate. Long-term strategic decisions need to be taken in the early weeks – for example, what sort of team will be set up and how long it will operate for – and these need to be adhered to. The stresses experienced by workers can easily be exacerbated by organisational problems affecting the work. Crucially, although some flexibility is necessary, workers need some indication of how long the service will be maintained and that the work is supported and valued by their department. Failure to provide a secure environment for the work is likely to undermine the extent to which staff feel they can work effectively.

- The voluntary sector in Liverpool was able to take over the running of the Hillsborough Helpline not only because it had a long history of co-operative working with social services, but because there was an identifiable group that had the skills to take on the job. Without such a group, it seems likely the voluntary sector would have been faced with the same logistical problems that the statutory services had to confront.

Notes

1. The slight over-counting results from the inclusion of some 'clients' in more than one category.

2. Quoted from unpublished internal briefing paper. Sefton Social Services Department.

3. Fuller details of this operation are available in Whitham, D. and Newburn, T. (1992) *Coping With Tragedy: Managing the Responses to Two Disasters.* Nottinghamshire County Council.

4. Relative support' at Walton hospital began in 1984. It was the brainchild of a hospital administrator, Mike Sobanja, who was moved one day by the sight of an elderly man walking down the hospital drive carrying a brown paper parcel containing his dead wife's belongings. This was a person who was now left alone to cope not only with his grief but with all the day-to-day arrangements that need to be seen to. The administrator set up a Steering Group consisting of representatives from the local clergy and bereavement groups, and they resolved to try to provide a service to assist people with practical arrangements after bereavement. The Steering Group advertised for volunteers and set up a training course. At the time of Hillsborough six groups of volunteers had been trained and despite the high turnover of people in voluntary work, had over 40 people they could call upon. The co-ordinator recently described the work of RSG in the following terms:

> ... simply a listening ear and a cup of tea, or we may be asked to provide transport to take someone home, or to accompany relatives to the mortuary, the chapel, the coroner, the registrar or help with funeral arrangements or social security matters.

Part 2

The Service Response to the Disaster
The User's Perspective

CHAPTER 4

The Impact of Disaster

Who is affected?

The ever-widening ripples caused by a stone thrown into still waters is one of the metaphors that is frequently used to describe the impact of disaster. Large-scale tragedies, it is held, do not just affect those who happen to be near the epicentre, but impinge upon a wide variety of groups as the effects ripple their way outwards. Indeed, such is the potential complexity of disaster impact that several authors have attempted to construct typologies of victims of disaster (Taylor 1987).

In the context of a disaster like Hillsborough, social workers and other carers provided help, support and counselling not only for those who were bereaved, but also those who were there and survived, to those relatives who found that the person who returned from the match that Saturday had been changed – sometimes in subtle ways, many times profoundly – by what they had seen and what they had experienced, and to many others who came into contact in some way with the tragic events that unfolded. Clearly, the needs that each of these groups of people manifest will not necessarily be comparable or even similar and, consequently, the way in which carers respond to them will need to be geared to their particular situations.

It is useful therefore, at least heuristically, to have some method which allows the various groups of victims involved to be separated and distinguished, although admittedly in a somewhat artificial manner. Perhaps the two best known typologies of disaster victims are those by Dudasik (1980) and Taylor and Frazer (1981, see also Taylor and Frazer 1990). There are similarities between the two for both categorise victims by their 'closeness' to the disaster. Dudasik offers four types of victim: 'event victims' who are those who suffer hardships directly attributable to the disaster; 'contact victims' who are those affected in some way by the consequences of the disaster; 'peripheral victims' who are those affected by reason of their close ties with the disaster area; and finally, 'entry victims' who are affected as a result of their contact with the disaster or disaster area during the aftermath, for example, rescue and recovery personnel.

More broadly useful is the six category system designed by Taylor and Frazer. Again, the general approach adopted is to separate groups according to their proximity to the emotional epicentre of the traumatic event. Thus, 'primary' victims are those who directly experienced the disaster, whereas 'sixth level' victims are those who might, but for chance, have been primary victims (for example those oil rig workers who were not part of the shift that was on the Piper Alpha platform when the disaster occurred), but escaped direct involvement and yet nevertheless suffered.[1] 'Secondary' victims covers the relatives and friends of primary victims, and 'third-level' victims are the equivalent of Dudasik's 'entry' victims – essentially those involved in the rescue and recovery, though there is some overlap between this and the next level. The 'fourth-level' of victims is the community involved in the disaster, though this category also includes those who come forward to help in the recovery operation. Those in the 'fifth-level' are not directly involved, but may nevertheless find themselves upset or distressed apparently as a result of the disaster.

The usefulness of such taxonomies should not be overstated. There is a need to categorise victims, for it is important that some conceptual models are developed that aid understanding of the 'ripple' effects that characterise the post-disaster phase. Furthermore, models such as the above, are likely to be helpful in the process of planning the recovery operation. They should allow consideration of who is likely to be affected by particular types or forms of disaster and, consequently, what sort of recovery operation needs to be put in hand, and what services need to be offered or set up. Importantly, perhaps, they ought to help guard against the possibility of ignoring or underestimating the potential effects on some apparently distanced social groups.

However, because both models are to some extent hierarchical in structure, aiming to reflect the 'closeness' of groups of victims to the disaster, they also contain an inherent danger. That danger lies in the assumption that this closeness is a clear reflection of likely 'need'. More particularly, whilst categories might reasonably be taken to reflect the proportionate effects of disaster – i.e. a larger proportion of primary victims are likely to require help or support than secondary victims – they do not necessarily reflect the 'depth' of need – i.e. it would be wrong to simply assume that secondary victims will be more profoundly affected than quinternary victims. In many cases such an assumption might actually be borne out, but acting on that assumption can lead to a possible situation in which a 'victim's' needs are not appropriately responded to. Far from helping, the carers' intervention may potentially exacerbate whatever problems exist.

Having suggested that a typology may be of some use, it is worth going one stage further and looking rather more closely at some of those studies which have considered one or more of the 'types' of groups delineated. Not surprisingly, the research effort has tended to concentrate on certain areas of disaster victimisation – particularly those 'closest' to the disaster – or, using Taylor and Frazer's (1981) definitions, primary, secondary and third-level or tertiary victims. Although there is much discussion and argument about what constitutes a disaster,[2] most such events tend to involve death or, at least, a severe life-threatening situation. Disasters, then, generally involve bereavement and survival, and it is the bereaved and the survivors who have been the focus of the bulk of disaster literature.

Much has been written about bereavement and loss (Kubler-Ross 1970, Bowlby 1980, Raphael 1983, Worden 1983) – though little of this literature has had disasters specifically in mind – and what has been written in relation to death and disaster reflects many of the concerns and received wisdoms of the more general bereavement literature. There is, by contrast, rather less known about the ways in which those who witness and experience the disaster cope with having survived it. Having said that, there is an ever growing literature on what is commonly referred to as 'post-trauma stress' and its more serious, long-lasting or entrenched corollary, 'Post-Traumatic Stress Disorder'.

Survival

A wide variety of reactions are associated with the survival of particularly traumatic events. Many of these are related in some way to the reliving or re-experiencing of the event – dreams/nightmares – 'flashbacks' often accompanied by heightened anxiety or panic. Phobic reactions associated with certain aspects of the traumatic experience have also been observed by those studying disaster survivors, as have a number of somatic reactions, including loss of appetite, disruption of sleeping patterns, inability to concentrate for any length of time, as well as a form of emotional numbness. There appears to be quite wide variation in the length of time over which such symptoms may persist, though Raphael (1986), reviewing the literature, suggests that 'for most people the reaction settles within four to six weeks'. A proportion of survivors, however, may go on to suffer what is now widely referred to as Post-Traumatic Stress Disorder (PTSD) as defined by the American Psychiatric Association (1980).

The difficulties of studying post-disaster morbidity mean that there is limited data on the patterns and levels of impact of PTSD. Perhaps the most thorough study of PTSD and peacetime disaster has been that by Weisaeth (1984). In his study of factory fire he found that approximately two-fifths of those most directly exposed to the fire exhibited symptoms equivalent to PTSD one week after the disaster, compared to a quarter of those not directly exposed and one-tenth of those who saw the fire but were not at the factory. He further found that those with 'a very high level of anxiety, traumatic sleep disturbances, startle reactions, fear phobia of the disaster area, and a degree of social withdrawal were highly likely to be suffering from the disorder seven months later' (Raphael 1986). Studies have suggested that upwards of 15 per cent of Vietnam Veterans have developed PTSD (Keane *et al.* 1985) and McFarlane's (1988) work confirms Weisaeth's findings that up to a third of people may do so after natural disasters. Nevertheless, evidence about PTSD is patchy at best and as Raphael (1986) says, 'many studies are bedevilled by their lack of appropriate methodology, their descriptive and retrospective nature, and a failure to use control populations and careful criteria of morbidity'.

There is considerably more data on post-disaster stresses and anxiety-related reactions. For many who survive, it is the encounter with death and the personal threat to their own life that forms the basis for the disturbance and distress that they experience afterwards. Studies of Hiroshima and Nagasaki (Janis 1951), Buffalo Creek (Erikson 1979), and the DC10 air crash in Antarctica (Taylor and Frazer 1981) have discussed in great detail the effect that witnessing the deaths, often horrific ones, occasioned by disaster can have on the survivors of the tragedy. It is perhaps Erikson (1979 p.122), in his perceptive study of the Appalachian community of Buffalo Creek, who most evocatively describes 'death anxiety':

> … death like this does not retreat into some discrete compartment of the mind, emerging now and again to haunt one's dreams. It remains with one… death lies out there at its inescapable worst… It's all there – an advance look at hell.

In addition to quite possibly having witnessed people die – sometimes relatives and close friends – or at least having viewed the remains of those who died, survivors are frequently left with an overriding feeling of guilt. 'Survival guilt' is primarily a response to not having died and yet being left with the feeling that one's survival may have been at the cost of another's life – as particularly evidenced after those disasters where there has been some form of struggle for survival. Guilt, therefore, may be focused upon what actions the survivors took in order to survive, whether or not they attempted to help or to save others and, related to those actions, whether or not they were successful in these attempts. At their most pronounced such reactions have been characterised as a 'survivor syndrome' consisting of chronic anxiety and depression as well as a variety of other somatic and psychological *sequelae*, and found with particular frequency among survivors of Hiroshima (Lifton 1967) and among concentration camp survivors (Eitinger and Askevold 1968).

Bereavement

In direct contrast to the relatively small literature on 'survival', there is a considerable disasters literature which focuses upon bereavement and loss. Part of the reason for this is that it has been 'natural' disasters, often involving death on a very large scale, that have drawn much of the academic attention. Indeed, although there continues to be considerable debate over what actually constitutes a disaster, generally speaking it remains the case that the term is used to describe situations where there has been death on a large, often horrific and unexpected scale. Also involved in this definitional process is the idea that the disaster is a 'public' event. In addition to provoking public sympathy and support, the acceptance of an event as a disaster also brings public attention in the form of the media, the statutory care organisations, voluntary bodies, community and neighbourhood groups, politicians – local and national – and so on. This transforms the experience of bereavement in a number of ways: first, the number of intrusions, however well-meant, is likely to be much greater than would be the case under 'normal' circumstances; second, the very public nature of the loss may make it difficult to grieve; and, finally, the socio-legal ramifications in the form of identification of the bodies, post-mortems, official inquiries, coroner's inquests and so on are likely to be especially burdensome and potentially traumatising in themselves.

A general pattern or process of grieving has been outlined by a variety of authors (Lindemann 1944, Kubler-Ross 1970, Murray-Parkes 1975, Bowlby 1980, Raphael 1983). This pattern typically involves the identification of a series of stages; for example, denial and isolation, anger, bargaining, depression and acceptance (Kubler-Ross 1970). Although there is some disagreement over the appropriate labels for the stages identified and over the components and chronology of the stages, there is nevertheless broad acceptance of the general pattern or process of bereavement. Consequently, there has developed a fairly substantial body of knowledge about counselling the bereaved (Worden 1983, Raphael 1986). Raphael (1986), for example, describes a variety of techniques that those in contact with the bereaved may use as a framework for care both in the 'crisis' period and in the months and years that follow. This framework includes *comfort* and *consolation* – helping the bereaved bear the pain of separation – *facilitating recovery* through reintegration into the social group and, finally, *therapeutic assessment* to examine the process of bereavement and check for malresolution and a variety of potential morbid outcomes.

Although the general process or pattern of grief – and consequently the techniques of bereavement or grief counselling – are held to be applicable to death as a result of disaster, there are, as was suggested above, several aspects of disaster that may require special under-standing and intervention. Worden (1983), although reflecting on the special character of 'sudden death', makes a number of points that are applicable here. First, death under such circumstances will often leave the survivors (the family for example) with a sense of unreality about the loss, and a numbness which may last for a considerable period. Second, there may be exacerbated feelings of guilt, and connected to these, a need to blame. Worden also mentions the involvement of the legal and medical authorities. The delay which often results from such involvement may serve one of two functions, he suggests. On the one hand, proceedings may distract the bereaved and prevent them from dealing with their grief on a 'firsthand' basis, while on the other legal interruptions may have a positive effect in cases where an adjudication helps to put some closure on the grief. Those bereaved as a result of 'sudden death' are also often left with a feeling of helplessness which results from a damaged sense of order and is often linked with enormous rage and a hitting out at those perceived to be responsible. Finally, there is frequently a much heightened need to understand, a very strong interest in finding out why the death happened. This again is linked with a desire to blame and consequently involves the search for a target or a focus for recrimination.

In addition to those bereaved and those who survive there are, as the typologies suggest, other groups who may be profoundly affected by disaster. 'Entry' victims (Dudasik 1980) or 'third or fourth-level' victims (Taylor and Frazer 1981) – rescue and recovery personnel and others who offer help in the aftermath – are increasingly recognised to be at risk from the reverberations of the disaster. Much of the research in this area has concentrated on the emergency services such as fire officers (McFarlane and Raphael 1984), and body-handlers (Taylor and Frazer 1982) rather than those who support or counsel the 'victims' of the tragedy. Raphael's (1977) research on the aftermath of the Granville rail disaster pointed to six aspects of the work as being particularly stressful: feeling helpless, the extent of disaster and the amount of death and injury, the suddenness and unexpectedness, the sight and smell of dead bodies, dealing with the suffering of the bereaved relatives and the injured, and having to cope with all these whilst working under extreme pressure.

Although researchers have tended to focus on the emergency serv-ices, there is now growing recognition of the potential effects of disaster on those who are tasked with providing support for or with counselling the 'primary' victims (Johnston 1990). Thus, Raphael *et al.* (1984), looking at the role stresses that disaster workers confront, argue that it is those who have the more clearly defined roles with associated practical tasks, such as police and ambulance workers, who are likely to have the better outcomes. Workers with loosely defined or vague roles – and in this regard social workers are specifically mentioned – are more likely to be associated with strain. Raphael (1986 p.232), summarising some of their results, says 'helpers who have been trained in their roles and have practised performing them are far more likely to perform without undue stress or with lower levels of stress. Past experience in disasters or other emergencies may also mitigate against responses, giving the helper a greater sense of command'.

The purpose of this brief introduction has been to point up the range of 'groups' that may be affected by an event such as Hillsborough. The bulk of the rest of the book is devoted to an analysis of the impact of this particular disaster and to an evaluation of the services set up in its aftermath. This chapter and the following one focus upon what, roughly speaking, Taylor and Frazer (1981) would take to be the primary and secondary victims of the disaster: the bereaved, the survivors, their relatives and friends. Chapters 6 and 7 focus upon the carers and helpers who were themselves affected by their experiences of Hillsborough.

The experience of disaster

It is impossible to convey the range and depth of the impact of something like Hillsborough without first considering the experience of the event itself. It is only by listening to the words of those who were bereaved or those who were survivors of or witnesses to the events that unfolded that Saturday afternoon that the power of the experiences becomes clear.

As with all disasters, the events were entirely unexpected; it was for most just a day out with family or friends:

> We all booked on the same coach... on the top deck me mum was there with me sister and the next door neighbour, so we all really went down together, my family and all me mates. (Male survivor)

> He left here, it was about 9 o'clock on the Saturday morning and his friend had knocked for him and they were going in my husband's car, he was driving down there. And they picked up another two mates and they went. I went out shopping with the kids, 'cause we'd booked to go on holiday. (Wife of survivor)

What happened in and around Sheffield prior to the match has become the focus of heated debate and considerable controversy. As has already been suggested, police attention and explanation for the disaster has focused on alleged misbehaviour and, in particular, drunkenness amongst the Liverpool fans. Although some residents and one publican made some similar claims, the testimony of the fans at the official inquiry and the inquests together with the police video of the events at Leppings Lane does not support the allegation of *widespread* misbehaviour. Our respondents highlighted the sense of fun that they had set out with that day and the impossibility of rowdiness in the crush that developed outside the ground:

> ... there were five of us... and we walked up there, loads were walking up singing, and it was a brilliant atmosphere, you know all the anticipation of winning and going to Wembley. (Male survivor)

> It just started like... it was just an ordinary day like, we dropped the kids... got the train... we didn't get on the football special... but we got the train that followed... We were like herds, it was like goats, off the train, out the station, couldn't even go to the toilet or buy a can of anything. (Female survivor)

> I think we got to Sheffield roughly about half-twelve to one o'clock. The season before there was a pub just up the road... that was open... only this season it was closed as was every other pub in the vicinity. As far as I could see there was not a great deal of time nor the inclination for anybody to go drinking. We did bring one large bottle [of beer] from the Co-op store... between three of us. (Male survivor)

The fans then made their way – for most, with great difficulty – into the ground. The survivors interviewed as part of this research were located either in one of the two central pens behind the goal, or in the West Stand above the Leppings Lane terraces. The West Stand spectators had an all-too clear view of the developing crush in the central pens:

> It was as if you were looking through binoculars. You could see people crushed, you could see... the shoulders coming close together and you could see them reaching out, sort of for help, and... dragging other people down because they wanted to get up and get some air. (Male survivor)

> The way everybody was standing, because we could see people's heads, this fella was lying at the very front on people's heads, and he was like right across... he must have been there for five minutes... I said 'he's dead', and he [a friend] said to me 'oh, don't be stupid'. (Female survivor)

> I haven't watched any of my relatives die, you know more like strangers die. I can still see them now... I saw this lad... trying to pull himself up, he just sort of disappeared, then came back up and I said 'that kid's dead'. Then a girl, just like a piece of wood floating on water. The copper in front of us was just looking. I shouted at him to do something, but he just sort of looked blank. (Male survivor)

It was, of course, in pens 3 and 4 that the crushing took place and where the injuries that led to the ninety-five deaths were sustained.[3] The following recollections give some idea of what the fans in this part of the ground survived that afternoon:

> You've come through a tunnel and if you look back there is just a high wall, and you've got fencing in the front, so you were literally penned in and you knew there was no way out, panic began inside. That's when the horror began really... it was very hot, the sun made it worse, claustrophobic was an understatement and the pressure on your body was incredible really. (Male survivor)

> You can't recapture the sounds on television, you can hear a deafening hum, but you can't hear the person next to you screaming in your ear and you can't hear people dying and you can't hear bones crushing and you can't smell the smell the smells that..you could smell people dying... combined with the actual sensation of being crushed as well, you've got every sense bombarded at the same time. (Male survivor)

> There was somebody lifted me up 'cause I was under a lot of people myself... eventually I could feel the pressure easing off and someone lifted me up and I just said, 'there's a lad here I've got to see to' and the bloke said 'He's dead mate, leave him...' (Male survivor)

> We couldn't get back through the tunnel... people were still trying to cram in... [and others] were trying to get back out because they realised how bad a crush it was. So you sort of stayed put. It was then that sort of kick-off time arrived... [and] the crush seemed to be worse again and we seen people trying to climb up onto the fence, trying to get over the fence... they were being told by the police to get back in... We tried as much as we could to try and sort of go backwards towards the stand... by then a couple of people had started to get pulled up into the stand which made a bit more room... so we edged towards the face of the stand, I boosted my brother up. I was lifted up and there was about four fellows leaning over the stand trying to pull me up. They got hold of my arms and lifted. As they lifted there was a bad crush again below me and my legs just jammed and these four able-bodied lads trying to pull me up and they couldn't... I was sort of suspended there, and it seemed like about five minutes, but it must have been one minute... Once we were in the stand we turned and looked at the pitch... you could tell people were very badly injured to say the least. (Male survivor)

> There was a bloke dying next to me. He was a really big bloke, like a docker. His mate was holding him up, trying to stop him from falling. The pushing from the back just forced you down. I was looking at the ground and thinking 'if you go down there you're dead'. The smell was unbelievable I can tell you. I was only at about armpit level of most people because of my size. I was trying to force my head up in order to breathe... I remember shouting at the bloke next to me 'move your

arm, move your arm, you're killing me!'. I looked around and it was obvious he was dead. His eyes, his tongue, I could tell... I've still got scars from the fencing. I had a black eye for months and criss-cross marks on my back from the wire mesh for ages. (Female survivor)

The escape was eventually either out of the back of the stand or onto the pitch. Once on the pitch the task, for those who were able, was to try to help those who were still trapped or in distress. Many survivors wanted to provide first-aid – indeed quite a number had first-aid qualifications – and large numbers became involved very quickly in the rescue operation:

I came to on the pitch. I wasn't quite sure where, but I do remember having white paint from the pitch markings on my jeans. I got up and tried to walk, but I kept falling over. I was barely conscious. I just couldn't do it. I could see the line of police across the pitch. I could barely breathe. They weren't allowed to break ranks. Anyway, eventually one did and his Sergeant or whatever tried to stop him, but he came over anyway. He asked if I was all right. I said I was and he rolled me over on to my side to see if I could be sick... I was moved over to the side of the pitch near the Forest end... Despite being in that state I got up, and with a lad started to break down the [advertising] boards to use as stretchers... I was carrying the stretcher with what turned out to be my crushed arm... I was taken to the gym and there were like these three piles there: the dead, the nearly dead and the injured but going to be OK like me. I was sat on this table, together with a lad who had broken his leg, and this St. Johns Ambulance lady comes up. She looked terrible, she was really upset. I put my arm round her and said you know 'it's terrible isn't it? You'll be OK'. (Female survivor)

I remember when we went over by the fence there was this old fella, he had a tie on, you know typical old man... so I was just like, trying to comfort him... every time he tried to talk it was like air... so I jumped on the fence... I could not get him out, but I'm not sure whether I broke his leg or what, the way I got him out... But when all the people in that pen saw me helping this old man out, all their hands started going up, and you know, help us up. (Male survivor)

Many who tried to help felt there was either little or, at least, insufficient they could do. Many felt impotent at the scale of what was happening in front of them and, despite their often heroic acts, they were often left with very strong feelings of guilt and failure:

As I was doing these compressions I was worried because I felt as though I was sinking further and further down... in the end we just lost the pulse and she was just dead. there was nothing we could do. I just felt, I felt a sense of failure cos that was my job. (Male survivor)

For those who had escaped the crush the feelings, understandably, were very mixed. Many were overcome by relief, some by anger and others were simply numbed by the shock and the grief:

> I was kneeling on the pitch gasping for breath. It was an incredible feeling of relief though, it really was. (Male survivor)

> The next thing I found myself running towards the Nottingham Forest end like some sort of hooligan, a man possessed... I was absolutely mad, and I was dying to get in amongst them and make them hurt, to let them feel the hurt we were feeling. (Male survivor)

> The memory I've got is of one lad who was dead on the pitch... he was uncovered and I just wanted to go out and put me coat over him... I couldn't and that hurt me for a long time afterwards – that I hadn't gone and done that. (Male survivor)

For those relatives and friends who were not at Hillsborough, news of the disaster generally came either from the radio or from television. There was live commentary on both local and national radio, and the BBC which was recording the match for television began to broadcast 'live' pictures from Hillsborough during its *'Grandstand'* programme. Indeed, sometime after the disaster, some relatives applied to the courts for compensation for the pain and suffering caused them as a result of watching that and other broadcasts. Hillsborough, like the Bradford fire before it, became a very immediate national event via the news media. For relatives, it was a particularly shocking way to find out that family members were in danger:

> I was ironing and I switched it on and I said, 'what on earth is this?' We didn't know what it was, because Liverpool wasn't being televised this week, and then we realised what it was, well it was just panic because I saw that our [son] was on the floor. (Bereaved mother)

> The television was on. And like I was pottering around... I could hear the noise in the background and when I looked around I realised what was happening then... it was just a feeling... but I just knew he wasn't going to come home for some reason. (Bereaved wife)

As is frequently the case in the immediate aftermath of disaster, the major initial problem was one of communication. How were fans in Sheffield to let their relatives know that they were OK? And how were relatives and friends who were not in Sheffield to discover what had happened to the people they knew had gone to the match? Emergency numbers were released but lines were almost immediately and permanently jammed. For many there followed an agonisingly long wait for news. Others – often thanks to the enormous generosity of the residents of Hillsborough and its environs – were able to make contact with their families fairly quickly:

We went back to the car, drove out of the housing estate that we were in and found a phone, and luckily after what I've heard since, we must have been so lucky, but we got through to my sister's house, and we left a message with her to say that we were all right and that the mates that were with us were all right. (Male survivor)

The security guy at the factory across the road [from the ground] said 'we've opened up. If you want to use the phones and toilets come on in'. (Male survivor)

It was just waiting then. I just sat there with me head on me Mum's shoulder and we just sat and sat and sat and then the 'phone rang about quarter to one in the morning and it was me brother-in-law and he said, 'I found him, he's dead'. That was it. (Bereaved mother)

We wanted to dash to Sheffield, but we were so convinced he would ring us up on our way, so we sort of hung around... we were all trying to ring that stupid number that you had no chance of getting through... (Bereaved Mother)

I started phoning at 7 o'clock and I got through at 1 o'clock in the morning... and they couldn't help me. (Bereaved mother)

I had tried all the emergency numbers all night for that, and that is more frustrating those emergency numbers, you know, no news at all really, you're just sitting there and waiting. (Wife of survivor)

Finally, for those who had either heard nothing, or had heard that their relative was, or was believed to be, among the dead, there remained the process of identification in Sheffield. The procedure for identification was described, and some criticisms of it were included in chapter one. Identifying a loved one is always a harrowing process. Over recent years, however, hospitals and mortuaries have developed methods of ensuring that the most unpleasant aspects are minimised and that things that might help the bereaved in the future are facilitated. It is now common, for example, to allow relatives to spend time with the body. No such courtesies were extended at Hillsborough:

... by three o'clock they said well just for last results will you come to the sports centre and look at these photographs and then you'll know we've not got him. He's either lost his memory, he's wandering around Sheffield... and then we went to look at these 95 photographs. And that's when we found him... I mean that was the only nasty part we had was like I found [son] on these photographs, took us out again then, to get in this queue again to wait to go, obviously, when you had found your children, whoever, they brought them to you. And we had gone out and I remember this lady saying this is Mr and Mrs... He said number XX, that was the only time I blew my top, I said 'my son is not a number'. Anyway they took us in there and they wheeled [him] to us... I said please just give me five minutes in a corner, he said oh, no, no, no, come on, come on. There's a queue waiting... and I thought that five minutes would have been so precious, and then that was it. They took us back then, took [him] away from us. (Bereaved mother)

My son-in-law said he would look at the photos and for an hour or more we waited for him to be called... we waited with a social worker and clergywoman who were... doing their best under dreadful conditions... the whole area was one of absolute heartache and emotional turmoil... those who were not sure if their relatives or friends were dead were subjected to the stress of witnessing the awful shock and grief of those who knew their loved ones were dead... It was in fact absolute chaos... my son-in-law finally came to me and said he had looked at the photographs and [son] was among the dead. I ran to the door to run out... I fainted. The police did nothing to help, my husband went for the social worker and he and my son-in-law eventually found a doctor... After an hour or so I went to see [his] body. I could hardly recognise him, so I checked his teeth which I could identify... and while doing so I noticed his body was warm as if he had only just died. The time was 2.30 am... spending time with the people who had died, we weren't allowed that, we truly weren't allowed. (Bereaved mother)

On the Monday, we went to Sheffield because as I thought, I just wanted to go and hold him and touch him... I had my brother and sister-in-law each side of me and I went in, and we were in this sort of corridor, and I was saying how are we going to get him in here?... I didn't notice at first, but there was glass at the side... All I wanted to do was get hold of him and kiss him and just hold him... I followed the curtain up, and then all of a sudden he, it was just as if he was asleep, and I was saying to myself I'll wait and see, and when he moves, I'll tell them they've made a mistake, that he's breathing... I know it sounds funny but I was saying to myself he really looked after his teeth, and look at them, they're black. And he loved his teeth... and he was just kind of blue... But then I noticed that he'd been cut from here to here, and it was like stitched up, but really like ragged, and I didn't know then, I thought someone had stood on him, and I just started saying they've stood all over him... they had to take me out then. (Bereaved wife)

The impact of the disaster

The section above provided a brief account of the experiences of some people who were either bereaved by, or survived Hillsborough. The intention in so doing was to give some feel for the power and depth of the experiences, and to provide a base for, first, an examination of people's needs after disaster and, second, an evaluation of the effectiveness of the social service response to those needs.

As was described at the beginning of the chapter, there now exists a sizable and growing literature on the 'impact' of disasters. Much of this material developed as a result of investigations of what was then known as 'shell shock', and has later been applied to non-military situations such as natural and man-made disasters. The bulk of the literature is not British – the majority being American or Australian – but research interest in the UK has been steadily growing over the last decade and was, not surprisingly, given considerable further impetus by the scale and number of domestic disasters during the late 1980s.

The data presented below differ in some important respects from much of what is contained in the extant literature in the field of 'disasters'. First, and most important, there is no attempt below to *measure* the impact of the disaster on individuals by using one or more of the psychological tools or techniques that have been developed in recent years. Rather, this, and subsequent chapters, are based on respondents' own evaluation of their experiences, their circumstances and their 'health'. Whilst there is reference made to the existing literature, there is no attempt made to impose explanatory schemata developed externally and prior to the collection of the data. Although data are categorised and, indeed, there is some theorisation attempted of post-disaster impact and intervention, the major research approach adopted throughout this work has been largely *qualitative* in character and informed by the assumptions of 'grounded theory' (Glaser and Strauss 1967).

Second, the data reflect a somewhat different research focus than much of the existing literature. On the one hand the data are not focused upon the rather specific – though of course very important – area of 'psychological effects', but consider the rather broader impact upon family, social networks, employment and so on. So, similarly, the aim has not been to measure which clinical psychological interventions are most effective at reducing stress or combating emotional problems, but has on the other hand been to consider the range of ways that social work can respond to the variety of needs that may be present in the aftermath of large-scale tragedy. Consequently, what is presented below is data collected from depth-interviews with and questionnaires completed by people affected by Hillsborough. What follows therefore is an account, presented largely in people's own words, of the problems and the needs that may arise after disaster. For example, the following quote from a young female survivor of Hillsborough gives some idea of the range of things that may happen during the aftermath of such an event:

> On the Monday morning [17 April 1989] I should have been at work, but the press were coming round and *The Sun* were camped on the doorstep. In the end I had to go and hide in the pub... What had happened was that the police had released the names of the injured... After that time things went from bad to worse really. I weren't sleeping, I lost my job, I near enough had a breakdown. I lost weight, I wasn't eating. I couldn't, I still don't go into town on a Friday or Saturday, it's too crowded. I went through a phase when I didn't give a shit... After [losing my job] I just drifted for a while... got involved in a variety of

criminal activities... I went on self-destruct. Still now I can get very aggressive. I was drinking a lot more. Not drugs, though there was the opportunity... Pushed my friends away. I wanted everyone to hate me. I hated myself so I thought everyone else might as well... I got glandular fever, cold after cold after cold... I was still having nightmares...

Though such a catalogue of 'problems' might be far from typical, the individual features are absolutely typical of what may beset those affected by disasters.

Practical impact

For the bereaved in particular there are a set of practical issues or problems that have to be dealt with fairly early on after the disaster and, of course, at a time when personal resources for doing so are likely to be very low. As the survivor's experience described above suggests, there are a whole series of problems stemming from the public nature of the disaster and the practices adopted by the news media – especially the press. The names and addresses of many of the bereaved families very soon became public knowledge and finding reporters camped on the doorstep or attempting to gain interviews using less than honest means was common. The funerals, for example, were intensely public events, frequently with television cameras present together with the by that stage ever-present London press.[4] The following bereaved mother's account is not untypical:

> And the door bell went. And I think it was a woman press [sic]. 'I'm from the somewhere'. And I went, and I just shut the door. And my husband said 'Who was that?' I said 'Someone from the press'. He said 'I'll answer the next one'. But I never gave it a thought. I answered the door two seconds later and it were just like mobs of them. And I was really frightened cos they were banging on the door. There was cars everywhere, they started knocking on my neighbour's door. And I'm just, in the end we had to phone the police because they were looking through the windows and everything. And I was just absolutely terrified... [It went on for]... about three or four days. And then they went to the school and started on [our son's] friends in the school. And they were picking upon kids in the street. The police moved them and they started going down the lane here to people there. They had to get police protection by the school for the kids to get out... my brothers had to go out and say 'If you don't go we'll make you go...' My brothers were getting pretty violent cos it was just, you know I've seen it myself on television, but till you've experienced it it's just frightening. Cos you just can't even move, you know. There's things you have to go out for and you're just literally terrified cos they're all swarms and swarms everywhere'. (Bereaved mother)

In a recent study, Shearer (1991) found that survivors,[5] of traumatic events consistently reported the press to be the most intrusive and least controlled of all the media and confirmed, as appears to have been the case after Hillsborough, that the local press and some sections of the broadcast media are the only ones who come out at all well.

For some families there may be immediate financial difficulties after the disaster due, for example, to the loss of the main wage-earner, problems with returning to work or, more straightforwardly, with the expenses incurred as a result of funerals, travel, solicitors and so on. Financial problems may lead directly and quickly to housing problems. Housing difficulties also arose because of relationship problems and, on occasion, due to the death of the named tenant. Finally, in terms of practical problems, the emotional and psychological effects of the disaster meant that merely carrying on with the usual day-to-day activities of shopping, childcare and so on was more than some were able to manage. A disaster such as Hillsborough, which although it involved death does not involve large-scale loss of residential property, nevertheless brings with it a host of practical problems and difficulties at a time when those facing them may be poorly equipped to deal with them.

Emotional and psychological impact

For the survivors of the disaster one of the most immediate and consistent experiences was a feeling of being totally preoccupied with the events (see McFarlane 1988) and, particularly, with the post-disaster reporting of events:

> I had no thoughts for anything other than Hillsborough whatsoever. And any activity that I was trying to involve myself in was just swamped by images and thoughts about what had happened... I just couldn't take myself away from Hillsborough and I was only comfortable really, ironically if I was talking about Hillsborough, because if I tried talking about something else, Hillsborough wouldn't let me. (Male survivor)

> He'd set the video up to tape Hillsborough, you know, the match. And for some reason I never turned it off... And I can remember him coming home that night. He sat here, pulled the chair round and just sat like that and... the swearing out of him as he watched that. And I kept saying, 'turn it off, turn it off'. But he wouldn't turn it off. He just kept as if he was glued to that telly and he was rewinding it and watching it again... it was [as] if he wasn't here. (Wife of survivor)

> Just couldn't stop thinking about it. It was on my mind all the time. Couldn't go out. Well I could go out but not and enjoy myself like I used to. It was just on my mind, just couldn't get it off my mind. (Male survivor)

It wasn't just the power of the experience, the difficulty in making sense of what had happened that drew survivors and others to the press and television coverage of the disaster, there was another factor, already briefly alluded to, that has been an almost ever-present theme since Hillsborough: the role of the fans. Although Hillsborough is just one of many disasters that have occurred in recent years, its aftermath is in one very important respect different from all the others. It is the only disaster in which there has been an attempt to present the 'victims' as the 'culprits'. From early on in the evening of 15 April 1989, there was a sustained attempt in some quarters to blame the Liverpool fans for what had occurred. The fact that it was a 'football' disaster made it all the easier to invoke images of drunken hooligans and ticketless louts:

> You feel you've got no-one to turn to. In other disasters the authorities were with them [the 'victims'] from the beginning, but that wasn't the case with Hillsborough. (Male survivor)

> I had to like in a macabre sense, I had to read what they were saying, because I thought they were talking about me. You're telling lies about me, but it used to agitate me, and the more I watched, the more upset I used to get. (Female survivor)

Although the preoccupation with the disaster diminished over time, it does not appear to be something that disappears. Many survivors continued to be 'drawn' to any newspaper, television or radio reports of Hillsborough several years after the event. Most expressed this as something that they felt they could not control:

> It still now comes back if anything comes up about Hillsborough. If I read anything about Hillsborough. If I see photographs, it still has that effect on me. I still cry and it's not something that I want to do. It's something that I'll just sit and I'll just read that, and you just can't stop yourself. (Male survivor)

One of the most common ways in which this preoccupation found expression, and one which was encouraged by social workers (and practised by them as well) and others as a positive way of getting control, was the collecting of reports and videos, and the making of scrapbooks:

> I didn't feel much like doing anything at all, going out or anything. I just wanted to collect all the information I could about it... I actually went over to the newsagents, bought all the papers I could which had pictures in, which I've still got. I made a video of the event and everything. (Male survivor)

Being preoccupied by the disaster meant, of course, that there was little time for or interest in other activities. As one of the survivors quoted above said, even 'if I tried talking about something else Hillsborough wouldn't let me'. This had a particular impact upon the families and friends of those who had returned from the match, for they felt excluded, ignored and alienated:

...he wasn't being rational, he did things mechanically. He got un-
dressed mechanically, sat down mechanically. He didn't respond to
people around him, even the children. Even [daughter] she said.. I love
you Dad and gave him a kiss. She loves you madly doesn't she? There
was nothing back, if she said Hello, how are you? It was just blank, so
he wasn't in a state of mind to do anything that a normal person could.
(Wife of survivor)

Bad I was, but... didn't associate with anybody, I just stayed in me room,
done that for about six weeks... didn't want to know nothing. (Male
survivor)

He wouldn't talk, he wouldn't, he just wanted to sit around. He
wouldn't do nothing, he wouldn't go anywhere and he wouldn't sleep
of a night. (Male survivor)

Many of the survivors felt emotionally paralysed by their experiences
and found that they were unable to do much other than cry:

...I was just crying me eyes out and everything like that. The more I
was talking to me friend, the more – just absolutely sobbing, you know.
I just didn't wanna do anything, you know, for a month whatsoever!
(Male survivor)

He just wasn't himself at all, he was very depressed, he wasn't sleeping,
he wasn't eating. he was crying and all that wasn't he? (Male survivor)

Sleep disturbance is one of the classic reactions associated with the
aftermath of a traumatic event and, not only in the short term, was
evident amongst many of the Hillsborough survivors:

I've ended up going out in the middle of the night, out walking. I was
up half the night, going to bed at five in the morning because I couldn't
sleep, and I was terrified to sleep, because I was having nightmares.
(Female survivor)

He wouldn't sleep of a night, he'd be in bed and then he'd jump up
and then he'd come back down here and then he'd come back up.
Cos I was that scared to go to bed sometimes... some nights I like wake
up in a cold sweat or find it hard to breathe.
He didn't use to be able to have covers on him in bed, quilt, says he
couldn't breathe.
Worried about getting tangled up in the quilt and when I wake up...
Panic and jump up and pull it off him. (Male survivor and girlfriend)

I was waking up screaming 'bully a policeman, be a murderer, go on
be a murderer'. It was really frightening... because the feeling was so
bitter, it was so awful. (Female survivor)

The last quote above makes reference to what was one of the strongest
emotions amongst both the bereaved and the survivors after the disaster: anger. There was, and for many there remains a burning sense of
anger and injustice. Anger is, of course, closely associated with grief

(Murray Parkes 1975) and was very clearly evident amongst those who were bereaved:

> I couldn't understand what was going on inside me, all these feelings and I would just explode for no reason at all... I hated everyone. I hated the woman across the road for having a husband, and if the woman next door had been laughing, I'd be saying 'it's OK for her to laugh, she's got a husband. (Bereaved wife)

> I mean I was just lashing out at everybody, anybody that talked to me, I was just picking things up and hitting them with them. You know, this was like in a pub if I had a bottle near me, I'd throw it at them. (Bereaved wife)

In addition, however, the survivors also remembered very strong feelings of anger and, on occasion, this was translated directly into a variety of aggressive behaviours:

> I've had two or three fights over it.. that's been with me mates and that, they just trying to tell me things like and they haven't got a clue what happened. (Male survivor)

> I was getting in to fights in pubs and all sorts... I mean at my age. (Male survivor – late twenties)

> I think if our Lord had walked through that door he would have argued with him. He wanted to fight everybody didn't you? (Female survivor describing her partner, also a survivor)

A sense of helplessness, a lack of motivation or confidence and an inability to concentrate were some of the other major and more immediate *sequelae* affecting both the bereaved and the survivors of Hillsborough:

> But everything goes a lot deeper now. And you know I'll phone places up and say, you know this is disgusting! And I'll write letters and I'm a lot, I'm very irrational you know, I'm always nervy and crying all the time. (Bereaved sister)

> I've lost confidence in myself in all aspects of my life. Even my wife says 'you haven't got the same, you know, sort of bounce about you'. And even people, my friends in my social life and that. It's like a spark, you know the spark's gone. (Male survivor)

> I was having memory lapses. I mean to be honest with you, you can go away from here now and I'll forget some of the things I've spoken to you about. (Male survivor)

The other emotion that survivors had in common was guilt. Indeed, 'survival guilt' is a well-documented part of the post-disaster experience for those who do not die but who have confronted the possibility of their own death and who have been in close proximity to people who did die (Lifton 1967). Hodgkinson and Stewart (1991) divide the guilt that may arise from such an experience into two main types. The first is 'existential guilt', which is a general questioning of why they survived and others died:

> It was guilt that I felt… Because it should be you and not someone else. Because you're so close to it and that you're thinking you should be with them, but you're not, you are not, you are still alive. (Male survivor)

The second was not given a name by the authors but is what might be termed 'role guilt'. Here, survivors question whether or not they did enough to help others or whether they did the most appropriate things. Survivors may question whether or not the actions they took (or the absence of particular actions) in an attempt to save their own lives, had a consequence for the loss of other lives. After Hillsborough, role guilt concerned both the actions of the survivor *during* the disaster (i.e. on the terraces themselves) and also in the immediate aftermath:

> I was starting to feel a bit guilty… how come we'd walked out and the other lads hadn't. In particular [a friend] had been standing in front of me, so it was me like who was directly crushing him and I felt like it was my fault and if I'd moved back then maybe he could have had a bit more breath. (Male survivor)

> I always felt guilty that I could never do enough and had I had the right equipment I could have done more. I know I could and there would have been more lives saved… I always felt guilty about that. (Female survivor)

> I'm qualified in first aid, and I was looking at people trying to carry out the resuscitation and that, and obviously they weren't sure what they were doing, and I wanted to get back down… find a way to get on to the pitch… I had thought long on that if I could've got down there… more lives might have been saved. (Male survivor)

Finally, there were a few survivors who articulated a slightly different form of guilt. This was not directly linked to survival itself or to their role during the disaster, but rather to the quality of their life after the disaster. In particular, it was difficult for some survivors to feel that it was reasonable for them to enjoy their lives when there were others who were either worse off (they felt) than they were – those who were bereaved for example – and others who had themselves lost their lives:

> I was feeling a bit guilty about getting better, sometimes I feel guilty about having a good time. (Male survivor)

On behaviour

There are those who feel at some stage after the disaster that they are increasingly unable to cope with their lives. Simply getting through the night or through the next day feels too great a task to deal with and, occasionally, retreat was the answer:

> There were times when I said I just can't cope... I couldn't explain why. I just can't cope... Somebody'll have to come and sit by me, because I just can't manage. (Female survivor)

> I had that many things to do that I just put my head in my hands and got into bed and put the bedclothes over me, because I felt as though I couldn't cope. (Bereaved wife)

Getting through the worst days was sometimes achieved through the use of drink or occasionally tranquillisers. Both men and women reported increased alcohol use, particularly early on after Hillsborough:

> I mean one of the worst things that you do, every one of us has done it because we've all said it, is you drink yourselves to oblivion for a while. (Female survivor)

> I just felt I wanted to get back and blot it out, if you like. But without realising it, I started drinking of a weekend. I went into a bit of a shell. (Male survivor)

> I was going in the pub at 12 o'clock staying there till 3 and coming home, sitting here, going at 7 o'clock drinking right through and I wasn't drunk. (Male survivor)

Feeling unable to 'cope' was sometimes perceived as a form of madness, or a precursor to breakdown:

> I'll be honest with you, at this present time (approximately two years after Hillsborough) I've got to go and see my own doctor again. Monday morning... I've felt I've been close to nervous breakdown. (Male survivor)

> ...days where the baby's in the pram, and I walk 10 miles out of the way. Didn't know how I got there. Just like, I felt like I was going mad. I really felt like I was going mad, or like an alcoholic stupor. (Female survivor)

> I bought me own car and I just went wild in the car, I slammed – just going mad in the car... and knew that I was daft doing it but its just something like, just snapped like and went wild. (Male survivor)

For others the problems that faced them, or the thoughts that beset them seemed either so intractable or so immovable that they contemplated their own death as a means of ending their suffering:

> On Monday I tried to hang myself from the loft. I had a rope up there when I tried to kill myself. I felt it's harder for me now because I've thought about it a lot and like something was telling me to do away with myself would save all the problems... I was sitting up in the loft with a rope round my neck and that was what I was thinking. (Male survivor)

I got to the point where I really felt like committing suicide and the baby was the only thing that actually stopped me from doing it. (Female survivor)

He tried to commit suicide when we went on holiday... It was on Father's Day and he couldn't get out of his mind, you know, about the kids who hadn't got any dads and the dads who hadn't got any sons, you know. And he tried to throw himself over the balcony when I was putting the kids in bed. (Wife of survivor)

I was on the verge of taking these tablets... and I went 'that's a mortal sin', I'll go to hell and our [son] will be in heaven and I'll never see him. (Bereaved mother)

A few 'victims' experienced such severe somatic effects that they felt physically unable to go out. Although such strong phobic reactions appear to have been relatively uncommon, there was considerable evidence of general avoidance of activities or situations that might prompt recollections of the traumatic situation. Such avoidance is found frequently amongst disaster victims and is one of the symptoms associated with PTSD[6] (Horowitz *et al.* 1980). In the case of Hillsborough, the places or situations to avoid were those where there was the potential for large crowds, confined spaces and crushing:

The last couple of months and that, I have been going out a lot more... if there's a lot of people there, like these, all me mates they go to clubs and that, we'll I'll go to the pub, I won't go to clubs... I just get paranoid. (Male survivor)

I still don't go into town on a Friday or Saturday, it's too crowded. (Female survivor)

The impact upon relationships

It is perhaps not surprising given the catalogue of practical, psychological and emotional problems facing those affected by disaster that considerable strain is often placed upon relationships. Family and personal relationships in particular frequently came under stress after the disaster. There were many that were quite radically changed and some that simply didn't survive. For the bereaved in particular this represented a 'double loss'.

A number of research studies have considered the impact of disaster upon family interactions and family functioning (*inter alia* Drabek *et al.* 1975, Erickson *et al.* 1976) and have identified both positive and negative consequences. For example, both in the immediate post-disaster and longer-term phases research has highlighted how family units turn to one another and to other kin for support and succour, and that closer relationships may develop as a result (Bolin 1982). Others, however, have shown how family functioning may become impaired in the aftermath of a major tragedy (Titchener *et al.* 1976), may have long-term negative consequences for children (Raphael 1986) and may, of course, disintegrate altogether.

There were positives and negatives evident after Hillsborough, though the positive aspects tended to be found rather more in the short than in the longer-term, whereas there seemed to be no time-limit on when the negatives might be reported. Negative or problematic consequences were reported both between partners and between parents and children. Relationships between parents and children were affected in four main ways. First, some parents felt that they were less tolerant of their children after the disaster. There was an increased tendency for parents to withdraw and to appear less interested in their children:

> After Hillsborough we lived on a knife edge. The kids couldn't look at him, he'd eat them, have no time for me, no time for the kids, just bad tempered. (Wife of survivor)

> And the holiday was – the holiday was OK – weather was nice, but he's, he's usually, he's a good dad, he plays with the kids – he just never had no time for the kids. Didn't wanna do anything. Everything was a chore to him, you know, there was no enjoyment anymore... All that stopped. (Wife of survivor)

Secondly, having suffered a loss or having survived the disaster but been brought close to the idea of loss through the experience, some parents became increasingly concerned about the welfare of their (remaining) children. This overprotectiveness put pressure on the relationships:

> I still tend to panic, you know, if he [son], if he says he's goin' out and he's not in by a certain time... all his friends went to Butlins on their own last year and I wouldn't let him go. (Bereaved mother)

> He became so possessive with the kids, you couldn't let them move. You know, where are you going, what time are you coming in, who are going to be with and they rebel against it teenagers. They don't like it you know. It definitely tears the family apart. (Bereaved step-mother)

Alternatively, there was the reverse fear that confrontation with the children would actually drive them away – and again that further loss would be stimulated:

> He's gone so completely off me, at the moment, I'm frightened to death of doing anything that will cross him... it was too big a gamble, that I could lose him completely. (Bereaved mother)

Third, there was some evidence of 'numbing' (Raphael 1983) amongst both the bereaved and survivors. This is an essentially defensive reaction common amongst 'victims' of traumatic events, particularly in the immediate aftermath of the event, which may distance them from the reality of what they have experienced. In terms of family relationships, it may have the effect of making the person concerned seem very withdrawn or distant. The potential consequences for families and relationships were devastating, with parents, at least temporarily apparently ceasing to care for or love their children:

> I thought those poor kids, you know... they've lost their dad and for a while they lost their mum. (Bereaved wife)

Finally, one element of the guilt experienced by survivors and referred to above concerned the difficulty of returning to the enjoyment of everyday activities after the disaster. As one woman said of her husband who had been at Hillsborough and had since become so depressed that he had attempted suicide 'he couldn't get out of his mind, you know, about the kids who hadn't got any dads, and the dads who hadn't got any sons'. The difficulties that some parents had in coming to terms with the fact that their children were still alive, reduced their ability to maintain positive relationships with these children. It was summed up in a feeling of 'what right do I have to be happy when so many others are suffering?'.

Relationships between partners also suffered, and often in similar ways to the parent-child relationships described above. For the partners of survivors the central problem most frequently for them was that the person they were living with after Hillsborough was not the person they felt they had been living with prior to the disaster:

> Our whole way of life changed completely. He went there as [his name] but he come back – I didn't know him, and that was very hard to live with. (Wife of survivor)

Such difficulties were often compounded by difficulties in communication between partners, particularly over the subject that was dominating their lives: Hillsborough. One of the very widely reported consequences of the power of such traumatic events (Raphael 1986, Hodgkinson and Stewart 1991) is that those who survive are left feeling that the only people that will be able to understand how they are feeling are those who have been through the same experience or something similar, i.e. other survivors. This, of course, creates a problem that carers such as social workers have to overcome, and this specific problem is returned to in the following two chapters.

Family and other close relationships may suffer because the survivor is either unable or unwilling to confide in their partner or other loved ones. Partners may therefore be faced not only with people who have 'changed and who they feel they 'no longer know', but they may be denied access to that person's feelings and with it the most likely means of reconciling themselves to the changes that have taken place. Furthermore, the inability of the survivor to talk to their partner about how they are feeling often goes hand in hand with a very strong urge to spend as much time as possible talking to other survivors – or occasionally uninvolved friends or acquaintances – and, perhaps not surprisingly, leads to resentment and misunderstanding:

> But you talked a lot to that girl at work hadn't you, who'd become a friend. And that made me – I hated her didn't I?… Cos he talked to her… he worked in an office with her. He talked a lot to her because she is a great girl isn't she – she will listen. And that annoyed me. (Wife of survivor)

The consequences may in fact be even more serious for the relationship, and several partners felt at times that there was simply no future for their marriage:

> It's very hard living with someone you know something's wrong and they won't talk, 'cos we – we're very open with one another. If you've anything on your mind, talk about it, get it out into the open, but it was very hard to live with that. I don't know how many times I told him to get out and leave us alone, you know, we'd be better off without him. (Wife of survivor)

In such cases the families often appeared to have 'survived', but the effects on the relationships were still visible and partners, despite remaining in the family home, lived more or less separate lives:

> Our sex life went out of the window. He wasn't interested in that anymore. (Wife of survivor)

Other relationships broke down seemingly irretrievably, and it was, on occasion, the survivor who made the decision to leave:

> I come down here and he wasn't here. There was a note in the kitchen to say that he'd left, he can't stand what he's doing to me and the kids, he was making our life a misery. We'd be better off without him and to let the mortgage company know and all this. There was no argument or nothing. (Wife of survivor)

> You know my husband was going to leave us, he was going to sell the house, what he was going to do was awful. We've always been so close, that was the sad part. (Bereaved step-mother)

In this way 'loss' was kept very firmly at the centre of concerns for families affected by the disaster. One of the very important lessons here for those who have to respond to disasters concerns the breadth of the impact of disaster and, consequently, who needs to be offered help. In particular, it reinforces the message that there may be significant negative consequences not only for those who were bereaved and those who survive, but also for the families of those who *survived* (adults and children). Close relationships may well be a source of support and succour after a disaster, but this cannot be relied upon. As a bereaved step-mother commented:

> I used to think when something traumatic like that happens... big families would stay together, but it doesn't, it tears them apart. It just literally tears them apart.

In addition to immediate family relationships, there are a variety of other areas of life that can change or suffer quite radically after disaster. First, there is the impact upon the networks of friends, neighbours, colleagues and acquaintances who may previously have been relied upon for a variety of types of more or less formal support. There were a number of cases in this study in which there was a very significant impact upon lifestyle. In the main this was visible through work, through life in the community or neighbourhood and in people's social lives.

It is generally held that we live in a culture in which death is a taboo subject, something that we have difficulty confronting and certainly that we have difficulty in talking about. There is a considerable literature on bereavement, much of which asserts that the bereaved in our society are poorly looked after, and that with the decline of local communities public mourning has all but disappeared (Gorer 1965, Aries 1981). Some of the mourning rituals evident particularly on Merseyside after Hillsborough have already been touched upon and Walter (1991) has used these to challenge some of these conventional wisdoms about death. His conclusion was that 'recent evidence from gays in London and from parents who have lost babies suggests that it is not just sentimental Liverpudlians who can, even in the late twentieth century, re-take mourning from the hands of pundits and professionals, and demonstrate that death need not be, and in some circles never has been, a subject that is taboo.'

Whilst not wishing to challenge either his view about mourning rituals or, indeed, the generally optimistic tone of his argument, the interviews with bereaved families and with survivors as part of this research suggest that there remain, at the very least, significant pockets of resistance to taboo-free attitudes towards death. The evidence for this lies in people's accounts of how they felt they were treated by neighbours and friends in the aftermath of the disaster. As with the impact on family relationships, both positive and negative consequences on social networks were identifiable. On the positive side, there were a large number of examples of support, of kindness and of sympathy, particularly in the weeks after Hillsborough when the disaster was still very fresh in everybody's minds:

> You know, to say it was a really beautiful funeral, it really was... my husband knows a lot of people who sing and they sang 'You'll Never Walk Alone' for him... It does help tremendously, you know people

themselves have been marvellous... But you just seem to open your door and people were there, they were tremendous. Neighbours and that. Really great. That helped... and having a couple of close friends of my own was really good for me because I needed them. You know, you have to talk to people you know, that you know is not going to go any further. (Bereaved step-mother)

However, this was far from being the experience that everybody had. Many of the bereaved and the survivors felt that people started to behave differently toward them after the disaster. The reasons for this varied, they felt, though one common theme appeared to be the difficulty of comprehending what had actually happened. This is particularly problematic for survivors for there is no common understanding of what 'survival' means:

People they just changed to me, people walked across the street, they just didn't want to speak to you... They're frightened to speak to you and you just feel like screaming at that... You can't handle all the looks and the questions, and you know people treat me as if I've done something wrong... even friends next door, they've moved now, but they treated us funny and you know they would see us come and they would go in... You wouldn't think they'd been friends... they didn't know how to handle it basically... They would just put their heads down and walk on... it was different. I think if it had been through natural causes they had died, I think people see them differently as it was a tragedy, it wasn't just affecting me, it was the way it affected everyone around us, the neighbours. (Male survivor)

My friends who hadn't been there had all like, it was virtually history for them... they couldn't understand why I was so down, why I was just not really part of them anymore, I was like an outsider. (Male survivor)

The bereaved on the other hand had to confront the difficulties that those around them had in talking to and knowing how to behave with people whose relatives had died in a football disaster:

I'd say 'well I lost him' and then they'd say 'how?' and I'd explain it, but like they'd all panic, you know really panic... So it was worse than that... for the first few months you know, they wouldn't mention [son's] name at all... some of my nieces wouldn't bring the children in case I got upset... so you were frightened to say anything 'cos you could see the panic in people's faces. (Bereaved mother)

Lonely, shut out, I think basically, shut out. Yes, shut out in the respect that if you'd walked down the street you'd hear you know, 'shshshsh'. And I'd snap and I'd say 'talk to my face, don't talk behind my back'. (Bereaved common-law wife)

Although there were indeed many very moving public rituals where some of the grief engendered by the disaster was expressed, and a widespread and very genuine sense of shock and sympathy throughout Merseyside, on an individual level many of those families affected by Hillsborough found that friends and neighbours had difficulty in understanding or empathising with their experiences. There were even instances when there was explicit 'community' disapproval if the family or the individual was perceived to be behaving in an inappropriate manner. In one case, a young woman whose common-law husband had died at Hillsborough found a new boyfriend. After he moved in with her he was attacked on several occasions by friends of the deceased and eventually she felt she was forced to move to a new home:

> I just had to get out. I had to get off that estate, had to. Because it was breaking me and him up anyway... he couldn't come... onto the estate without getting trouble... they just didn't want me to be happy.

The development of difficulties with social relationships was by no means a one-way process. The psychological and emotional impact of the disaster had an impact on the ability of some who were affected to relate to others, and the most common reaction was to withdraw, temporarily, from such contact. The length of time that this was maintained varied considerably as did the extent of the withdrawal. For some it was very short-lived, but others had not picked up their social contacts some two years later. In addition, a certain strain was sometimes placed on relationships by the behaviour of those affected by the disaster. At first, for both survivors and the bereaved, there was the difficulty of appearing (and quite possibly actually being) obsessed by their experiences and being consumed by a desire to talk about it, or about specific elements of it such as the role of the police. Others, as was suggested earlier, found that their difficulties in communicating with their friends – especially if the friends had not been at the match – led to anti-social or to violent behaviour:

> I used to be classed as a happy drunk and now I felt embarrassed because I got my friends into trouble a few times... got banned from a club smashing windows... I stopped going out, I didn't see my friends any more and a little while after that when I made an occasion to go out with them, I got into trouble and got them into trouble and I felt bad about that. (Male survivor)

The impact on work

One of the areas in which there were noticeable short- and long-term consequences as a result of the disaster was work. All the bereaved that were interviewed had taken compassionate leave of varying lengths in the immediate aftermath. Of the survivors, those who had physical injuries were obviously unable to return to work immediately, but many of those who had not required or sought hospital treatment were also away from work for some period. On the other hand, some survivors felt it necessary to return to work in order to occupy their minds or because they could see no reason for having time off work. For some, the consequence of this was relatively lengthy periods of absence at a later stage where they found that they were no longer able to cope.

> On the Monday I was still stunned, so... I said, 'No, I'll have a couple of nights off 'till I feel OK'... I just went upstairs, got meself ready, got me bag packed and went to work...just to escape... I should've had them couple of weeks off, cos 12 months later I had to take time off.

The full range of personal consequences of Hillsborough – the emotional and psychological, practical, physical and somatic – all had an effect on people's abilities to continue in their jobs. One young woman, for example, who had been a nurse prior to Hillsborough and had been one of the many fans who had been actively involved in offering first aid at the match, found that she was unable to return to work at all:

> I've never been able to go into a hospital. Just couldn't bear it. The thought of it makes me physically sick, going anywhere near it. (Female survivor)

Although there were few others who found that the disaster and their work were too closely connected in their minds, there were a number of indirect links between Hillsborough and an inability to continue at work. The first was the extent to which people's psychological health interfered with their ability to do their jobs. The breakup of eating and sleeping patterns had a tendency to undermine daily routines:

> I'd arrange to meet someone at 10 o'clock, just couldn't do it, I was what you call it, I was being awake all night...just some mornings I tried to get myself into a routine but I just couldn't keep to it. (Male survivor)

Those who managed to get to work frequently found that their ability to concentrate on the task in hand was so significantly diminished that they felt unable to carry on with their jobs:

> It's as if like I can't do the job properly, I don't know if it's just playing on my mind or I'm a bit paranoid, but with joinery I can't do it. No more. (Male survivor)

In addition, there was the question of how to cope with the large number of practical and time-consuming matters that occur after a disaster. One woman who lost her husband was forced to give up work because she had to stay and care for her children who required a lot of time off school afterwards. Whilst employers were generally sympathetic to the need for compassionate leave in the immediate aftermath of the disaster, memories were short, and requests for leave at later dates did not necessarily receive a similar response:

I've had to ask for time off to attend the inquests. I did write a letter first explaining about me needing time off and the last time I phoned up... they said 'Oh is this still going on, when is it likely to end?' That hurts. (Bereaved mother)

But they were very good at the beginning, but I mean after a while [they said] 'not that again'. You know, because I had a couple of days off, and I had a day off when the police came. (Bereaved father)

This assumption that because a certain amount of time has passed 'Hillsborough must be over' was something that many of the bereaved, survivors and others affected by the disaster came up against time and time again. Despite the widespread sensitivity over Hillsborough, particularly within the Liverpool community, there were still those who remained stubbornly resistant to the requirement for such sympathy – especially where survivors were concerned. One described how the attitudes of his work colleagues prompted him to leave his job for good:

I heard a few jokes, stupid jokes, even when I went back to work someone said to me 'it should have been 96', the bloke I work with, which made me feel really bad and a little while afterwards I actually broke down in work... I felt really stupid when I started crying. I didn't want any of the blokes to see me, the boss saw me, I felt stupid when I went back in because everyone was looking at me, no-one said any more jokes. (Male survivor)

With Hillsborough occurring in April, one of the most significant groups affected were pupils and students who had to sit exams within a matter of weeks of the disaster. Some school headteachers were reported by social workers to have been unsympathetic to the idea of getting support for their pupils who had been at the match because 'they should be concentrating on their exams'. The story is far from completely negative for there were many success stories of students successfully completing exams despite the difficulties they experienced. Furthermore such problems were by no means confined to the year in which the disaster occurred. There is an important lesson here which bears continued repetition: disasters are not simply isolated or one-off events which recede into the background as the years pass. The disaster is followed by a series of events – official inquiries, anniversaries, inquests – which are not only a vivid reminder of the tragedy but which, because of their nature, may be a form of secondary victimisation (Shapland *et al.* 1985). Hillsborough – like, no doubt, Lockerbie, Kings Cross and others – is an ongoing tragedy.

The following case study of a 40-year-old male survivor, married with two children, sums up many of the problems with work that occur in the aftermath of disaster. Interviewed approximately two years after Hillsborough, he reported that he had worked for the first 16 months after the disaster, but toward the end of that period the introduction of a new element in the work had led to a significant increase in the level of stress he was feeling:

> where I'd been able to bluff it through, I just couldn't bluff it any more... trying to hide away from responsibilities. [I had] reached a block where I couldn't go any further.

In August 1990 he was sent home from work and told to see his GP.

> The very next morning I had a person round from work here asking what was wrong with me and why I wasn't in... they were hounding me for weeks.

He had some counselling at this point but felt that his employers were far from sympathetic:

> I was in a very distressed state at the time because work were really hounding me and threatening to fire me.

He had seven weeks off work and was very anxious about returning, partly because he was worried about what his colleagues would be thinking, but also because he was not confident about being able to do the job. He spoke to his employers about this but found them still to be largely unsympathetic, with any jobs offered to him involving a significant drop in income:

> I realised I couldn't manage on that, I felt that would have give me bigger problems if I'd to sell the house and put my wife and kids through something else.

Consequently he returned to his old job, but felt increasingly depressed about it:

> I really am struggling, I'm under pressure, going to work is tying a knot in my stomach. I'm not doing my job and I try and tell them and it's frustrating that I'm not getting through... And to be honest with you, at this present time, I've got to go and see my own doctor again, Monday morning. I don't know whether I'll go back to work. I've gone in this week and, I'll be honest with you, I've felt I've been close to a nervous breakdown. Only for my family, it's only for what I've put them through that I'm going in, 'cause for me, I would never go back there again.

Conclusion

The central aims of this chapter have been threefold. The first aim was to look at the question of who is affected by disasters. As disaster is generally held to involve loss of life there are obviously bereaved families and other relatives who are centrally caught up in the consequences of such tragedies. In addition, there are also those who are involved in the disaster, whose life is threatened and yet who survive.

'Survivors', as the term is used here, is also taken to include those present at the disaster – with the exclusion of the emergency services – but whose lives were not at risk, i.e. 'witnesses'. In addition, the consequences of disaster for survivors are potentially so traumatic that their relatives may also be taken to be 'at risk'. Some of the most intractable problems face those whose relatives are severely injured as a result of disaster. Although such cases were relatively few in number after Hillsborough, the long-term consequences for these families, as was suggested above, were extremely profound. Finally, although their experiences have not been reported in this chapter, we know that those who are tasked with trying to provide care for any or all of the above groups are themselves likely to be, to a greater or lesser extent, affected by their indirect or vicarious contact with the disaster. They too may have needs that have to be met, and this question is considered in Chapters 5 and 6.

The second aim was to attempt to convey, using the words of those caught up in the event, what the disaster actually consisted of. There were a number of reasons for doing this. First, it helps to put into context the impact that Hillsborough had and continues to have upon people's lives. It brings out into the open what lies behind the term 'disaster'. Second, it helps make sense of the breadth of the impact of disaster. Although, for anyone who has not been through such an experience, it is impossible to imagine the full horror of losing a loved one suddenly and unexpectedly in a disaster, one can nevertheless empathise to some extent with such a bereavement. Death, after all, is ubiquitous. Survival, on the other hand, is in some senses an altogether more difficult concept to grasp. Those who come back from disaster are often greeted by something akin to a 'you were lucky' attitude by friends, colleagues etc. As this chapter has attempted to show, the consequences of disaster for those who survive them mean that many such people are far from 'lucky'. Indeed, as was suggested above, some are so badly affected and so far from being pleased that they survived that they feel that their lives are simply no longer worth living. In discussing the impact of disaster then, the aim of this chapter has been to put survival as much at the forefront as bereavement.

The third aim was to look in some detail at the actual impact of disaster. What are the consequences for those who are bereaved, those who survive and those who are otherwise affected by such an event? In addition to the practical consequences, three major areas of impact were identified. The first was the emotional and behavioural effects which included anger, depression, irritability, aggression, changes in eating and sleeping patterns as well as an increased propensity to become involved in accidents or to suffer from ill-health. There are also the 'cognitive effects' (Shepherd and Hodgkinson 1990) which include problems with concentration as well as 'flashbacks' and nightmares. Second, there is the impact of disaster on relationships and, in particular, the impact on 'family' relationships, i.e. those between partners or between parents and children. Finally, there was also evidence of a considerable impact on work relationships.

- The disaster had an impact on people's lives in five main ways: practically, emotionally, on behaviour, on relationships and on work. It is the emotional consequences of disaster that are most usually discussed but, given the catalogue of practical, psychological and emotional problems facing those affected by disaster, it is perhaps not surprising that considerable strain is often placed upon relationships. Family and personal relationships in particular frequently came under stress after Hillsborough. There were many that were quite radically changed and some that simply didn't survive. For the bereaved in particular this represented a 'double loss'. Negative or problematic consequences were reported both between partners and between parents and children.

- Relatives and partners often need as much support as those directly involved for two reasons. First, just as 'professional carers' require supervision and support, so too do non-professionals and, second, because they are 'victims' in their own right.

- Engaging in practical support early on is of crucial significance, not only because it can be of significant value to families and survivors at particularly difficult times, but also because it may enable the worker to establish some credibility and trust.

- Many of those affected by the disaster found that their working lives were disrupted. Whilst employers were generally sympathetic to the need for compassionate leave in the immediate aftermath of the disaster, memories were short, and requests for leave at later dates did not necessarily receive a similar response. There is an important lesson here which runs throughout the study and which cannot be repeated too often: disasters are not simply isolated or one-off events which recede into the background as the years pass. Disasters are followed by a series of events – official inquiries, inquests and so on – which are not only a vivid reminder of the tragedy but which, because they are not geared to the 'needs' of those affected by disasters, may exacerbate rather than mitigate suffering. Hillsborough – like other disasters – is an ongoing tragedy for many of its 'victims'.

- Special provision (including training) needs to be made to enable social workers to provide support for families through the difficult and often extensive legal processes following disaster.

- Intervention at the point of crisis may avert the longer-term consequences of broken relationships, and reduce the chances that those who are vulnerable will get into negative work and behaviour patterns.

Notes

1. Tumelty (1990, p.23) noted that 'Piper Alpha, like most oil rigs, worked a two week on, two week off shift system. This known as a 'back to back' operation with each man on the rig having an opposite number on shore. Some of these men suffered quite traumatic reactions, as they came to appreciate the arbitrariness which seemed to decide that they should be safe, when in some cases they had been at work only hours before the platform disintegrated, killing the men who had replaced them'.

2. So important and so resistent to definition is the term 'disaster' that many of those involved in the study of such events or in responding to such events have themselves attempted to a classification of disasters. The recently published report of the CRUSE/Department of Health Disasters Working Party uses the term 'major incident' as defined by the Association of Chief Police Officers:

   A major incident is any emergency that requires the implementation of special arrangements by one or all of the emergency services for:
   a) The rescue and transport of a large number casualties.
   b) The involvement either directly or indirectly of large numbers of people.
   c) The handling of a large number of enquiries likely to be generated both from the public and the news media usually to the police.
   d) Any incident that requires the large-scale combined resources of the three emergency services.
   e) The mobilisation and organisation of the emergency services and supporting organisations, such as the local authority, to cater for the threat of death, serious injury or homelessness to a large number of people.

3. As has already been stated, one of the deaths occurred later in the week following Hillsborough. Although the vast majority of those who lost their lives would have appeared to have died on the terrace itself, this was not the case for all 94 of the victims of Hillsborough who died on the Saturday afternoon.

4. Newspaper reporters, photographers and editors do not come out of the Hillsborough episode at all well. Only the local press (*Liverpool Echo* and *Daily Post*) appear to have behaved well throughout, going as far as to

keep their photographers away from the funerals so that the national press could not claim they were local.

5. Within this definition of 'survivor' she includes those who have been bereaved as a result of a traumatic event such as a criminal act or a major disaster, as well as those who were present at the event and 'survived'.

6. The most commonly discussed aspects of post-disaster 'functioning' are the psychological and emotional *sequelae* of such events. Before proceeding, however, it is important to mention two points about the state of current knowledge. First, despite the existence of a significant body of work on the subject of the consequences of disaster, there is still considerable disagreement about the extent of and particularly the persistence of reactions to such events. Second, the notion of 'Post Traumatic Stress Disorder' (PTSD) (DSM III 1980), which has developed a very widespread currency in recent years, is often used glibly and inaccurately, especially by the media, but also by professionals, and consequently often obscures more than it illuminates.

Without going into too much detail it is worth providing a brief explanation of the notion of, and the boundaries of PTSD. The disorder, which may not appear until several months after the traumatic 'event', is defined by a number of criteria which include: the existence of a recognisable stressor; re-experiencing of the trauma; diminished interest or involvement with the external world, together with a number of other symptoms of 'increased arousal', including sleep disturbance, irritability, anger, difficulties with concentration and so on (APA 1987). The crucial point about PTSD is that it is a construct which aims to help distinguish between *normal* and *abnormal* reactions to stress. It is important therefore – and this is where confusion most often arises – that the 'disorder' (PTSD) is distinguished from post-traumatic stress *reactions*. There are a variety of reactions which are normal responses to stressful situations or experiences and which 'like the wound's response to injury or the grief response to loss, [may be] essentially adaptive and healing' (Raphael 1986 p.80). It is only when they become entrenched and particularly severe or long-lasting that the reaction(s) may become defined as a 'disorder'. To repeat, the existence of post-trauma stress reactions is neither necessarily indicative of the presence of a psychiatric disorder, nor should it be interpreted necessarily as 'abnormal'. The reverse of this, of course, is that even though such reactions are 'normal responses to abnormal events' it may still be possible that there is something abnormal present which requires 'treatment'.

CHAPTER 5

Help, Support and Recovery

As more is discovered about the effects of the losses that disaster brings, so increasingly the caring organisations, agencies and individuals in our society have sought to provide help, comfort and support for those in need. Social services, because of their resources and their pivotal position in local communities, have been crucial to such responses. This chapter focuses upon the sources of help available after disaster. It looks at the question of who people turn to for help in such circumstances, what help they need and in what form help is acceptable. Crucially, given the overall focus of this book, what is the role of social workers in the aftermath of disaster? Can they and do they help?

In an otherwise rather eccentric review of the literature on disaster theory, Richard Brook (1990) quite rightly commented that the development of social work practice in relation to work after disasters has been haphazard and too dependent upon a sharing of experience rather than an evaluation of method. He quotes Rosser (in Burningham 1988 p.7) in support:

> Although it is clear that there is a far greater need for counselling than we were previously aware of, we still have no information on the nature of distress incurred, who is most vulnerable, who is most likely to respond to help, and what form this help should take... In the past few years we have built up a great fund of expertise but we still do not know how to channel our resources most effectively.

The previous chapter provided a considerable amount of data on 'the nature of the distress incurred' and this chapter considers the nature of the help available. The chapter begins, however, by looking at the important questions around recognising 'need' and requesting help, for it is clear from previous experience of disaster work that acknowledging the need for help or support is one of the major hurdles that both those affected and those offering support have to overcome.

Hodgkinson and Stewart (1991) in their 'handbook' of disaster management discuss the importance of 'selling' a social work service. That they do so is a consequence of the widespread reluctance to accept help. In day-to-day social work 'clients' are either referred by another agency or individual or they refer themselves. Rarely, will social workers 'seek out' clients. As was suggested in the Introduction, however, disaster work has tended to involve considerable proactive or outreach work. It therefore casts social workers into somewhat unfamiliar territory, and certainly places the 'victims' of disaster into a most unusual position – being approached without request by social workers offering help. How this works in practice, and the consequences of it are explored below.

Recognising Need and Seeking Help

As was suggested above, we live in a society in which there are strong cultural and other barriers to requesting professional help, particularly help in relation to feelings and emotions. The data from this research suggest that there were five general reasons that underlay people's reluctance to seek or to accept help after disaster. The first was *recognition*.

As we have seen, for many of those affected by disaster the period immediately after may be characterised by an emotional numbness which not only blocks out much of the pain that is felt but also many other things that are going on around them. In this study, words like 'dazed', 'shocked', 'stunned', 'calm', were common descriptions that both the bereaved and survivors gave of themselves at this time. As a consequence, they did not take on board the full impact of what was happening to them, were not necessarily aware of how they were behaving and, in many cases, attempted to carry on with their lives as if unaffected:

> He'd get up in the morning and never say a word, go to work, come home never say a word. Basically, he'd eat his tea and go to bed... [He] turned round and basically said 'there's nothing wrong with me. No, I have no problems, go away' I couldn't believe it, I just couldn't believe it. (Female survivor)

> I just put it to the back of my mind to be honest with you, that was the worst thing, well since I've been to see people, it was the worst thing I could have done. I tried to black it out. I didn't believe it. (Male survivor)

The second barrier, and one that is related to recognition is *acceptance*. Whilst there were some, particularly in the immediate aftermath, who appeared largely unaware of their predicament, there were others who, whilst recognising that the disaster was having an impact upon them, did not accept that this meant that they might benefit from some help with it. This was particularly the case amongst the men and was in many cases a reflection of their self-perception or self-image. More specifically, this tended to be based upon their pre-Hillsborough self-image and, when and if help was eventually accepted, this tended to have resulted from or to result in a changed perception of themselves.

Central to the 'acceptance' was a strong self-image, someone with the ability to cope without the help of others. This is far from being a particularly new or surprising finding but it is, nevertheless, of considerable importance. There is a small but growing literature on masculinity and although little of it considers male victimisation, much of the literature touches on emotions, feelings and rationality. Reduced to its simplest message, what much of this literature suggests is that there are a variety of problems that men experience in relation to their feelings and emotions and that contemporary masculinity (Seidler 1991) and machismo (Segal 1990) emphasises strength, control, rationality and objectivity. Feelings, especially strong and explicit feelings, are not accorded legitimacy:

> I've never admitted weakness... I've always got on with the job and I've always looked at myself as a strong person. (Male survivor)

> I thought it was better to forget about it, not to keep reminding myself of it. (Male survivor)

> Me own sort of counselling, just forgetting it, well people saying it's bad for you and that, suppose it is but you forget, well you try to forget. (Male survivor)

This is not to say that there weren't elements of such denial amongst the women in the study, rather that attempts at denial by women were on the whole much less common and rather less successful:

> Most people think, 'oh I can manage, get through it and what have you', but I think most people, everybody needs help sometimes. And I think you've got to admit it. (Bereaved wife)

The problem for many of those people affected by Hillsborough was that they continued to behave as if they were unchanged by the disaster and, more particularly, to believe that because they had 'coped' before, they would cope now. This presented a number of challenges for social work. It meant that workers were frequently confronted with people who were very resistant to the idea of professional support and, indeed, others who saw themselves as quite unaffected despite evidence to the contrary. It meant attempting to present a service that would understand the nature of these resistances, would acknowledge them and yet would, in as unintrusive a way as possible, continue to be offered. As a consequence, the service had to continue to be available until such time – and there was no way of judging when this would be – that it was perceived to be required and to be acceptable.

The third of the barriers identified in this research is what might be termed *worthiness*. This was related to the individual's perception of whether they were deserving of help or not. What is interesting here is the method by which individuals judged 'worth', or 'legitimacy'. By and large, the key was some sort of *hierarchy of worthiness* – the closer one was to the top of the hierarchy, the more deserving of help and support. At the beginning of Chapter 3 some models of disaster victimisation were outlined. Such models tend to distinguish between types or levels of victims. Unintentionally, however, they tend to reinforce the unspoken idea that there are 'hierarchies of victims' and that some victims are more 'needy' than others. The intention of such models is in fact quite the opposite: it is to illustrate just how widespread the impact of disaster may be, and that it isn't confined to those close to the epicentre.

Amongst the 'victims' of Hillsborough, there was some evidence of an implicit hierarchy in operation. The survivors, in particular, frequently viewed themselves as being less deserving than the bereaved. Similarly, relatives of survivors sometimes felt guilty that they were feeling bad when there were others 'much worse off'. On occasion such feelings were reinforced by the attitudes or the behaviour of others who failed to recognise the legitimacy of their needs. The idea that there was some sort of 'pecking order' was widespread:

> I thought social services were for next of kin. I know we were bereaved but not sort of, we were simply too far, you know, we weren't sort of direct line for social services, they were for people who had lost children or husbands not us. Or people that were injured. (Bereaved sister-in-law)

> It really annoys me because I said well I go out of my way not to say how bad myself and my sister and brother are, I mean [brother] still sleeps with my mum. You know the main concern is my mum. I mean I know, you know, she, she is like the centre of the family, but you know, it's affected us all in such a big way. (Bereaved sister)

> I felt like my problem was just minor compared to [friend's] and compared to people who had lost relatives, friends... I just felt like there were people who needed help more than me, and I felt if I went I was thinking of myself rather than people who really need it. (Male survivor)

Fourth, and perhaps crucially, there was the importance of access to *information* about the availability of help. Outreach work is time-consuming and labour-intensive and therefore has to be targeted. The decision after Hillsborough, like most disasters, was that first of all an attempt would be made to visit all the bereaved families. Making contact with relatives other than immediate family was more problematic and outreach to survivors was done by visiting places of work, schools, through the football club and so on. In addition to such work, leaflets were distributed as widely as possible, announcements were made through the media, and some networking was undertaken. Inevitably, therefore, there remained many survivors particularly who were largely unaware of what was available and for whom a decision about seeking or accepting formal help from social services was not an issue. For some of those who were aware that some services had been put in place for people affected by the disaster there remained the somewhat frightening prospect of something called 'counselling':

> I didn't know what counselling was, I didn't even, I had no idea, I hadn't the foggiest, and I just thought it was people just trying to tell me I should pull myself together. (Female survivor)

Finally, there was a barrier to the take-up of help that was linked directly to the source of that help: the *stigma* attached to social work. Very few of those interviewed had had any previous first hand experience of social work, yet there were quite strong and widely held views about social work and social workers. Perhaps not surprisingly, given the general tenor of the media portrayal of social work in the past few years, the preconceptions held about social workers were largely negative. As was suggested above, little of this appears to have been based on direct experience, and it is probably fair to conclude therefore that the views of those interviewed had been quite significantly influenced by the widely-held public image of social workers framed by successive child care tragedies and media investigations of social services' 'failures'.

It is worth exploring respondents' attitudes towards social work and social workers in some detail as they have a significant impact upon the likelihood of offers of help being heard and being accepted. The most common view of social workers was that their primary concern was the safety of children. It was child protection work that respondents most commonly associated social workers with, and this formed the focus of many of the worries about the purposes social workers had when calling after the disaster:

> I thought that's it, once a social worker's come in I've got no kids 'cause they're going to take them off me... That's all that was going through my – if a stranger knocked on my front door, I'd throw the kids in a room, I wouldn't let them in, because I'd think they were going to take them off me. I wouldn't let no-one near my kids. (Bereaved wife)

> I just thought social workers were there for people who batter their children up, abuse their children. That's what my thought of a social worker was. (Wife of survivor)

> They, how can I explain, they would come and be all nice, but then they would go back and say well I think, you know, she's not looking after the kids properly or whatever. And that was the idea I had of them. (Bereaved wife)

One of the respondents made a very clear link between this view of social workers and her initial refusal to have anything to do with them:

> I think it, maybe thinking back if they hadn't said they were social workers. Maybe if they would have said we have come to see can we help here. They did say that really... when you think of social workers you do think the worst. You know you only hear of social workers when they've neglected their job and a child's been murdered or abused some kind. (Bereaved mother)

There is something of a quandary here for social workers. They are faced with a situation in which there is a need for them to work proactively, to offer help, and yet many of those they approach will assume that their purpose is not to help but to investigate and, if necessary, to remove children. As one of the respondents said of the workers that called at her front door 'I thought they were being nosy. I thought they were down-right nosy'. One potential solution to the problem is to avoid the term social worker completely and find some alternative description of the job, or the work. Some workers described themselves as 'counsellors' when first visiting families after the disaster, and then only at a later stage when some rapport had developed, letting it be known that they were social workers. The services offered were also often described as 'counselling' and for at least one of the respondents interviewed in this study, this would appear to have been a successful strategy:

> I suppose it did because if it had just been advertised on the radio as a social worker will come out and visit, I think I would have thought 'Oh well, I'm not having a social worker in my house seeing if I batter my kids', you know. But it was classed as a counsellor, which did seem completely different. It seemed someone who was trained in dealing with this kind of thing. But I don't think I would have thought a social worker would have been. (Wife of survivor)

There were other elements to the negative stereotype held of social work, though little that was as specific as investigating child abuse. Other respondents talked more about their perception that there had to be something wrong, or that social workers were some slightly strange breed who would be unlikely to understand people's everyday problems:

> I think, a lot of people I have spoken to since have agreed that they felt that if you went to see a social worker that maybe, you know there'd be something wrong with you and that you were going to sit in a small room and talk to some strange fellow who not really had any idea about what you were talking about and be very philosophical about everything. (Male survivor)

Recognition, acceptance, worthiness, knowledge and *stigma* all act as major barriers to fuller use of the types of services that are set up in the

aftermath of disaster. It is not enough therefore to put services in place
and to publicise them. One of the keys, as Hodgkinson and Stewart (1991
p.109) describe it, is to sell the services, to present the 'service to the client
in a certain way so that they understand what is being offered and they
can make an informed choice'. The selling of social work is considered
in detail below but, first, it is clear that a considerable number of people
who do not seek help early on, do so at a later stage, and do so for reasons
other than face-to-face outreach.

Other 'triggers'

Some people make contact, 'refer themselves', because the service has
been publicised either on television or in the press or, alternatively, they
have seen publicity leaflets or other materials. All the social work teams
set up after Hillsborough put some of their efforts into publicising their
existence and their work. This was found to be especially important over
the summer of 1989 when there was a fairly general decline in the
number of referrals following the early surge after the disaster. Such
campaigns met with varying degrees of success. For teams such as those
on the Wirral and in Knowsley it led to a perceptible increase in the
numbers of referrals coming through and to a rise in the profile of the
team. The Lancashire team based in Skelmersdale, on the other hand,
felt they had been unable to conduct the type of publicity campaign they
would have liked because of constraints imposed by their department.
As a result, these attempts at outreach were perceived by the team as
having largely failed.

The one service that required considerable publicity to enable it to
work was the telephone helpline. The helpline number was printed on
posters and leaflets that were distributed around Merseyside, Sheffield
and Nottingham and, where possible, in other areas. It was also publicised through the media, including newspapers, radio and television.
The number was given out, for example, after the 'First Tuesday' documentary programme that was broadcast in February 1990 and which
contained some harrowing video material. The phones started ringing
almost as soon as the number was on the television screen, and
prompted a large number of extra calls for the rest of that week.

In addition, there were a variety of other 'triggers' which prompted
the search for or the acceptance of help. One of the more common, for
example, was a public event which led, directly or otherwise, to the
receipt of support. Again, there were a number of reasons for this: some
of these events such the memorial services, the inquests or events to
mark one of the anniversaries provoked feelings and emotions so strong
that they broke the barriers of 'recognition' or acceptance. Also on a
practical level there were social workers and other helpers present at

some of these occasions, and contact was made then and followed up later.

For others it was the problems that they experienced at work that led to them seek help. The feeling that they could longer continue to hold down their jobs in their current state was, on occasion, an incentive to look for help. These cases were few, however, and the more commonly expressed experience was of work as a barrier to accepting or seeking help:

> I knew it would mess my job up if I went for help, I knew it would affect my job, so that was one of the reasons I wouldn't get help in the first place. (Male survivor)

Seeking help at a later stage after a period when there had been resistance or reluctance was often associated with some form of crisis, of 'not being able to take it any more'. The *it* in question might be the behaviour or feelings of the person themselves:

> I walked into the kitchen and said to my mum, 'I need to get some help and that was the first time I really come to grips with and realised I needed help. (Male survivor)

A further trigger, on occasion, was the behaviour of someone else; often a partner or, less frequently, a child:

> I got to the stage of I couldn't cope with how I was feeling and the pressure he [partner] was putting on me. I could manage one or the other, so in the end I decided if I got help for myself, maybe I could cope with him, but I couldn't cope with everything. (Female survivor)

For some it was a question of time. Many were unable or unready to accept help immediately after the disaster. Indeed, as has been suggested, there were those who did not recognise that they had been badly affected by the disaster. However, the passage of time led to the emerging realisation – or just the opportunity to realise – that there were things that it might be helpful to talk to someone about. For at least one specific group, the passage of time lessened the practical constraints on emotional concerns. For example, the carers of the long-term injured are a good example of the importance of the timing and the continued availability of support. These parents were overtaken by the calamitous impact of the disaster on their children, and it was only later that they began to have the time, the space and the energy to consider themselves:

> You're more interested with what's going on with your son. You're not interested in what's going on with yourselves. (Carer of brain-damaged son)

Finally, and centrally in this regard, there is the role of relatives and friends in the process of seeking or accepting help. For many of those affected by traumatic events such as disaster, it is often family, friends or others in close contact, who recognise the need for help or support before they do themselves. After the disaster, this most commonly involved some element of persuasion by the relative or friend, varying from encouragement to 'threats':

> Mum organised [contact with a social worker] cause my mum had been in contact with her, talking to her for a while because my mum noticed a lot of changes in me because I got violent when I drank and I used to drink, I just wasn't happy at all... it's not until now that I really look back and my mum said she saw these changes in me and that is why she wanted me to get help. (Male survivor)

> I think it was sort of when it all came to a head that made you realise wasn't it, because after I had done all this screaming and shouting... I was calm. And I sat quite calmly that night wasn't it, or the next morning I can't remember now, I sat quite calmly and I said I'm leaving tomorrow with the kids. Normally I shout and I think that's what done it really I was so calm and I said it. And you said 'where are you going'? and I said 'I don't know I'm going'. I didn't know where I was going, but I think that was what, yeah, I think it took something like that for [husband] to realise that something had to be done. (Bereaved sister-in-law)

It is no coincidence that in the two quotes above both involve 'reluctant' men being persuaded or forced to seek help by their female relatives. Many of the young men in the study who had survived Hillsborough described their resistance to seeking help and the role their mothers played in making them overcome this. The women interviewed appeared to exhibit less reticence and fewer problems in relation to making an approach for help from social services or other agencies offering support. However, they frequently found themselves living with men who found it difficult to talk about their feelings in relation to the disaster, who they felt were slow to realise that Hillsborough was having a significant impact on their lives and were often reluctant to consider looking for help with any problems that had been identified. The woman's role – either as mother or partner – was, under such circumstances, a traditional one of support, facilitation and sharing, even occasionally at significant personal cost:

> No, he [husband] won't talk to me about it. It's taken me nearly two years to get him to go to the [Hillsborough] Centre and go to a group. Just over 18 months to go to a group and I mean eventually, I had to start going with him, and I didn't want to go because well, I go to a group on my own. I have space and I know what I want to talk about and what I want to get rid of. But to go with him... because I always got the feeling that he wanted to say something but couldn't because he felt he was going to upset me... (Wife of survivor)

In summary then, there appear to be a variety of barriers which lie between the caring agencies and those whom they seek to help. The general ones discussed above concerned the ability of those touched by disaster to recognise that they needed help, the difficulties they – particularly men – had in accepting help, the impact of the widespread perception that some were more deserving than others, and the importance of knowledge; it is not only necessary to know that help exists and where it can be obtained, but that the help that will be offered is open to all and that it is a safe and non-threatening process. In addition to these general barriers social work and social workers face other problems stemming from the less than perfect public image of the profession.

Social work after disaster

Those included in the interview sample varied considerably in terms of the point at which they came into contact with social services. The primary determining factor appears to have been their 'relationship' to the disaster: the bereaved, for example, were almost all contacted by social services within a week or two of the disaster and many had been contacted within 48 hours of Hillsborough. By contrast many of the survivors did not come into contact with social services within the first year and a few not at all. The bulk of those interviewed were drawn from social services records and, consequently, the sample is heavily weighted towards those who had some contact with a social worker. Those survivors responding to the questionnaire by contrast had come into contact with the formal services provided after the disaster only infrequently.

As was suggested above, the social work teams set up after the disaster made a policy decision to contact all the bereaved families in their region irrespective of whether or not help had been requested. Given the number of deaths that had occurred, this was a reasonably manageable task, though the amount of work that it might bring in the long-term had not necessarily been thought through. Contacting survivors was an altogether more problematic prospect. One of the support team leaders was quoted (Brook 1990) in the first few weeks as having said that his team aimed to contact each and every one of the fans from its region that had been at the match. Even if this were a realistic prospect – and, given that the number might have totalled upwards of 5000, this seems unlikely – it is difficult to imagine how they might all have been traced. The means by which tickets were distributed for the match meant that there was no register of who attended, and although a sizable proportion might have been traced *via* supporter's clubs and so on, just the administrative task would have been massive. Not surprisingly, this appears to have been the only occasion on which contacting *all* survivors was mentioned or seriously contemplated.

The consequence of all this is that only a small proportion of survivors – based on the referral figures to the teams the proportion was probably fewer than one in twenty – were contacted formally by social services. Indeed, only 11 per cent of those responding to the survey had been contacted by or had contacted social services. Clearly much depended on the survivors themselves for unless they prompted contact, or someone close to them did, they were likely to remain unknown to the support teams. Many, of course, will not have required support. Others, as was outlined above, might have been quite badly affected by Hillsborough but unable or unwilling to seek help. Some will have been on the margins of these two groups and a few described their desire to remain 'anonymous:

> They asked how did it happen, and I said I fell off my bike and they strapped me up and that... 'cos I knew they would have just carried on about it and they would have said 'Oh were you there' and things like that, so I said I fell off my bike. (Male survivor)

Outside Merseyside

Much of the discussion so far has concentrated both on the services set up in Merseyside, Sheffield and Nottingham and on residents from those areas who were affected by Hillsborough. The reality of the disaster, however, like many disasters, is that its impact was geographically widespread. A considerable proportion of those who died at Hillsborough were not from Liverpool and its environs, yet no formal services were set up outside the regions already mentioned. In addition to the bereaved, there were also large numbers of survivors from other parts of the country. Liverpool Football Club has a national, even international, following and consequently the supporters at the semi-final were from all over the UK. There is no reliable way of estimating what the proportion from outside Merseyside might have been, but it is likely to have been sizable.

Contact with survivors from outside Merseyside appears to have been sporadic and haphazard. Little criticism of the support teams should be implied from this, for they were not only fully occupied providing a service for those affected in their own regions, but none of them appear to have had outreach outside their region as part of their brief. The fact that some did take on such work, and even went to considerable lengths to publicise their existence and to encourage those outside the region to come forward, is to their credit. It is fair to conclude at this juncture, however, that most survivors that were contacted lived in or near Merseyside, that most of those who did get support from social services were not contacted until some time after the disaster, and that those who lived outside Merseyside often came into contact with social services very late after the disaster.

First contact and first impressions

The majority of interviews conducted for this part of the research took place between 18 months and two years after Hillsborough. Asking about first contact with social services therefore required many of the respondents to recall something in the fairly distant past, and in a past coloured by very strong traumatic memories. Consequently, recall of such 'first impressions' may not be an entirely accurate reflection of what was felt at the time. Interestingly, the overall impression of first contacts was largely positive, though it is important to view these impressions within the context of the expectations of social services that were held by respondents. Expectations were themselves influenced by which party had initiated the first contact, and the likely response to an unsolicited approach from a social worker was dependent upon when and how that contact was made.

First contact with almost all the bereaved relatives was made as a result of the initiative of social services. For those relatives who were themselves at the match, or who travelled to Sheffield to search for their loved ones, contact with a social worker often occurred at one of the hospitals, at the Boys club or at the temporary mortuary. Whilst quite understandably memories of such contacts were very hazy, some quite strong relationships were established in Sheffield that first weekend, and these had an impact on families' responses to subsequent approaches from social workers in Merseyside or elsewhere.

One of the crucial determining factors in the impressions created as a result of the first contact with social services after the disaster, was the nature of any previous contact with social workers there had been or, alternatively, preconceptions of what social workers were like and what they were for. Even if the generally held reticence that existed about social workers that was described above had not existed, the behaviour of some sections of the media after Hillsborough made the task that much more difficult. Stories of media excess are not uncommon in these days of high tabloid competition, but the inherent newsworthiness of disasters does appear to bring out some of the worst in British journalists.

A number of respondents were extremely critical of the behaviour of journalists and photographers in Sheffield, and the campaign in Merseyside against *The Sun* newspaper is well known (Coleman *et al.* 1990, Walter 1991). Even more disturbing, perhaps, were the calculated attempts that were made by some journalists to gain access to the homes of the bereaved and thereby secure a story. Take the following account given by one mother:

> When I met him [their local social worker] in the office first... we'd had a bad experience in Sheffield with somebody, he said he was a social worker and turned out he was a reporter for a newspaper and L... I was suspicious of everybody because there was an awful lot going on. I mean even at home here the press... they were saying they were other people. This fella up in Sheffield, he even told me his son went to school with [son], he said 'I'm from Liverpool.. he had a clipboard with everything on it... papers and he invited me and my sister to his house... I thought he was being nice and he brought a photo in one day of his supposed son and he knew the state I was in... But this fella invited me and [sister] to his home to sleep, shower, nice meal, really relax and everything... the phone rang in the ward... because all the phone calls had to be vetted because we were getting some terrible phone calls. This person just said 'Mrs—would you like to tell us how you feel, how you found out it was your son' and she was saying things that we'd said to this man. So I said, 'excuse me who are you?'... she said... 'We're the [name of local newspaper]... one of our people who acts as social services department [sic] for the newspaper has been spending time with you and he's told us all this'. They wanted the full story. (Mother of severely injured survivor)

Not surprisingly after experiences such as this, people were very wary about who they let through their front door, and about what they were prepared to tell others about their experiences and feelings. Whilst many were, at best, reticent about the prospect of a social worker visiting, there were a few who had had experience of social services before and were sanguine about what the experience might be like:

> See me mum used to foster kids so that's only, we had to get inter-viewed a few times... As I say we've always had social workers come in the house, I know what the job is... (Male survivor)

> Me mum is in a wheelchair so they, well me dad's dealt with social workers and welfare workers... So it never bothered me getting in touch or having, you know, them phone me or anything. It never frightened me. (Bereaved wife)

In addition to the widely-held often negative views of social workers, a number of other factors appear to have been crucial in determining the likelihood of the first approach leading to further contact and to some form of relationship being established. The two most important were the extent to which and the manner in which workers made clear what their purpose in calling was and, the time and the way in which the first contacts were made. Whilst it is hard to separate one out from the other – or indeed from other factors which played a part – it does appear that the workers' ability to present a straightforward and positive reason for calling was crucial in overcoming resistances.

Not surprisingly given the way welfare services are generally organised and offered in the UK, some of the bereaved families were, to put it mildly, surprised to find that their local social services department had sent someone round to see them. As well as often being in a state of quite profound shock, these families, as has already been made clear, were frequently besieged by the media, and inundated by offers of help and expressions of sympathy from relatives and friends. In one important sense, therefore, having a social worker arrive on the doorstep was a potential recipe for further confusion and possible resentment. It was vital in such circumstances that social workers should be clear about what they were there for, what they could offer and how they should behave. Uncertainty only exacerbated distress:

> I wasn't sure what they were actually here for. I just, they would say 'How are you feeling today?' and I'd say 'Why ask a stupid question like that?'... we didn't know what they were actually for. I think really, if it would have been explained a little bit what they were for, it might have been better... They'd sit on that couch and just stare and ask me questions, but look, look frightened. It probably must have been hard for them to come into a situation, situation like Hillsborough and have to face someone like me at the time, who was angry and thought that they were asking me stupid questions. (Bereaved mother)

Social workers, as will be described in Chapter 6, tend to describe this element of the work as one of the most difficult parts that they have to confront. Most of them were extremely nervous at having to approach members of the bereaved families or survivors of the disaster and offer them help and support. What was most problematic for them was being the initiator of the contact. The fact that the potential 'client' has not requested the call, but that the service provider is anticipating the 'need' puts both the social worker and the 'client' in an unusual position. Not only this, but the worker is reaching out to someone who is likely to be profoundly distressed, suspicious of their motives and, perhaps, angry about other intrusions they have suffered. All in all this adds up to a potentially stressful and unsatisfactory encounter, and it is the responsibility of the professional through his or her approach to mitigate the most difficult aspects of the interaction. Their ability to do this depends on a number of skills but, crucially, it depends upon their feeling secure about the reasons they are there. Many of the problems that occurred at this stage appeared to be related to confusion on the part of the worker about their role and doubts about what they could offer.

It is important to re-emphasise that the word 'offer' is an extremely important one here. Certainly as far as most of the bereaved families were concerned, but also a certain proportion of the survivors, the service was an outreach one; they had been the ones approached. Consequently, there was nothing more undermining or confusing than being asked what they wanted, what they needed, or how best they could be helped. At this stage, they had not identified that they 'wanted' anything from a social worker. Workers who attempted to put the emphasis back on the client merely ensured that the person they had approached felt that the whole experience was unsatisfactory:

> Well after he'd come, I seemed to lose faith again, 'cos I thought – when I spoke to him I felt better, but when he said 'If you need me again, just ring me', and when he went I thought – hadn't really helped... thought 'that's not all the help you can offer, like'... so I never phoned again. (Male survivor)

> What do you want? I said 'I don't know what I want'. I said 'I genuinely don't know what I want'. (Male survivor)

The timing of an approach is also important. Hodgkinson and Stewart (1991), in drawing a general picture of responses to offers of psychological help, suggest that in the immediate aftermath people may be so shocked and stunned that they will simply not hear the offer. As the shock turns to anger the more likely response is resentment followed, in some cases, by a sense of euphoria where help may seem unimportant. Their argument therefore is that it is only in the longer term that offers of psychological help may actually be fully considered. There is some evidence from this study to support such a view, particularly amongst the bereaved who reported being in such a state in the first days that they just couldn't take in what was happening. Several respondents reported having had phone calls, letters or visits from social services in the days after Hillsborough which they didn't respond to and which they could remember little about. In one or two cases there was some resentment of what was felt to be an intrusion:

> I think it was on the Monday, a lady came here. I don't know who she was, and I still don't know who she is... and she was insistent... she pushed herself, and in the end I had to say to her – 'well I'm sorry, I cannot' I said. 'You leave me your card and I'll phone you if I need you'... pushing herself on us... you can imagine the state we were in. (Bereaved mother)

> I think if we'd had a phone call or, you know, a card through the door first, we could say 'well alright these people are coming'. But at the time there were all sorts of press come knocking at the door and things... And then all of a sudden there was another knock and it was... the two social workers... if there had been a phone call... we could have arranged, well, you know, stay in the back kitchen, or just let us be on our own with them... But you know there was just so many

people, My Mum was... I mean she didn't really know what was going on anyway to be honest. (Bereaved sister)

There were very mixed feelings about the visits that were made during the first week or so after the disaster. Although many seemed only partly aware of it at the time, when they eventually came to accept help it was viewed at least as a positive gesture, and as having been important in the long-run, though perhaps somewhat intimidating at the time. In these cases the early visit was of *symbolic* rather than direct practical importance. In other cases, however, the respondent approved of there having been some delay in the approach from social services:

I think it was a few weeks after that, you know, the people started to come like and I can't even remember who it was now... but he was a social worker... if he'd have come the week after it happened, I'd have probably have slammed the door in his face, give him a load of abuse. Even worse, I'd probably have hit him, I don't know. (Bereaved wife)

By and large hostility appears to have been avoided, although there were a few cases in which the particular approach adopted by the social worker caused some resentment. Timing in these cases does not appear to have been important, rather the manner of the worker – 'he had a briefcase on his knee, he was doing his job' – determined whether or not the person they were visiting felt able or willing to talk to them about what was happening to them. Almost irrespective of the time at which the first contact took place, initial communication was reported as having been largely 'awkward' or 'difficult', though a few respondents did feel ready to talk at length about how they were feeling. Encouragement was required in most cases for subsequent contact to take place. Letters were sent, telephone calls and follow-up visits made by social workers and in a number of cases relatively long-term relationships established:

But after seeing her for a second time, I realised that I needed help... She's got a lovely comforting, calm voice... she wanted to help right from the start.

User's views of the social work service

The social work service provided in response to Hillsborough from the day of the disaster to the time of writing (some three years afterwards) represents the most comprehensive welfare response to any of the disasters over the past decade in the UK. Once again, the bulk of the evidence presented below will be the testimony of those affected by the disaster. It will be their perception of the usefulness of the services that were provided and that they had contact with. It is not, therefore, an *objective* evaluation of the social work service – assuming that such a thing were possible – but is rather an examination of the service from the user's point of view. The discussion begins with a general description of some of the work undertaken in the three years after the disaster and an examination of the nature of the relationships built up between 'workers' and 'users', before moving on to the evaluation of the 'users' views of the workers and the work.

A wide range of activities were undertaken under the umbrella of social work – so broad is the range that it is impossible to describe it fully in the space available here. In essence there are four general elements that may be defined: *practical support, personal support and befriending, individual counselling,* and *group counselling.* There are, no doubt, certain bits of the work that do not fit easily into any one of these categories, and the categories themselves are certainly not mutually exclusive. They do, however, provide a structure within which it is possible to look analytically and critically at the social work undertaken after disaster.

The bulk of recent literature on the subject (see, for example, Hodgkinson and Stewart 1991, Gibson 1991, Tumelty 1990) tends to concentrate on the psychological and emotional aspects of disaster aftermaths. Whilst this is perhaps understandable, the discussion of impact and needs contained in the previous chapter highlights the rather broader range of *sequelae* that are evident after disaster. Indeed, it is probably fair to argue that the most pressing needs after disaster are practical – money, transport, housing, childcare, legal, financial and other professional advice – rather than psychological or emotional. Furthermore, it seems quite clear that many of those most immediately and severely affected will at best be likely to be suspicious of offers of help at this early stage.

Practical support

Practical help may, therefore, be not only the most *useful* avenue at this time, but the offer of practical help is most likely to lead to acceptance. This was certainly the case after Hillsborough, and the importance of it cannot be overstated. The offer of practical support and help was much less threatening – not only for the client but also for the social worker – than any talk of counselling. It represented something concrete that the worker could do and showed that they were prepared to help and that they would respond to what the individual person wanted. The potential consequences of engaging in practical support were twofold. First, through such contact some people began to overcome their suspicions of social workers and to develop a rapport with the individual worker who was visiting them. Second, it enabled the worker to undertake some largely non-threatening and achievable tasks before beginning to think about taking on the less concrete and inevitably more frightening work associated with psychological trauma.

The range of activities that come under this heading is very broad and the boundaries set in each case were generally determined by the individual's preferences and their family circumstances. For some the contact was therefore fairly minimal and confined to small tasks like sorting out tickets for memorial services, the FA Cup Final, organising travel arrangements and so on. Others, by contrast, were willing very quickly for the social worker to become quite closely involved in very personal matters such as the organisation of the funeral, paying household bills and ensuring that other aspects of day-to-day household business continued, negotiating with employers and so on. It is here that the boundary between the first two categories – 'practical' and 'personal' support – become somewhat indistinct.

The friendships, as one might expect, tended to develop over quite extended periods of time, whereas the practical assistance tended to be concentrated towards the earlier stages when relationships were yet to be established and clients were some way from being ready to accept other types of support. Despite this pattern, there is a strong vein of practical support running through all the social work service at whatever stage help was being offered. To take just one example, with the large number and generally cumbersome legal proceedings that take place after disasters, there is continuing need for transport to be provided or to be arranged and sometimes to be paid for. The practical aspects of the social work role certainly diminish over time as counselling begins, but they never disappear entirely. Such tasks are not only important in themselves, but also because they help facilitate the trust that is important if other work is to be undertaken. It is all the more ironic therefore that these aspects of the work are often accorded relatively little importance in analyses of the social work task after disaster, if they are discussed at all.

Personal support and befriending

By contrast, 'counselling' is assumed to be so central to the social work 'task' that the role of the post-disaster social worker is often described as 'counsellor'. The reality is somewhat different, and many of such worker-client relationships did not involve much counselling[1] at all, whereas more generalised forms of personalised support were ubiquitous. A large number of post-disaster activities can be subsumed under this heading. For example, people were accompanied to a wide variety of public and private events. From the funerals in the first week after the tragedy to memorial services years afterwards, social workers – amongst very many others of course – have attempted to provide a supportive and friendly presence. In addition to these two types of formal event, there were a number of other activities at which survivors and family members might be escorted by a social worker. For example, some of the respondents in this study had arranged – or a social worker may have arranged for them – to revisit Hillsborough at some stage after the disaster. Revisiting the 'site' of a disaster is often undertaken by those affected and can help in the process of accepting the reality of the tragedy. Visits to Leppings Lane and Anfield, attendance at services, and the official inquiry at the inquests, were all occasions at which relationships with social workers might potentially be cemented. Not all experiences of the presence of social workers at such events were positive and there were occasions when it was felt to be intrusive or unhelpful.

In a few cases quite quickly, and many others over a more or less extended period of time, quite strong personal relationships developed between workers and clients. In such cases the nature of the practical tasks being undertaken often tended to resemble the types of activities that one might associate with a family member rather than with an outside professional. Thus, some of the social workers did things like taking the children for days out, such as taking them to the cinema, to play sport or out to eat; they went shopping and for days out with adult clients and in one case helped finish some decorating that a survivor had felt unable to complete. Personal support was in some cases really very extensive:

> When A [social worker] comes here, she's not – I know it's her job, but when she comes through that door, she stops doing her job, she's like a friend. (Male survivor)

> There are a lot of things that I can talk with to P [social worker]... that have nothing to do with Hillsborough, even private things in the house. [He] is involved in everything with me now. There is nothing that goes on that P... doesn't know about. If I was not able to, if I were sick or something the first person I would think of is P... because there are maybe things he would know more about than maybe someone in my family... [He] spends a lot of time here and I have really gone through everything with him. (Mother caring for injured son)

This type of support – which was very much at one extreme of what was described by users – raises questions about dependence and potential over-involvement. Some workers clearly felt that they went beyond what they would view as 'professional boundaries', and it is undoubtedly the case that the relationship described above would be viewed in some circles as evidence of 'bad practice'. Certainly, the intensity of such a relationship underlines the importance of planning the termination of such involvement well in advance and negotiating the end of the work with all the parties involved.

Individual counselling

Where something akin to counselling did take place, those on the 'receiving end' tended not to talk of counselling, but more usually referred to 'talking', 'chatting' and so on:

> I needed to talk about what happened. (Female survivor)

> I needed to talk and express my feelings. (Bereaved sister)

What actually took place within 'individual counselling' was, in itself, quite varied and appears to have depended very much upon the philosophy and strategy of the individual worker. Some were quite directive in their approach, basing their counselling work around models of bereavement or grieving, whereas others adopted a less structured approach. One survivor, who had had experience of two social workers with contrasting styles, described it as follows:

> He just kept saying 'It's a normal reaction', or 'you will feel like this'. That's not what I – not what I wanted really, but when she come out, it was just completely different. She wasn't pushing me or nothing... She listened to me feelings more than what I was actually saying. What I was actually saying to her didn't matter.

Both these workers came from the same social work team, yet the differences described in this account were in some ways indicative of what different teams were doing. Another survivor who had had support on different occasions from social workers from more than one of the core teams described his experience as follows:

> Two different schools of thought really on the approach of social work in dealing with a disaster... Team A took a view that the only people who really knew about the disaster and about the effects that it had were the people themselves and that they would determine the course of the help that they received, in so much as they spoke and the social workers responded to that using their experience and their training, but in a way which the survivors and the families wanted, and it was very much in the hands of the people who were receiving the help... whereas Team B had got a structured plan as to how they were going to help us and that any deviation from that agreed approach was really not very helpful. Team A was certainly far more flexible in their approach and I would say they were far more down to earth as well. I know of a number of people who were quite alienated by the formal Team B approach. (Male survivor)

The contrast was at its most stark, he felt, in the group sessions that were run by each of the teams:

> The Team A group, for instance, was certainly far more relaxed and it enabled people... to open up far more than anybody at the Team B groups were prepared to do... perhaps simply because they were allowed to... At team B they were putting up sheets on the wall with lists

of your symptoms and saying this is what's happening to you isn't it? This is what we're all going to go through... you know this is normal, this is what we would expect to happen because we know, because we're the experts and we're telling you what's wrong with you sort of thing.

Despite such differences, there were a number of underlying features that were broadly characteristic of the work undertaken by each of the main core teams. As was described in Chapter 3, many of those affected by the disaster found that their thoughts became utterly dominated by what they had experienced for some time afterwards. In response to this some social workers encouraged the people they were seeing to write accounts of what had happened, to write poetry, to put together scrapbooks and so on. Although there was some initial reluctance, many of the respondents found that such 'creative' ways of expressing their emotions were much easier than simply sitting and talking. In the short-term it gave them some way of putting their own story together and in the longer term helped facilitate communication with someone like a social worker.

Group work

Most of the core teams ran groups at some stage or other, but some placed far more emphasis on that work than others. As one of the survivors quoted above suggested, the nature of the groups varied considerably and the experience of those who attended them varied as well. The majority were set up by one or more social workers but, depending on the attitude of the individual worker, on the approach of the host team and, more importantly, on the views of the group, the social worker might withdraw after a certain period of time.

We don't have social workers, but there was a Wednesday group... was originally started by two social workers. They decided, the group themselves made the decision they didn't want the social workers in it. They wanted to run the group themselves, and its happening more and more and more. (Female survivor)

Attitudes towards such groups, and particularly on the presence of social workers, ranged from the supportive to the hostile. There were many instances where the attendance of a social worker was felt to be important and almost invariably the role of these workers would be described as being facilitative rather than directive:

If the group wanted a social worker to be there they would be happy to turn up and we would, we were all happy for T [social worker] to come along because we all got on pretty well with him and he was just adding to the sort of conversation, he wasn't sort of dictating the way the conversation went. (Male survivor)

The problems that people experienced with groups were broadly of three sorts. First, as has been suggested, there were problems associated with how the groups were run by social workers. Some simply found their presence intrusive, others objected to what they took to be the overly directive way in which such groups were run. Second, just the anticipation of 'having' to talk in front of a group of strangers about feelings and emotions was enough to put some off. Furthermore, a few of those who overcame such fears sufficiently to attend a group found that the experience was just as frightening as they had imagined it would be.

Third, there were some difficulties associated with the composition and concerns of the groups. People joining groups some time after they had become established sometimes felt that they didn't belong, that they weren't welcome, or that they didn't fit in some way with what was going on. This was particularly the case for those who attended groups on Merseyside but lived outside the region. Their sense of alienation from the group concerns was often quite profound and very much reflected the peripheral position that non-Merseyside families and survivors felt that they had occupied ever since the disaster.

Use of the media

Perhaps the most inspired of all the pieces of work undertaken after the disaster was the positive use to which the media coverage of Hillsborough was put. As has been suggested, the media, and particularly certain sections of the national tabloid press, caused considerable upset and anger in the way they portrayed the Liverpool fans who had been at Hillsborough. The use of close-up photographs of the dead and dying with apparently little concern for the effect this might have, caused particular disquiet. However, some of the material was put to good use.

The newsworthiness of the disaster and the presence of outside broadcast cameras meant that there was an enormous amount of material documenting what happened that Saturday afternoon. For many of those affected, however, what had happened to them or to their loved ones was uncertain and confused. Relatives were unsure of where their loved ones had been standing, survivors often could not remember when how they had escaped from the pens. For these people, handled in the right way, the photographs and especially the video material that was available meant that they could quite possibly trace where they had been standing and what had happened to them. Although upsetting, this was very important for those who primary emotion was guilt; guilt that they did not do more to help others, that they did not save more lives. Most of those interviewed as part of the study had seen all or part of the video material, most in the company of a social worker. These techniques worked as an addition to, a precursor to, and helped facilitate more formal one-to-one counselling. Although new to most of the social workers at the start of the Hillsborough work, they became one of the central planks of the work, and perhaps the one element where almost all concerned – whether worker or client – felt positive about it.

> I'd blamed myself for a long, long time until I actually seen that police video, for the death of that lad, you know. (Male survivor)

> I was given access to newspapers, videos, news reports on the tragedy, as a means of exorcism if you like. It was very helpful to me, as I wanted to see myself on tape/film at the Leppings Lane end, morbid though that may seem. (Male survivor)

Users' views of social workers

Those who had established a relatively long-term relationship with social workers tended not to be particularly critical of their workers. Indeed, overall criticism of the skills and qualities of social workers was generally muted though, perhaps not surprisingly, those who had had shorter term involvement with social services after the disaster, were the most critical. There was more criticism of certain features of the service, rather than of social workers – though there were negative feelings about the attitudes, approaches and actions of some individuals.

Respondents were questioned about the qualities of the social workers they had come into contact with. Overwhelmingly, it was age, gender, personal experience and interpersonal skills that were identified as important by users. In respect of age, users expressed a preference for social workers who were of the same age or older than they were. This appears to have been very much a reflection of the type of 'relationship' that was viewed as most beneficial: one of 'friendship'. People of a similar age were assumed to be able to empathise and understand how their client was feeling, and to allow them to talk on the 'same level':

> I would have spoken to a younger one first. Probably would have spoken to them a lot earlier than what I actually did... I don't know maybe somebody, classing them as a mate type of thing, I don't know. My own age group and that. (Male survivor)

> She was probably only what, the same age as me. Obviously the same feelings, she knew what I was going through. (Male survivor)

> I do think there's a need for at least one, that you relate, because you pick your own don't you, there's always one that stands out and you feel you can really open your heart out to them... Because I'm older you see. These younger ones to me, I thought they're only starting their lives, if their children are young they're career people, my children have been my life. So how would they understand what my loss is... So an older person when I was talking to these more or less the same

age group as me, at least I thought, they've brought theirs up and
understood. (Bereaved mother)

Age was in this way also associated with life experience: having been
through a sufficient amount in their own lives to have some feel for what
their client was going through:

I wouldn't have felt the same if she'd have been some just newly
qualified [worker] with no experience of life... You know people who
have – as I say – have had no experience of life and then try and preach
life to other people. (Male survivor)

If it had been a young one, I'd have just said, you know, 'you're not
even out of nappies yet', you know, go away basically. (Bereaved wife)

There was strong bias in favour of women undertaking such work
amongst both the men and the women in the sample. There appeared
to be a number of reasons for this. First, the empathy factor: some of the
women simply wanted to talk to other women, just as people often felt
most comfortable talking to someone of the same age. Second, women
were generally perceived to be less threatening, which was especially
important given the general view of social workers that existed. Finally,
and crucially, the preference for female social workers reflected fairly
strongly held traditional views of the roles and the characteristics of men
and women: men are strong, reliable and disciplined, women are caring,
sensitive and empathetic:

I felt easier crying in front of a woman than a man... it is a womanly
thing to cry you know... I think I'd have tried to bite my lip and keep
it in if it had been a man. (Male survivor)

I think a woman social worker has got an easier way about than a man
has... He had a rough edge about him, some of his questions were, he
would just come out with them, whereas... would go all around with
them... she built it up better, whereas he just went straight for it. (Male
survivor)

The different experiences of men and women in relation to seeking help
and particularly with regard to their relative abilities and willingness to
articulate their feelings and their needs were described in some detail
above. What this reflects are some of the differences between traditional
conceptions of masculinity and femininity, and the quite highly gen-
dered views that users had of the qualities of social workers illustrates
how powerful the effects of such stereotypes are. Not all men felt easier
discussing personal matters with women, although again the problems
that experienced were related to the traditional views of gender roles
that they held:

Now and again I've had to stop myself from cursing, you know, when
I've been angry at a session sort of thing, you know... Well it's a woman

you know. I've been brought up you know not to swear in front of a woman like. I mean if I slip out, I always apologise to a woman. (Male survivor)

I mean I'm going to find it hard to say this to yourself [female interviewer], but I mean at the time all this was going on, the sex life with my wife, you know, went by the board and I just mentioned it quickly [to a female social worker] and got onto other things, you know. Maybe if it had been with a man. (Male survivor)

Nevertheless, it would be quite false to create the impression that respondents were not happy with the service that was generally provided by the male social workers. Although there was this sense that it was *easier* to talk to a woman about such emotional issues, those who were visited by male social workers tended to be satisfied with the experience and did not express any desire to change. Strong relationships were built up between male social workers and their clients and, on occasion, there were those who suggested it was easier in the longer term to establish a relationship with a man:

I think the first time it's easy to sort of pour it out to a woman than to a bloke, but I think once you get to know a bloke then it does make it easy, you don't hold back as much. (Male survivor)

Although gender cut across all the other issues identified by users as having been important, there was nevertheless, a significant other factor in user's accounts. Developing a relationship was largely perceived to have been dependent upon the opportunity to find some point of similarity, or something around which the worker could be seen to have the ability or the experience to empathise. Thus, having a social worker of a similar age was important and, for example, for the bereaved, so often was seeing someone who had children of their own, or even who had themselves lost a child:

She could relate to kids and homes... the main thing was that she reacted to the things I was saying, I don't think I would have, say like when I took off on the kids, I mean I was throwing bedside lamps at [daughter]... I don't think I would have told C [social worker without children] that... [Other social worker] would say things like 'oh I remember throwing such and such at our [son]', you know, *she was sort of just like me*. (Bereaved wife, emphasis added)

He sent this young girl down, which I really liked, because she had lost a daughter. Now I really felt I could talk to that lady. (Bereaved mother)

Of all the personal and interpersonal factors and skills mentioned by respondents, the skill that was mentioned more than any other was being able to 'listen'. This meant different things to different people, but was described as 'not interrupting', 'listening to what I was really saying', 'listened to me feelings more than what I was actually saying', 'good at letting me talk and talk and talk'. This is discussed in more detail below, but it is important to make the point here that listening appears to have been not only the central activity at almost all stages of the social work task, but also, therefore, the crucial skill necessary for undertaking such work successfully.

Being sensitive and caring, 'gentle', 'soft-spoken', being calm or confident and having some religious faith were also mentioned with some frequency. The absence, or particularly the reverse of any of these attributes diminished the chances of success. For example, social workers who were perceived to be nervous, timid, or ill at ease by their client – and not surprisingly this was most likely to occur at the first meeting – tended to make the client feel nervous and unsure and consequently unlikely to feel willing to talk openly. Finally, given the nature of the disaster and the community that was primarily affected, having an interest in football was important, especially for the survivors:

> He was a Man United fan, it was sort of friendly rivalry talking about the teams, and that sort of set us at ease at the end of the session... And he used to stand on the terraces, be a fan himself... it's naturally a male sport I think and you don't tend to believe that women do know a lot about it. (Male survivor)

> It would actually help if they actually went to the football, or they at least like had been to a football game, because if you don't understand, only we ended up some people having to explain it like, the stands, the ground, where you stand, you know what I mean, it just seemed ridiculous. (Female survivor)

The end of the service

One of the major sources of criticism focused upon the ending of the social work service, though occasionally the social worker became the scapegoat for the shortcomings of the service. Some problems came when decisions were made to close down the team that had been providing support. As was outlined in Chapter 2, so strong were the feelings of users when the announcement came that the Wirral team was to close, that a campaign was started and the team eventually saved. Although there were criticisms from respondents about the closure of specific teams, there was no consistent message about how long they felt teams should be kept going. Rather, the impression was that there remained quite a number of people who felt unprepared for the withdrawal of the service when that finally happened in their area. There were a number of reasons for this.

First, there was a widespread impression that the decision about the closure of the teams was an administrative or financial one, rather than being based on some evidence that the work had been completed. For those affected by Hillsborough, the disaster was something which did not go away after a short period of mourning or adjustment. Not only were there the everyday personal reminders of the tragedy, but the official *sequelae* of the disaster – seemed set to continue long after the second and possibly even the third anniversary. The majority of the core teams were closed down before two years were up, and some clients and indeed workers (see Chapters 6 and 7) had difficulty in reconciling these timetables:

> We weren't ready for it to stop because we had so much still going on, 'cos there's claims still going on to the – against the police and that. (Male survivor)

> Well we had an idea that it was going to be the 18th November, they told us. But the inquest was starting on the 19th, so we were trying to get it held over through the inquest. So that hope was there that it would, but it ended up it didn't. It finished and it was a great shock. It's terrible… we was left on our own again, you know, it was sort of like well, you've got to go and cope now, go and get on with it. (Wife of survivor)

Several of the teams had closed by the time the final inquests were held in Sheffield. It seems clear in hindsight, however, that some of them handled the closure rather better than others. There was a consistent message from the clients of one of the teams that the closure had been abrupt, had been poorly communicated and had consequently caused considerably more anguish than might have otherwise been the case. Other teams, where this was possible, were very careful to communicate the decision to close as early as possible, and then to begin to work with clients towards the cessation of the relationship. Where strong relationships had been built up, it was all the more important that considerable effort and forethought be put into how and when it would be terminated:

> Very abruptly which er, was quite upsetting, mainly because um,… our social worker became ill herself, but it did end very abruptly. From seeing a person I regarded as a friend, I used to see her every Tuesday and then it went to er, say perhaps fortnightly but never any more than fortnightly er, then it was just finished, you know, nobody came or nobody was in touch or anything. (Bereaved mother)

> It's surprising really 'cos it was like, at first, it was like every couple of weeks and then every four weeks, then every whatever. But I haven't heard nothing. I don't know whether she's moved or, whether she's – I don't know whether it's all finished, I don't think it's finished, but you know whether she's been moved on or whether it's 'cos I've got my money and she thinks that's it now. (Male survivor)

The other major source of criticism came from those who lived outside those areas where the core services were provided. They felt particularly resentful of the amount of help they believed was available for those living in Merseyside, especially when contrasted with what was available to them. Isolation was a key problem, and it is not difficult to understand how problematic this might be when one reflects on how important being with others experiencing similar problems and feelings is felt to be by those affected by disaster. This is not to suggest that those living away from Merseyside did not receive any help or support, merely that there were clearly far greater numbers of people 'falling through the net' in areas where core services were not set up.

Because they were reasonably easy to trace, many of those who were bereaved but who lived in other parts of the country were contacted either by one of the core teams or by someone from their local social services. Where it was one of the core teams, closure was again a problem, particularly where it had taken some time to establish a relationship. By contrast, where local social services became involved, different patterns were sometimes set. In some cases, there appears to have been relatively short-term contact made with the family, yet in others social workers continued to visit long after most of the core teams had closed. By and large this was rather more a reflection of the dedication of the individual worker involved, than it was a specific policy adopted by the department, although the activities undertaken by the worker clearly had to be continued to be sanctioned by their employer.

Users' views of the impact of social work

Although there were critical comments made both about the role or approach of individual social workers and of social services departments more generally, on no occasion did anyone who had had lengthy contact suggest that, overall, social workers had been unhelpful or that social services were unimportant in the aftermath of disaster. Those who had been in contact with social workers for briefer periods of time were somewhat less fulsome in their assessment of the service. Whilst the majority of those who had had very little or no contact with social services generally presented this as having been their choice, there were some – particularly those living outside the regions that had established core services – who felt resentful or angry that they had not been offered a similar service.

This is an area which requires attention, if planning for future emergencies is to be tackled more effectively. Whilst using the Hillsborough model will ensure that teams will be set up in the regions deemed to be primarily affected, unless specific measures are taken to set up an 'away' team (Hodgkinson 1990) as was done after Piper Alpha and the Herald disasters, it is likely that large numbers of those affected but who live outside the main areas will fall through the net. The likelihood is that local authorities that have few bereaved or *only* survivors in their area will perceive themselves to be largely unaffected and will do little in response. Hillsborough, for example, was clearly viewed as being a 'problem for Liverpool' and yet, leaving aside the thousands of survivors who came from other parts of the country, over a fifth of the deceased did not live within the boundaries of the nine authorities at the time of the disaster.

In their evaluation of the social work service the respondents in this study divided their comments into what they saw to be the qualities of the service and how they felt the service had affected them. There was appreciation of the wide variety of tasks that had been undertaken in the name of social work, from the mundane and practical to the longer term counselling that many received. As was highlighted above, it was the listening skills allied to the role of the social worker as 'outsider' that was felt to be most helpful. Outsider, in this case, does not imply a neutral or impartial role – except that the social worker was perceived as being outside family jealousies, squabbles and so on – but rather someone who did not know their prior history and who they did not have to take any responsibility for.

One of the central problems that many people faced was the feeling that they were placing too great a burden on other family members, or that they were boring them or upsetting them. By contrast, social workers were there to listen to their experiences however often they felt the need to repeat them:

> I realised I had to try to see somebody else who was prepared to listen over and over and over again and who I wasn't going to subject to the same, um, distress that I was actually going through myself. Because there was a danger that they would get drawn into what I was going through really. (Male survivor)

Feeling that the social worker could 'cope' with what they heard was vital in allowing people to unburden themselves of their feelings and emotions in relation to the disaster. There is increasing evidence, however, and this is discussed in much more detail below, that undertaking such work may actually be quite traumatic for social workers and other carers. It is important therefore that there are support mechanisms in place for welfare staff, for if they begin to find that they are unable to cope and communicate this to their client – and there was one such case in this study – then the whole basis of the social work role is undermined.

In terms of the impact of the work, there was appreciation both of the short-term and the longer term value of the work. Some referred to the immediate help that they had received from social workers and others in Sheffield that helped them simply 'get through' the first 24 hours, or the practical support that they had had in the first few weeks after the disaster. Most though made reference to the longer term impact that 'support' had for them. Such comments fell broadly into the following six categories: *advice, support, validation, reconstruction, facilitation* and *mitigation*. Users particularly valued *the provision of advice and support at difficult times*. Many respondents felt that it had been important to have an 'extra' person to turn to at especially difficult times, from the funeral and other early events, to later anniversaries, legal proceedings and so on.

Furthermore, they singled out the role social workers had played in helping them *validate their feelings* or in helping them *make sense of feelings and emotions*. Crucial for those affected was finding some way of normalising the very strong emotions they experienced; help in finding out that what was happening to them was not the first sign of impending breakdown, but rather a normal response to a powerful and traumatic event. 'Victims' frequently feel that they are alone, and a number of respondents in this study described the importance of discovering via their social worker that they were one of many feeling the way they did, or that there was a reason for the way in which their relative was behaving:

> I could accept it better you know. I could accept it, it didn't stop me from feeling guilty, but it was just basically you've got to learn to accept things, that's what I learnt. Learnt to accept it. And I'll accept that I'm going to be guilty all my life. (Bereaved mother)

> It sort of helped me to clarify my feelings, to sort of put them in sections and go that's why you're feeling guilt, that's why you feel ashamed, that's why you've lost your confidence, that's why you daydream. They helped me identify my feelings. They helped me sort of realise that some of my feelings were unwarranted, you know, as regards the guilt and that. (Male survivor)

'Reconstruction' refers to the help people received in *piecing together the experience of the disaster*. One of the key activities undertaken by social workers was to help those affected piece together what happened to them, what happened to their friends or relatives and what their role in it all had been. By allowing them to talk, often at great length and on many occasions, and through using materials like the video recordings produced by the BBC and by the police, personal accounts of the tragedy could be constructed. However awful the experience, feeling sure rather than unsure about what happened was important in enabling those affected to move on and was, almost without exception, appreciated by them:

[it was] a continuation of the process of building up a complete picture of what had happened to me which was probably the most important thing really. Because every time I watched the video it brought back something new and every time I spoke about what happened to me that again brought back something new. (Male survivor)

The facilitation of self-help was also viewed positively, especially when it was simply supportive and non-directive. The most successful means of facilitating self-help was via the mutual support of some of the groups that were set up. Many felt that they alone had such experiences, and many described the importance of discovering (sometimes as a result of contact with a social worker, or through a group set up by social services – though in many other ways as well) that they were one of many feeling the way they did, or that there was a reason for the way in which they or their relatives or friends were behaving.

Finally, many of the respondents referred to what they took to be the vital impact of social work intervention on their long-term functioning. Over a third of those interviewed who had had lengthy contact with a social worker felt that this had helped mitigate some long-term and potentially serious consequences of the disaster. These ranged from the purely individual (emotional or psychological problems) to wider questions of relationships and employment. The following quotes are indicative of how important many of the respondents in this study felt the support provided by social services had been:

I just dread to think because as I said we didn't know. We didn't know nothing, we had never been in that position... I think we would have cracked up completely. (Female survivor)

I don't think I'd have been, well I wouldn't be like sitting here now talking to you. I think if it had gone on, if I hadn't of seen anyone, I'm not saying I would have topped myself, but I might have got into serious trouble, through either like fighting or... through drinking too much. (Male survivor)

When I think back, if I hadn't sorted that out with [social worker], I don't know what I would have done... she pointed the danger things out, the warnings, so that when I would be like that [angry with the children], although no matter how angry I was or whatever, I would kind of see what [was happening]. (Bereaved wife)

In a similar vein, social workers who had used the staff support service also identified significant long-term benefits for themselves, those they were working with and their organisations:

Somewhere to offload a lot of emotion. An opportunity to begin to stand back and to look in a more objective, detached way at the issues that were affecting me. Something that challenged me to face up to some realities, some of which were about Hillsborough, and some that were about things that had been triggered by Hillsborough. A lot of growth and a lot of personal development, and a more realistic expectation of myself. (Hillsborough social worker)

Conclusions

- The key aspect of the work undertaken in the aftermath of the disaster is simply the process of listening to relatives' and survivors' painfully explicit accounts. It was the fact that this work was so intensive and yet repetitive that many workers singled out as being the key to separating disaster work from the mainstream jobs they had done before (and since).

- Not everybody sought out or accepted professional help. The five major barriers to accepting or requesting help – recognition, acceptance, worthiness, information, stigma – have important implications for the organisation and running of a post-disaster service. Self-evidently, given the above, services need to reach out to those affected by the disaster. The majority will not seek help without being prompted. Services need to be provided by staff who feel confident about what it is they are offering. Services need to be available over an extended period of time – at least two years – and it needs to be clear at the outset to all concerned – staff and potential users – that this will be the case.

- The next of kin of those who die in disasters are likely to be relatively easy to trace, as will be many other relatives. The outreach task in such cases is therefore – at least in terms of making contact – relatively straightforward. However, with a disaster like Hillsborough, there will be many thousands of survivors who cannot be traced. Offering a service is somewhat more problematic here. This was borne out in the research which found that only about 10 per cent of survivors appeared to have been in contact with social services since Hillsborough.

- This confirms the importance of having 24-hour, 7 days a week helpline as the major back-up to a proactive counselling service. It also suggests that those responsible for the organisation, management and provision of services after disaster need to review how such services are brought to people's attention. Hillsborough workers were generally of the view that much more 'outreach' work could have been undertaken, for example, in schools and places of employment – two sites where considerable resistance was often encountered. One particular area where help might have been expected to have been forthcoming was from General Practitioners. However, although a small number of respondents mentioned having had positive support from their GP, this did not appear to have been the case in the vast majority of cases and, indeed, was mentioned as having been particularly unhelpful by some.

- Considerable efforts need to be made to make GPs more aware of the impact of stressful events such as disasters, and to encourage them to consider referring patients to social services or other organisations rather than relying on medical intervention alone.

- Two factors were identified as having been crucial in determining whether the first approach made by a social worker would be likely to lead to further contact and to some form of relationship being established. These were, the extent to which and the manner in which workers made clear what their purpose in calling was, and the time and the way in which the first contacts were made. Workers' ability to present a straightforward and positive reason for calling was central in overcoming resistances to social workers.

- The work that is undertaken in the aftermath of disaster is not adequately described by using the term 'counselling'. In some cases very little counselling will actually occur, and in the vast majority a variety of activities in addition to 'counselling' will take place. Practical support is likely to dominate in the early stages, together with or followed by a strong element of 'personal support': accompanying people to a wide variety of public and private events and adopting a befriending role – essentially 'being there' for people, not just in early days, but later on when other sources of support have disappeared or when particularly stressful occasions arise.

- Early on, practical help tended to be not only the most *useful* avenue, but also the most likely to lead to acceptance. The offer of practical support and help was much less threatening – both the client and for the social worker – than any talk of counselling. It represented something concrete that the worker could do and showed that they were prepared to help and that they would respond to what the individual person wanted. As was suggested above, such tasks are not only important in themselves, but they are also valuable because they help facilitate the trust that is important if other work is to be undertaken. It is ironic, therefore, that these aspects of the work are often accorded relatively little importance in analyses of the social work task after disaster.

- Counselling – individually or in groups – does and will take place. Absolutely central to the work undertaken after Hillsborough was the use of video and newspaper material. The published records of a disaster, in newspaper and television coverage, can be vital in helping people to piece together what happened to them, and to encourage them to talk about their experiences.

- In a similar way, groups were valued because they allowed people to meet and spend time with others who were in a similar position to themselves. For many it was in such circumstances that they were first able to realise that they were not alone in the way they were feeling, and that perhaps they weren't 'going mad' after all.

- Social workers must be clear about what they can offer to people affected by disasters.

- Both workers and users confirmed that listening skills, empathy and flexibility were the keys to building up a successful working relationship. Users made direct reference to the importance of services taking account of what *they* wanted, and what they felt they would benefit from. Comparisons of different practices between teams suggested that workers who presented themselves as experts or who insisted on a highly structured approach to the work were, as far as the users were concerned, likely to be less successful. Thus, one of the most novel areas of work undertaken by Hillsborough social workers was the use of video and other photographic material with survivors and others affected by the disaster. There never appeared to be a set pattern to when and how this would take place, but rather it tended to be geared to what the user, in collaboration with the worker, determined was appropriate. Watching the video material, although frequently harrowing and extremely distressing, was almost universally agreed to have been a positive thing to have undertaken.

- Providing practical support is at least as important a function in the aftermath of disaster as counselling.

Notes

1. The Barclay Report (NISW 1982 p.41) described counselling as 'a range of activities in which an attempt is made to understand the meaning of some event or state of being to an individual, family or group and to plan, with the person or people concerned, how to manage the emotional and practical realities which face them'. With specific reference to bereavement and loss the Working Party went on to suggest that such feelings 'which are inevitable in any society can be tolerated and accommodated so that, while it affects one's life, it does not become destructive or debilitating'.

Part 3

The Experience of Disaster Work

CHAPTER 6

Doing Disaster Work

> I must admit to having doubts about whether the skills we have would be any use in a situation like this. I'm convinced now that we do have something to offer. It actually rekindled my faith in the profession and what we do. (Hillsborough social worker)

The purpose of this chapter is to look rather more closely at the impact of 'disaster work' on the workers themselves. Chapter 7 will then examine the sources of support available to workers and consider the effectiveness of such services for staff. As has already been suggested, the bulk of the academic literature in this area has concentrated upon the role of and the stresses suffered by emergency services staff. Little attention has hitherto been paid to other 'welfare' staff. How do social workers experience working in the aftermath of tragedy? Do they feel prepared for such work and, if not, why not? Are there aspects of the work that were more difficult or more rewarding than others? To what extent and in what ways are they affected by the work? By using the Hillsborough experience as a case study this chapter addresses these questions and others. In particular, it focuses upon the experience and the impact of the work, and it poses a number of questions, taken up at greater length in Chapter 7, about providing care not only for the 'primary victims', but the carers as well.

Before considering the specific questions about the experience and impact of the work, it is worth looking at the background of the Hillsborough workers. Data was collected on age, gender and seniority of workers, their experience prior to taking on disaster work, and details of any relevant training they had received.

Of those responding to the questionnaire, over two-thirds (71%) were women and over four-fifths were aged between 31–50 (32% aged 31–40 and 50% aged 41–50). Almost one-half of the respondents were either level 2 or level 3 social workers, approximately one-third were either senior social workers or team leaders, with the majority of the remainder being drawn from more senior grades. Only four of the respondents did not have a social work qualification. Of those that did, almost all had CQSW (88%) with others having CSS, CSW etc. Of those with the CQSW qualification about a quarter were also Approved Social Workers under the Mental Health Act. Finally, not only were they qualified but the majority were quite experienced: less than a fifth had fewer than five years post-qualification experience, almost a fifth had between five and ten years experience and over a fifth had spent between 11 and 20 years in social work.

Respondents were asked to what extent they felt that their professional social work training had prepared them for disaster work. The response was as follows:

Table 6.1 Extent to which social workers felt prepared for disaster work

Whether prepared or not	Number	Approx. %
Unprepared	10	15%
Slightly prepared	44	65%
Well prepared	14	20%
Totally prepared	0	-

Although it is by no means surprising that none of the workers reported feeling 'totally prepared' for such work, it is significant that only one in five felt 'well prepared' and more than one in seven said that they felt 'unprepared'. The ways in which they felt underprepared are considered in more detail below.

These were, of course, qualified and experienced social workers. Measuring *relevant* experience is problematic, for it is not entirely clear what it is that might be relevant in these circumstances. However, in the absence of other indicators respondents were asked how much experience of bereavement counselling they had. Less than a quarter reported having had 'considerable' experience of bereavement counselling, over a third (36%) reported 'some' experience, almost a third (29%) reported 'little' and approximately one in eight (12%) reported having had no experience of bereavement counselling. Ironically, it tended to be those who had been most peripherally or temporarily involved in the Hillsborough work that had most experience of counselling, whereas those with no experience had frequently been involved in the long-term response.

Almost all of the respondents had had no specific 'disaster training' prior to their involvement in the Hillsborough work. Of the few who had, all said that they had found it useful to some extent. Workers were then asked whether they had received any relevant training after the disaster. Almost exactly half of the respondents had received some training after the disaster. The amount and type of this training varied considerably, as did its availability. As was explained in Chapter 3 the Merseyside authorities (in conjunction with Sheffield and Nottinghamshire) made arrangements very early on for a private training organisation to set up sessions in the region for as many staff and managers could be catered for at short notice. Consequently, many of the Merseyside respondents had received training, whereas those from other parts of the country frequently had not.

Respondents were asked a series of questions about the training they had received, ranging from a general assessment of its worth, to more specific questions about its content. On the basis of the in-depth interviews that had been conducted with workers prior to the survey, four elements of the work were identified and respondents were asked to assess how helpful the training had been in each of the these four areas. They were asked to assess how helpful the training had been in 'explaining the nature of disasters', in 'preparing you emotionally for the work', in 'informing you of potential pitfalls', and in 'providing you with new skills'. It has already been suggested that workers generally felt favourably towards the training they had received and, indeed, as will be described in more detail below, workers were frequently resentful if they felt they had missed out on any training that had been available to others.

Although there is not the space here to consider workers' evaluations of all the training sessions that were provided, it is worth considering their views of the most comprehensive programme set up in the aftermath by the consortium of authorities responding to the disaster – that provided by Michael Stewart and the Centre for Crisis Psychology (CCP). In all, 26 social workers who responded to the survey had attended training sessions run by Stewart in the immediate aftermath of Hillsborough. They were asked to rate the training in relation to the four aspects outlined above, using a five point scale ranging from very unhelpful to very helpful. The results are interesting in that the ratings for each element vary quite considerably. The training was rated as being most successful in 'explaining the nature of disasters' – four-fifths of workers found it either very helpful or helpful in this regard. Approximately two-thirds found the training helpful or very helpful in informing them of potential pitfalls, and three-fifths suggested that it was helpful in preparing them emotionally for the work. By contrast, less than two-fifths found this training helpful in providing them with new skills, indeed a small number rated the training as positively unhelpful in this regard.

The results are quite enlightening for they illustrate the qualities and content of the training. Most of the training that was provided was necessarily short-term in character, usually no longer than one day, although Stewart and others from the CCP did provide some 3-day sessions for social workers. It is perhaps not surprising, therefore, that the provision of new skills was rated somewhat lower than other aspects of the training. In fact, the elements of this training that were highlighted in interview were the emotional and motivational aspects. Where workers felt that Michael Stewart and his colleagues had been successful was in convincing them that they could undertake this work. His presentations were charismatic, galvanising and often uplifting. Workers were clearly impressed that he 'had been through it himself' and that he was aware of many of the difficulties of undertaking such work. For the majority of those who were able to attend, the training sessions helped them to understand what might greet them when they began the work, enabled them to focus on what their immediate tasks were, and pointed out to them some of the longer term problems that they might face. What, by and large, was not on offer after the disaster was skills training. It might reasonably be argued, as it was by one senior social services manager in interview, that such training would have been impractical at such a time and that what was needed, and provided, was something that would 'gee up the troops'. The workers themselves confirm that this was the essence of what they received. By and large this was not perceived as problematic in itself by social workers, but they *were* critical of what followed.

More accurately, social workers were critical of what did *not* follow: further or follow-up training. Although they found the Stewart sessions useful, particularly in terms of persuading them that they were the right people to be undertaking the work, many continued to feel ill-equipped for the tasks they were confronted by. Consequently, they felt that further training – training that would be rather more focused on providing or refining particular skills – should be provided as the work went on.

These qualified and experienced social workers said that they felt 'deskilled' in the face of the immediate impact of a disaster, and continued to feel in the months and years after, that they were presented with tasks that they would tackle more effectively if they had received specific training. The following worker who said that she felt confused frequently about her 'disaster role', summed up the feeling of many:

> Very often felt totally out of my depth. I didn't know how to proceed. Wondered if I'd cause more distress.

The remainder of this chapter explores workers experiences of providing support in the aftermath of the disaster, the difficulties they experienced and the impact that it had upon them. First, then, how did the workers experience providing support in the aftermath of a disaster?

The experience of disaster work

> [In mainstream work] it's not the same thing all the time, but with Hillsborough it was. It was to do with hearing personal accounts of the same incident, watching the video numerous times, literally time and time and time again. With different people but watching the same events, watching the same trauma, watching people suffer. (Hillsborough social worker)

There were a number of significant respects in which the work was felt to be rather different from the mainstream activities that workers had been engaged in prior to Hillsborough. The unusual aspects of the work were also frequently identified as having been the sources of considerable stress, but some at least were also the basis of considerably increased levels of satisfaction with the job.

The outreach nature of the early part of the work was something that separated this from much of the worker's prior experiences. Those who were involved in the first two weeks reported a number of difficulties in relation to making contact with bereaved families for the first time. There was apprehension at how they would be greeted, what they would find when they knocked on the door, and how they would respond to any hostility that might be shown. Several workers said that they could still remember very vividly almost every aspect of the car journey they made to the first family they visited after the disaster. During the journey they were preoccupied with what they would say first of all and then what they would do if and when they were invited inside. As the evidence in the previous chapter suggested, it was the workers who were comfortable or were able to appear most comfortable in their role at this difficult time who made the most positive initial impact. This element of the work was not only viewed as unusual – actively seeking out potential service users – but was also found to be very stressful. One worker described her first experience of responding to Hillsborough in the following words:

> The phone call came in the morning... [from] the Director... He wants people to go out like about 10 minutes ago to support the families and see what we can do. My reaction was to say, well hold on a minute, I'm not really prepared to go out [immediately]... lets get some more information... I was directed to get out there... I went, arrived in [local town] to see this family. Couldn't find the address and the locals were sort of very hostile and saying 'What do you want them for?' Thought I was more of the press and clearly they'd had a bad time over the weekend... When I got to the house the door was opened by one of the brothers. Again very hostile. The door opened, peeping, 'what the fuck do you want?'. Said I was from Social Services and was there to offer whatever sort of support, help or counselling that was appropriate or needed. I got inside the door and these two brothers looked absolutely

ghastly. Really in shock and grief, everything was awful. Just said that their mother was in a bad way. She was sedated. They took my name and address and said they would contact me.

Once some form of relationship had been established, then the most basic and, reportedly, the most stressful element of the work itself began. At its crudest, this merely involved spending time – frequently a considerable amount of time – listening to people talk about their experiences and their feelings. This was, of course, not in essence different from much of what is undertaken on a daily basis by social workers in a wide variety of different types of work. However, there is one crucial respect in which disaster work is not comparable with mainstream work, and that is the magnitude and intensity of the experience. Most people caught up in the aftermath of a disaster have some sense of the extent to which it is different to other experiences, although invariably they find this difficult to explain. The reality is that the public nature of disasters, the scale of them and their highly visible and public nature means that they are experienced as being a much more powerful set of events.

This *intensification* was visible in a number of different ways. First, it was the sheer scale of the consequences of the disaster:

> It was the enormity of it. It was the scale of it, and it was the mass destruction, death and grief... I dealt with bereavement a lot and I was not prepared for it. I didn't feel very skilled when it came to it. It differed seeing people in a mass act of grief... from work seeing people in a private room, holding a baby... that had just died. That is different, you can handle that, even hysteria, but mass hysteria was quite hard.

> Just the sheer numbers, that was what I hadn't taken into account... But then the numbers of people that you began to see one after the other. I think the sheer size and enormity of it began to hit home... seeing people one after the other, it was pretty awful really. The feelings of being overwhelmed, of sheer helplessness faced with all this pain did at times feel just like a sense of drowning.

The final quote above also alludes to the other primary difficulty that social workers faced at this time: that was feeling that there was nothing that they could do to make anything better for the people they were seeing. That they did not have any skills or powers that would change anything, and that the emotions that they were dealing with were simply too powerful to cope with. In all, over four-fifths of the Hillsborough social workers said that they had sometimes or even frequently felt helpless in the face of their clients' experiences of the disaster. They described the feeling in the following ways:

> Just listening didn't seem enough

> What do you say when faced with these appalling stories?

As a social worker I'm not used to doing things where there was nothing I could do to take the pain away.

It was more intense both professionally and personally. Very little social workers can do... we're used to doing things, having the answers. In disaster work there are no answers.

I have often felt powerless in the face of such strong, seemingly everlasting feelings of pain and anger, frustration and despair.

It is difficult to say anything to make it OK.

Such feelings on behalf of the workers were, in the main, confined to early days and weeks of their involvement in disaster work and it is positive to be able to note therefore that such helplessness did not seem to continue – certainly at this sort of level – as the work progressed. Indeed, as relationships developed between workers and users this feeling of impotence declined. No doubt this was partly due to the, albeit slight, lessening of the intensity of the public emotion being expressed, although it is also clear that workers began to feel more comfortable in the role necessitated by disaster work. As one worker commented:

Initially some of the experiences were overwhelming – though this feeling diminished with experience.

The feelings of inadequacy underpinned and fuelled social workers' expressed need for further training. As was described above, the majority of workers involved in the response to the disaster felt that their professional training was an inadequate preparation for such work – particularly in terms of the limited grounding in counselling it gave them – and that some further training would be beneficial. To an extent the initial training that was organised and provided in the immediate aftermath did confront one of the major sources of difficulty that workers experienced, in that the organisation that provided this training was run by people who had been disaster workers themselves and so were, familiar with what the Hillsborough workers were likely to be experiencing. The training was therefore geared to reassuring social workers that their basic skills would see them through and that much of the helplessness that they experienced was an unavoidable aspect of working with such a major tragedy. However, neither the initial or later training were able to do anything about one of the more fundamental problems that workers felt they faced in the longer term they continued to feel that there were specific counselling skills that it would be helpful to possess, however, little further training was forthcoming and despite a number of requests none of the authorities supported their workers in advancing their skills in the areas they had themselves identified as likely to be of greatest use to them.

As time moved on there were other aspects of the post-disaster work itself that were reported as having being particularly stressful. Although there was a general lessening of public emotion and, particularly, a diminution in the public profile of the Hillsborough work, it is clear that this was not necessarily parallelled by a lessening of the emotion that was expressed in contacts between workers and users. Some workers continued to find the extent of the grief, the guilt and the shame that they encountered all but overwhelmed them on occasion. Many found themselves spending a lot of their time thinking about the accounts of the disaster they had heard or reliving their experience of other's grief, and some discovered that at certain points this was almost impossible to control.

In addition, there were a number of activities that were central parts of the post-disaster social work role that were reported as having been a source of stress and difficulty. One of these was accompanying relatives and survivors back to Hillsborough for the first time since the disaster in order that they might see where their loved ones had died or where they themselves had stood that afternoon. Not surprisingly, such visits were very painful for those returning to Hillsborough and, on occasion placed a significant burden on the accompanying carers. For the social workers based in Sheffield, liaising with the Football Club, making arrangements for visits and accompanying relatives became a regular part of the workload, and whilst on many occasions they reported that it appeared to have been useful and valued it was, nevertheless, an emotionally enervative experience.

In some respects the anniversaries were experienced in a similar way. There was often a lot of organisational work to be undertaken, a lot of anticipation about what the experience would actually be like, followed by what felt like a thorough examination of their social work skills. In one important sense, this got more difficult rather than easier as the years went by. The more time the workers spent involved in Hillsborough work, the more they tended to identify with the disaster as something that they were involved with themselves, rather than simply as carers of others: crudely, they identified with it *directly* rather than *indirectly*.[1] Consequently, there was a feeling for some that they wished to attend anniversary memorial services and so forth for their own needs, and that supporting others – at least in anticipation – felt increasingly problematic.

Finally, and this is by no means an exhaustive list, a large number of the workers reported having found the inquests particularly difficult. The final inquests that were held in Sheffield Town Hall began in November 1990 – some 18 months after the disaster – and continued on a daily basis for five months. A number of relatives attended every day for the whole of this period, and many others spent a considerable period in Sheffield. One can only imagine the strain this must have placed upon them. As was outlined above, most of the core social work teams had closed by the time the full inquests were opened and consequently much of the social work burden fell upon the Liverpool team, which was still running, and a number of Sheffield workers and volunteers who provided cover for the full period. Workers from other teams did attend the inquests from time to time in order to accompany relatives or survivors they had been working with, or when other pressures allowed.

Perhaps the major sources of frustration for the workers were the organisational impediments to providing a service at the inquests and the lack of acknowledgement they felt they received from their employers. The more general organisational problems are discussed in rather more detail in the next section. However, there is one further aspect of the role of the social worker that needs to be raised here. That is, what is the role of the 'professional' and are there boundaries which distinguish the worker and user which need to be maintained at all times? This rather vague question arises because of the different experiences that workers appear to have had at the inquests. Stated at its baldest, some workers identified so closely with the relatives that they accompanied that the proceedings began to upset and anger them in a way that appeared to parallel the upset and anger of the relatives. The extent to which such workers remain in a position to provide support, comfort and advice – other than that of a 'we're all in this together' fellow-feeling – is questionable. Both workers who found themselves affected in this way, and others occupying a more 'detached' role commented on the consequences of this type of (over)-identification. First, the 'identifiers':

> It's a double-edged sword. Being able to see and understand the sheer frustration of people... was helpful. Sharing that and feeling some of that frustration was negative... We found ourselves in a position whereby to try and maintain too great a distance would effectively exclude us from working with [the families]...

> ...a sense of frustration sitting there [at the inquests] listening to what was going on. Almost feeling, I suppose, feeling a victim is too strong, but being able to identify very strongly with the feelings of the survivors and the families. A great deal of anger I associate with the inquests. At how people were treated as witnesses, and the dismissive way in which their feelings were dealt with. The judicial system... is not there to deal with people's emotions. But the fact that so little thought was given to it all, when simple measures could have made it so much easier for people. The fact that the victims had to defend themselves makes me angry... I still... feel angry.

and, second, a rather different point of view from a worker from a different team:

> ... it felt as if the social workers from—... who I think got very involved with their families, they were getting very angry about things that I didn't feel they needed to get angry about. They were saying [the Coroner] is favouring certain witnesses rather than others... I hadn't seen that, I hadn't picked that up... They seemed to have spent so long with their families, and it was so important to their families – and of course I understand that – that they seemed to have taken that on board and it was almost as if they had become families themselves.

Clearly *empathy* and *identification* are likely to be key aspects of the type of work undertaken in the aftermath of disasters. Nevertheless, the extent to which one can 'take on' the frustrations, the anger and the priorities of the users and continue to provide a professional service is a practical question to which there are no easy answers. What this situation does point up, however, is the pressing need for there to be reliable supervision of workers undertaking such work, for it is clear that if nothing else such close identification can lead to a number of emotional problems at that and a later stage.

The power of disasters does lead to a very high level of involvement amongst social work staff, and echoing Shepherd and Hodgkinson's (forthcoming) research (reported in Hodgkinson and Stewart 1991), the majority of workers responding to the survey conducted as part of this research found that they identified closely with the experiences of the users.

> ... it was totally absorbing. It became *our* disaster, certainly for [a colleague] and I Hillsborough became *our* disaster – we never claimed to have gone through what they all went through, but you owned it because it sucked you in. They were *our* families, and we'd refer to *our* families and we'd refer to *our* survivors. We'd come in and sling the newspapers on the table – 'have you seen this?'. Livid, angry, because that's how we felt.

Almost 90 per cent said that they had at some time imagined how they would have coped if they had been one of the victims themselves. A quarter of the workers said that this occurred 'frequently', and over a half 'sometimes'. Workers were especially prone to such identification during the first year after the disaster, and although a significant number continued to report such feelings up to three years after the disaster the proportion doing so had declined to approximately a quarter. In almost all cases workers imagined either being in the crush themselves or losing a relative in the disaster:

> As a long-time football fan I can appreciate what the experience of Hillsborough might have been like for those who were there – and for

those at home. It is something I think about still, both because of my background and the continuing involvement in the work.

The thought of losing my son who is a football supporter and just weeks younger than the son of one of the families. To a lesser degree the fear of losing one of my daughters – I was not involved directly with anyone who lost a daughter.

I did some work with the sister of a lad who died... my son at that time was the same age and he is a football fan, so you talk to someone for a couple of hours and on the way home you're saying 'it could've been my son'. Because of that my husband found it quite difficult. I mean usually I go home and he listens... children and death he has trouble with, and that made it difficult.

Working with parents who had lost children the same age as mine I found initially difficult. because I'd lost a child, so initially I think I identified with them in terms of my own children's mortality.

Furthermore, four-fifths of the workers said that they sometimes found themselves preoccupied by their clients' experiences of the disaster. Although the work with the full range of users appeared to have this effect, it was primarily the experience of working with survivors that was reported as having led to preoccupation by workers. It was having to sit and listen to large numbers of very detailed accounts of near-death experiences, of survivors talking about what they saw and heard and smelt at Hillsborough that ingrained itself on the worker's minds:

In the first year of work I frequently found the experiences very hard to forget. Especially when I ran an evening survivor's group on my own.

I personally experienced secondary flashbacks from the most stressful experiences of a particular client.

In the evenings I became preoccupied with work – distanced and emotionally remote from my family

... felt drawn into their emotional distress and the injustice of the whole situation.

Finally, such feelings also triggered off a number of memories or experiences that had occurred at an earlier stage in the worker's life. In all, three-fifths of the workers said that the disaster work had reminded them of earlier unhappy memories, issues or incidents, although very few suggested that this had been frequent:

It has raised issues about my past; about how and why I deal with some feelings less easily than others. Thus it is not specific experiences that I am *reminded* of, but previous experiences that I have needed to look at and work through.

Assisting nursing staff in the presentation of dead babies to parents in my last job recurred constantly in my mind whenever dealing with the bereaved. Photos of the dead stirred memories of the coolness of the touch of death and made me deeply aware of the transiency of my relationship with my own child.

A loss I suffered [many] years ago. It took my work over Hillsborough to realise what this meant to me, and how it had influenced a lot of what I have done since – both in terms of what career I went into, how I progressed and also in terms of a desire to prove people wrong.

The personal impact of disaster work

There are some respects in which the issues which are raised under this heading are not separable from the issues discussed immediately above in any real sense. However, in order to obtain a little analytic clarity it is easier to consider the experience of doing the work and the personal impact of that work separately. This section concentrates on the physical, emotional and social well-being of the disaster workers, and examines the extent to which they felt that their well-being was disturbed by becoming engaged in disaster work.

In terms of the emotional impact workers reported a number of issues that caused them to question how well they were functioning and, in some cases, to actually look for help. One significant area raised by workers concerned aspects of their own life-histories which they had not resolved, and which their disaster work brought into renewed focus. Perhaps not surprisingly, the bulk of these personal difficulties were themselves related in some way to loss. Workers reported difficulties related to bereavements of their own – particularly in childhood – separation, divorce and other family problems, and sexual abuse, both in early childhood and in adolescence. For such workers it was the stirring up of emotions in relation to these issues in their lives which either caused them difficulties or added to the problems they experienced with the work. As one commented:

What actually happened is I surfaced very very young child sexual abuse... I didn't really have a clue that it was there. But I heard my reaction to something and I thought this is over the top... The disaster opened that up... Doing the work... because I'm working at quite a deep level with people... Then I'd realise, yes this is taking me into something in my own life...

In this case this aspect of the worker's personal history was not the sole cause of the problems that were experienced. A number of problems to do with the way the disaster work was organised and managed exacerbated the other difficulties:

I felt very bad about the organisation and about them abusing me. It was not just about the sexual abuse [in my past], it was about mistreatment by the organisation which tapped in to the sexual abuse.

Not surprisingly, many of the workers referred to the emotional character of many aspects of the work and, in particular, to the impact of the first few weeks of work and then to the incremental pressure of the work in the following months and years. The following worker became involved on the weekend of the disaster for a few days and then joined a team several months later:

The first week I think I was probably in a state of shock. I spent a lot of time crying. I was fortunate in that I'd got a very supportive husband who was very protective. The crying lasted maybe a few weeks. The feelings, the slight depression lasted for longer than that – a few months, by which time I was doing Hillsborough work again... I think for the whole year there had been experiences that we had had where you were constantly putting a lid on your feelings and your emotions, and there was one incident at the inquests where, in the last week... which... had been quite difficult for me. Again, during that day, I'd been sort of in control of myself. I'd been supporting other people, the police, the family, all the rest of it, and driving back [to the office]... because I had a meeting... I thought how can you be like this? How can you have seen and heard, and have done what you've done today?... You should be getting out of social work because it's just not touching you... And I got back... and I said 'I'm going upstairs'... there was nobody up there, and I sobbed and sobbed and sobbed. And that was like the lid was off and I thought I could put it back on again but I couldn't... I ended up having three weeks off work with nervous exhaustion.

As has already been discussed in some detail, one of the key aspects of the work undertaken in the aftermath of disasters is simply the process of listening to the painfully explicit accounts of the relatives and survivors. It was the fact that this work was so intensive and yet repetitive that many workers singled out as being the key to separating disaster work from the mainstream jobs they had done before (and since). It was often easy for workers feel somewhat preoccupied with such accounts and to find it difficult to 'switch off' after this type of work. Many also reported rather more significant emotional and somatic consequences that they felt were associated with this area of the work, including sleep loss (a number reported that they found themselves waking up at six minutes past three at night), nightmares, weight loss, difficulties in concentrating and so on:

I was very aware at that time (about three months after the disaster) I was starting to have nightmares. Not just not sleeping but having nightmares... very, very disturbed about something. Also some of the information that the lads had given me about the sights, the sounds, the smells of Hillsborough were beginning to... I couldn't pass... I couldn't talk to anyone about them, and I was stuck with them.

Predictably such effects had a wider impact than just on the individual worker him or herself:

> [My partner] was trying to help all the time and finding it really difficult I'm sure, because she was saying to me 'it's that bloody job, you've got to give it up. It's no good for you, it's not doing you any good, and because it's not doing you any good, it's not doing me any good'. So it had like a knock-on effect with our relationship.

What workers then reported – having realised that the work was having some sort of effect on them – was a more or less extended struggle in which they attempted to control their feelings and emotions, to keep going, keep doing the work, and not let anyone down. The general assumption was that they were OK really, that the feelings would pass, and that although they might be struggling the people they were working with needed them and that they therefore had to stay strong and stay working. Despite all they had heard about the potential impact of the disaster on them as workers many ignored very explicit signs that they were not functioning properly. Not only did they want to carry on working under such circumstances but in the vast majority of cases they were allowed to do so:

> It was really strange because I'd been conscious I'd not been particularly well for about three or four weeks. We were backwards and forwards to Sheffield every day. The inquest finished on the Friday... I'd been there every day that week. Going out six o'clock in the morning, coming in at nine o'clock at night, because most often you'd stop to have a meal with whichever family [you were with]. I remember coming in, just going straight up the stairs to bed... I remember getting out of bed Saturday morning feeling awful... It just came on suddenly. There's something that just keeps you going... I had to get to the Friday and that was my last one... I remember feeling... that's it, I've done it. The inquests are over. We were disbanding the following Wednesday... I spent three weeks sleeping (and had ten weeks off work).

Another of the workers reported the consequences for him in the following way:

> I thought I was dying. I was convinced I had a tumour. Really did think I was dying. It was a pain that I'd never experienced before. It was pains that were shooting up at the back of my neck into my head, across the top of my head, and across the front of my forehead. There were times I just felt that my head was going to burst open and everything spill out... I really felt at rock bottom... After that I just didn't go anywhere... I just closed the curtains, opened the windows and just sat there in the shade for about seven weeks. I had a lot of time to think

about it. I was convinced by what my doctor said, and by what other people said, that it was the job that was really the stress factor that was pushing me over the top... As the tablets started to work, and as being at home, being away from the job started to take effect, so the pain began to subside, so that I could relax. I could just flop a bit, whereas before I'd been so tense and just couldn't get comfortable anywhere.

Almost two-thirds of the Hillsborough social workers said that they felt vulnerable 'more than usual' since being involved in the work and almost half reported an increase in their consumption of alcohol. Indeed, few of those who had been involved over an extended period of time did not feel they had been profoundly affected by the experience. For some, like the following two social workers, it was perceived as having been life-changing:

There's lots of times that I would love to be the person I was two years ago, and I know that will not happen.

The tiredness... sort of takes over you life. I just can't remember what I did before Hillsborough... It's like your whole life just takes a whole new course.

Consequently, there are occasions where the boundaries between worker and victim can become very blurred:

To be honest I think when I was going along [to the inquests] I was going along because I wanted to be [there], I wanted to hear what was coming out... Maybe to begin with, the first week or two I was... getting stuck in... after that I went along for the ride. Part of me wanted to be there, but it wasn't as a social worker, it was as someone who had been through Hillsborough.

Organisational pressures and role stresses

Whilst there remains little discussion of the potential impact of post-disaster social work on those providing long-term support, there is, at least, some acceptance these days that providing a social work service in the aftermath of a disaster is potentially a source of stress. This is confirmed by the small amount of research that has been undertaken, and the departments that find themselves responsible for the provision of such a service that acknowledge that their staff may need to be both protected and supported whilst undertaking such work. It is ironic to find, therefore, that it is precisely these employers who workers report as being the *source* of many of the stresses and difficulties that they encounter (see Newburn 1991). In addition to the nature of the work itself, many workers found that it was the organisational context in which they worked that presented them with their greatest problems or was, at least, as one worker suggested, 'the straw that broke the camel's back'.

The bulk of the difficulties related to either the perceived mismanagement of the worker or the worker's team, or to lack of support for or lack of acknowledgement of the work by their employer. Many of the problems related to the lives of the disaster support teams set up in the aftermath by individual local authorities. These lives, and the experience of these lives for team members, illustrate some of the organisational pressures and role stresses facing disaster workers. Although the situations, settings and circumstances of the teams set up after Hillsborough varied considerably, there are a number of common themes in relation to their histories that may be identified. Each of these themes relate to a specific aspect of the organisation of post-disaster work and each carries with them a number of tensions that may act to increase rather than decrease the likelihood that workers will experience some negative consequences as a result of their involvement in the work.

These themes – of which five are identified here – may be viewed as a set of stages. The five stages – *entry, engagement, establishment, ending* and *re-entering the mainstream* – follow one another in rough chronological order although they are not necessarily temporally distinct. They are neither all-embracing nor mutually exclusive. To reiterate, each of these themes or stages is associated with particular stresses – some of which, once identified and recognised, should be within the power of the host organisation – in this case social services departments – to mitigate.

Entry

The first stage is *entry*: the point at which social workers begin disaster work. Although for many workers such work begins when they arrive at the scene of the disaster, often, as was the case at Hillsborough, in response to a call for help, support teams generally come into being sometime after the event, though for most of the Hillsborough teams this was only a matter of days. This period of entry may be problematic, and workers experiences and expectations will be influenced by the manner of their recruitment. The British Psychological Society's Disaster Working Party, for example, recommended that an 'appropriate selection process for professionals must... be established' (BPS 1990 p.7).

In relation to the Hillsborough teams, three different procedures were employed. Some teams were selected by 'management' – most usually the person who was to be the team leader – others by accepting volunteers, and for two of the teams, staff were selected through the more usual appointment procedures of advertisement and interview. Of the workers responding to the survey, approximately two-thirds said that they were either invited or selected, the other third having volunteered. The majority of those who were invited said that they would have volunteered anyway, and almost all the social workers – irrespective of their method of entry – felt that the fact that they thought they would make a good contribution was the most important reason behind their decision. This was followed closely for many by the feeling that they possessed the right skills to help (which is interesting in the light of what they said once they actually were involved in the work) and a strong desire to help.

Each method of appointing had its attendant problems. Managerial selection, for example, sometimes appeared autocratic. As one team leader commented:

> We contacted people we knew could cope with it. We took some flak for that at the time I remember. There were other people in the office who wanted to make a contribution. At the beginning we focused on the appropriate qualification. What we didn't take on board was the fact that we had unqualified staff who were perhaps trained counsellors. It was very rigid really.

In a similar way calling for volunteers was sometimes inefficient and potentially chaotic. Traditional methods of filling job vacancies were time-consuming and consequently not necessarily well-suited to crisis-response. In addition two further problems in the selection procedures were identified by team members. There was a significant issue in one of the teams about equal opportunities and, in particular, that the advertisement of the posts and the selection process had produced a team without any ethnic minority members. This was set against the fact that the city in which the team operated, Liverpool, has a large and long-standing black population:

> We didn't have any black candidates... Knowing what I do now I think it probably should have been advertised differently... We actually tried to rectify it... put [two workers] into Toxteth... and tried to find out what they needed and what we could do within our team to fulfil some of the needs of the areas. There's a lot of bad feeling about the black community and the black workers not being consulted in the beginning...

Given the history of Liverpool's ghettoised and segregated black population (Small 1991) and of the virtual exclusion of this population from much of its footballing culture (Hill 1989), there can be little surprise that scant consideration was given by the authorities to the possible needs of this significant and long-standing community. That the team attempted to do something about this situation is laudable, but given that it was by this point rather late in the day – the team, remember, was not established until several months had passed – the efforts were probably destined to fail. The 'bad feeling' that was alluded to by the worker above is the sign that at least one section of the community affected by a major tragedy feels that, once again, it has been ignored.

The other problem that cut across many of the teams was the lack of adequate thought that was given to the appointment of administrative staff. This is not to suggest that the wrong people were appointed, rather that the types of difficulties experienced by social workers also affected administrative staff and were even less likely to be recognised. Thus, problems associated with moving jobs in a hurry, not knowing how long one would be required for, yet quickly finding that it was going to be important to have consistent administrative cover, caused problems for staff. The general experience also appeared to be that the needs of administrative staff were the last to be considered and the least likely to be dealt with.

Selection procedures for such specialist or core teams are further complicated by the fact that they occur during the 'impact' phase of the disaster (Powell 1975, Raphael 1986) when considerable goodwill is still present. At this point, when 'arousal' is high and 'heroic' activities are undertaken (Erikson 1979, Cohen and Ahearn 1980), large numbers of workers may wish to become involved and to help in the response to the disaster. Hillsborough was no exception to this. One worker who was at Hillsborough on the day and later became a member of one of the teams described his feelings in the following way:

> What I was surprised about... was how desperately I wanted the job, because I... felt some belonging to it. I would've felt very angry if I hadn't got it. When I was interviewed I actually didn't feel like they spent as much attention to the fact that I could've been a victim and shouldn't have been doing the job, as they should've. I was prepared for that. I was prepared to say how I felt like I had dealt with it... I was quite relieved because I wanted the job, but I could've been much more damaged and much less use to people than I hope I was.

The widespread altruism which exists in the early days may itself lead to problems for those tasked with putting together disaster teams. Under such circumstances, there is a much increased likelihood that, for example, unexplained managerial selection will lead to resentment amongst those who are excluded, or that calls for volunteers will result in too many people coming forward, thus leading once again to the necessity for managerial selection.

For those who are chosen, they often begin this difficult, taxing and especially unusual work in the knowledge that some of their colleagues feel resentful about the process by which the appointments were made and even about the necessity for the work. In this situation the core team member may have no effective means through which to counteract such feelings, for the appointment procedure is, more often than not, opaque, even to them. Not only were there colleagues outside the teams who questioned the procedures by which teams were appointed, but there were also some who questioned the work itself. This was particularly felt by those undertaking disaster work outside the main areas affected by the tragedy:

> A lot of people couldn't actually see the relevance of [our] involvement. I think if we'd been in Liverpool or Sheffield colleagues would have had more sympathy... 'There's no real need, what are they doing out there?' Also I picked up the 'well OK it's a disaster and people have suffered, but there are a lot of individual disasters out there and people haven't had this sort of attention.' There was a lot of anger around about that... It was quite stressful.

Such criticism was unusual in the immediate aftermath of the disaster, but there was a tendency for it to become more explicit at a later stage, generally when the period of goodwill had passed.

For some workers the problems they face at this stage are exacerbated by being unsure of how long they will be called upon to occupy their new role. As one team member said:

> when I called in that first day I didn't know whether I was going for two hours, two days, two weeks or two years, and I wasn't sure I wanted to be there at all.

Under such circumstances, the experience of the transfer from one job to another was for many Hillsborough workers enormously stressful. Nevertheless, it remains the case that the effects of what Erikson (1979) has called the 'honeymoon' period of the response, the sense of 'goodwill', the desire to help, are so strong at this point that they appear to offset many of the less positive experiences of beginning disaster work.

Engagement

The 'entry' and 'engagement' phases are difficult to separate for both tend to occur before this honeymoon period has passed. The *engagement* phase is a period in which workers first confront and then begin to come to terms with the task they are faced with. It is a time of considerable pressure, role strain and role conflict. Enormous demands are made upon workers both emotionally and physically in terms of the numbers of hours they work. More than four-fifths said that they had overworked in the immediate aftermath of the disaster, and although this proportion declined as time passed 70 per cent of workers said that they had overworked at some period since. In the immediate aftermath it would appear to be a combination of the amount of work to be done together with a strong sense of urgency:

> I overworked immediately after joining the team through a combination of enjoying the work and the manic atmosphere in the team at the time.

Such a response was by no means confined to the social workers themselves. As one senior manager responsible for his department's response to the disaster commented:

> In the early weeks there was such a lot of work to be done that we did all that was possible throughout the day and then slept.

Under such circumstances it is particularly important that there is someone who can take control and make sure that some order is maintained and that workers take breaks, for it is clear that the pressure to work combined with the desire to help will make some continue far beyond the bounds of what is reasonable or, indeed, professional. The reality is that there quickly comes a point where workers cease to function effectively and far from being a support to those in need, may themselves become a casualty. Whilst many are able to recognise when the time to stop has come, this will not be true of all, and the expectation that individuals will take care of themselves in this respect is not a realistic one. One of the most important managerial functions in the immediate aftermath is to stop staff working at specified intervals and make sure that they go home and do not return until a reasonable period has passed. If there is a lack of clarity about the nature of the organisational response or about line structures and responsibilities, then an unreasonable onus will be put upon individual workers. One worker described her initial foray into disaster work in the following terms:

> I went out at half past eight on the Sunday morning not to reappear until two o'clock on the Monday morning, having only popped in briefly to tell my husband where I was. That in fact went on for three days at that pace. It was only when my husband said 'when are we going to see you?' [that] I actually considered my family and myself.

Many Hillsborough workers talked about the extent to which their personal lives took a backseat during the early days and even weeks of the disaster. There is much interesting and important research work to be done in the future with the partners of disaster workers for their lives too may be profoundly affected by the consequences of events like Hillsborough.[2] When the above social worker's line manager also attempted to put a stop to this excessive activity the worker reported feeling very angry and disappointed. This is a common feeling and makes it all the more likely that managers may attempt to avoid the responsibility of taking control in such circumstances. Nevertheless, even extremely experienced social workers found themselves caught up in this way:

> She said, you know, 'you must go home, you've done your bit, you've done enough... its over to the rest of us that weren't involved at the weekend' – other social workers had been called in to cover for us... I know some people felt well that's fine but I'll go when I'm ready to go

and not when I've been told. I found it very difficult I must admit because there was a bit of me that didn't want to go... I was on this sort of high I suppose.

Further role conflict resulted from the very quick transition from one job to another. For many Hillsborough workers this meant dropping, often without warning, their complete caseload, leaving their previous teams and clients and hoping that their already busy colleagues would cope with the extra burden.

[The management] asked people to apply for the jobs. There were some difficulties initially in that they were asking people to apply but weren't agreeing to cover the post you were leaving. That made it difficult for people.

For other workers there was at least a transitionary period where they were expected to maintain their existing caseload whilst taking on disaster work. One team leader commented 'I was panic stricken when the first batch of referrals came in and I had to start juggling the caseload'. A team member commented:

I did part-time in my old job and part-time with the team I think for two or three weeks... That was bloody awful, that part, to do it. And I did do it but it was like cutting yourself in half'.

Many workers felt they were breaking commitments to existing clients by leaving to do Hillsborough work, with no guarantee that their employers would ensure that their work was seen through. For others, like the person just quoted, the continued demands of their existing jobs made it difficult for them to engage with Hillsborough families and survivors as fully as they desired. These conflicting demands were a source of considerable extra stress for social workers, under circumstances that departments frequently failed to recognise or respond to. More than one team felt that the amount of work they were able to do – particularly of a proactive or outreach nature – was restricted because insufficient space in their workloads was made available.

This is an area where considerable pre-planning and thought by departments is required for, as has been suggested, both workers who were able to do solely Hillsborough work and those who had to continue pre-existing work alongside the new demands, experienced considerable difficulties. That this is a complex and difficult transitionary period for social services departments to manage is illustrated by the fact that even some of those workers who made an almost immediate and complete break from their previous posts also felt partly unsupported or unprotected. Many felt that their absences, and the nature and importance of the work they had left to do, were not properly explained to the teams and colleagues they had left. This is not only a problem for workers when they begin such work, but the resentment they experience often continues – and at times increases – during their period in the disaster team. It is a particular source of concern for them when they approach the point where they anticipate re-entering mainstream work and possibly rejoining old teams and colleagues.

Establishment

Relations with colleagues, be they peers or managers, continue to be a potential source of role stress in the third phase – *establishment*. This phase occurs roughly between the end of the goodwill or honeymoon period of the disaster and the end of the life of the team. For some teams whose lifespan was very short and confined to the 'impact' phase of disasters, establishment is not an issue. For teams with an extended existence, this period is a lengthy one in which staff settle into their role as disaster workers. Crucially, however, the period of goodwill ends; just as the disaster workers are settling into their new roles, almost everyone else in their department is attempting to get things back to normal. This resulted in some instances in quite strong feelings of isolation amongst disaster workers. Far from being lauded and praised for the work they were engaged in, they often felt defensive and under attack. One worker described it as a 'backlash' and said 'the team you left are asking what the hell you're still doing engaged in this. People begin to say you're not doing much anyway. [They say] we've got kids in danger here from the lack of a child protection team and these clowns are there... in a purpose refurbished building sitting around and drinking cups of tea'. As one senior manager commented:

> For many people not closely involved, the disaster was soon forgotten, and I sometimes felt I was viewed as a nuisance or an irritant when I was still pursuing relevant matters some time later.

This backlash comes at a time when workers are becoming established in their new roles, which are often outside normal social work assumptions and boundaries. Disaster workers are frequently given considerable freedom, at least early on, to develop their work in the way they see fit. They are given, at least early on, some of the freedom, resources and power, normally denied to them. To an extent they become detached from the normal mainstream hierarchy of the organisation they belong to. One of the team leaders observed:

> We've certainly been able to do lots of things you wouldn't imagine you'd be able to do in an ordinary team. From taking a couple of kids ten-pin bowling to giving people money... We've been given a great deal of leeway... [and] we haven't had bureaucratic requirements. So there's not that degree of control... We don't fill any forms in and no-one really asks me what we're doing.

As a result, workers' identities become very much focused on the team and the work of the team, and this, allied to the heightened emotional nature of the work, reinforces the massive commitment, identification and involvement social workers develop for disaster work. At such a time, perceived lack of support for such work by management or, as was the case for at least one of the Hillsborough teams, by local politicians, is very keenly felt.

One of the observable consequences of the way in which the social services response to Hillsborough was managed was that some of the core teams became increasingly isolated from their departments. As has been suggested, such is the desire on the part of the authorities to respond, and to be seen to be responding quickly and effectively, that teams are set up, resourced and housed with little thought to the long-term consequences for that team and its members. The setting up of teams and the way that this was managed after Hillsborough was not overly problematic in the short-term (i.e. the first few weeks after the disaster), but sadly some aspects appeared to have increasingly deleterious consequences in the longer-term. Central to this was the siting of the teams, both physically and symbolically, outside the everyday structures of the host department. As one team leader described it:

> [Team spirit] was always undermined, I felt, by the lack of support by the Department. Saying, well we've given you a nice little building, we've given you X number of workers, we've given you the freedom to choose the way you do the job, get on with it. That's the extent of the support that I feel the Department wanted to give.

The early autonomy that teams required to respond fluidly and creatively to circumstances as they unfolded became entrenched and dysfunctional as time passed. As the disaster work became less newsworthy and less time-consuming for senior managers, so the teams tasked with responding certainly perceived themselves to be cut off from the day-to-day functioning of their employing body. Workers and team leaders felt that their work was not understood, that their efforts were not appreciated and, in some cases, that their work was not *managed*. The 'hands-off' approach that was established at the outset was rarely changed as circumstances altered. Communication between teams and their departments was always likely to be difficult given that the usual line-structures appeared not to be in operation for much of the time. The simple lesson here is that just as disaster workers need to be closely supervised and managed, so core teams – and in particular the team leaders – need to be closely supervised by their departments. This issue of supervision and management is returned to in the following chapter.

Ending

If it has not already been decided, at some point during this stage a decision about when the team is to close will have to be made. This is a difficult decision to make, and one that will inevitably cause resentment and indignation if the ending is imposed by managerial or political dictate. Walker Smith, in her report on the work of the Kings Cross Support Team (1990), says that they were greatly helped by the knowledge that they would be in existence until the second anniversary. For many of the Hillsborough teams having a recognised closing date which they were, to some extent, involved in choosing was of importance for two major reasons.

First, such teams were able to fit their closing date into a convenient point in the chronology of the disaster aftermath: after the first or second anniversary, after the end of the inquests and so on. Second, knowing in advance when the closing date was to be, allowed the team members to plan the way they wished to finish. This involved not only the extremely difficult job of bringing to a close the work they were still doing with families and survivors, but also planning how they would cope with the termination of disaster work and re-entry into mainstream social work. Recognition of this difficulty led Hillsborough teams to adopt a variety of approaches to this further transition, such as the use of counsellors to aid their understanding of the process and to provide extra-departmental debriefing, writing up and producing accounts of their work, holding some form of celebration with those who had used the services they offered to mark the closing of the team, and so on. Peter Hodgkinson (1988 p.123), writing about the work of the Herald Assistance Unit, describes the importance for them of group support, and of external support to cope with the termination of disaster work:

> Bearing in mind that our work was so closely connected to bad endings, a totally external group was brought in to help us 'say goodbye' to each other, the work, and a very specific role to leave the pain behind, and to reintegrate into previous or new jobs. It was inescapable that we returned different people – survivors, but not victims.

Experience from this and previous disasters suggests that it is very important for the future well-being of support team members that the team is not allowed to slowly collapse or fragment, but is able to work towards a concrete finishing date, that the 'ending' is not one of dissipation but decision. As has already been suggested, one of the greatest sources of anger and stress for workers was the lack of clarity about how long they would be able to continue with the post-disaster work. For the workers in more than one team it quickly became apparent that despite all the 'hype', as they perceived it, there did not appear to be a commitment to maintaining the response. One worker who had gone on holiday just prior to joining the core team returned to find that at the first team meeting she attended one of the items on the agenda was the future of the team. It became apparent at this point some four months after the disaster, she suggested, that the department was seriously contemplating closing down the team.

One of the problems that affected several teams was that after the initial rush of the first week or two – there was quite a lengthy period in which relatively few referrals came through. This prompted two general types of response: on the one hand some managers viewed this as evidence that there was relatively little need for the service; as one worker said:

> When we started up and there weren't queues of people at the door looking for help, it seemed the [team leader] interpreted that as meaning that people were OK and that we weren't needed.

On the other hand, there were those – particularly the workers themselves – who saw this as an opportunity to build upon anything that had already been achieved and to work at bringing the service to those who might need it. It was, in some senses, a clash of cultures between those responding to 'demand' – as they would be expected to with regard to other areas of social services work – and those who had taken the message about the importance of outreach to heart and were convinced of the need to publicise the service:

> It was very different to any other team I joined in that in other teams the work was waiting to be done... [with the Hillsborough work] you didn't get a caseload and say, there you are, go and see Mr and Mrs Bloggs. It was about selling social work, selling ourselves, selling what we had to offer really.

Once this crisis had been seen off, for several teams there was a continuing struggle to keep the work going. In one authority the pressure to close came directly as a result of financial restraint measures adopted as a consequence of poll tax capping, whereas in other cases the decision-making process appeared to be rather less clear:

> We never really knew where the pressure to close down the team was coming from. We assumed it was coming from higher up [the department], but it might have been [the team leader].

Staff who were working very hard, often under very difficult circumstances, felt frustrated and sometimes bitter about the actions of their employers. One worker, describing the battle she and her colleagues had to keep their team going in the face of opposition from some quarters in their department, said:

> I'm quite angry about [it] because I think [it] masked some of what we were going through. We were caught up in it, and it wasted some of the energy that could have been put into the work.

and this was confirmed by another colleague:

> It was almost that our *raison d'etre* was to survive, because we felt that there was a lot we needed to do. So we put a lot of energy into justifying our existence, which was very frustrating – you couldn't get on with the job you'd been set up to do.

The experience and its potential consequences were neatly summarised by one worker:

> What was a problem was the fact that we felt very much unsupported by our department. On top of everything else that made the job very difficult. I can remember going home and being in tears. It wasn't the Hillsborough work that was upsetting me – though that was upsetting – I could have contained that, but what seemed to push it over the edge was the fact that you weren't getting any support. Not just personal support, but even worse you were having your job taken away from you.

In terms of the pressures placed upon workers by their organisations, it was the difficulties that surrounded the closure of teams that caused the greatest resentment and distress. Whilst it is difficult for departments, particularly in these times of severe economic restraint, to commit resources for definite and lengthy periods of time, clear thought needs to be given in the future to the possibility of making commitments to the staff who take on the disaster work. Many of those interviewed as part of this research said that without a written contract they would not consider, and they would advise any colleagues not to consider taking on work of this sort in the future. Indeed, even if the conditions that they felt were necessary were available it is doubtful that many would undertake disaster work again.

Re-entering the mainstream

With the end of the team there is the question of re-entering mainstream work, and possibly returning to old colleagues and teams. How do ex-disaster workers cope, and what sort of support do they get? Of the disaster workers who had been involved full-time in the work and who had returned to mainstream work by the time of the survey, just over two-fifths said that they had found the transition back difficult. The majority of these felt that little had been done to help smooth this transition and that little support had been forthcoming, particularly from their new colleagues and line manager. For some, the problems stemmed from the inevitable comparisons they made between the work they had been doing, the environment they had been working in and what they experienced when they returned:

> ... the teamwork and sense of purpose and commitment of colleagues, which was a really positive experience, are lacking in mainstream work with some colleagues. We also had more freedom and autonomy to make quick decisions.

> There were some acerbic comments from non-involved peers. New skills were not capitalised on – frustration knowing what one could/should do with general clients, but are neither encouraged nor able through time constraints... Eventually I was off [work] for two months with anxiety.

Some workers simply found that they were still so affected by the Hillsborough experience that moving back into mainstream work was problematic on both an emotional and practical level:

> The other big issue for me was I lost my confidence when I came back. Having never particularly been a person that had a problem with that... I don't know where that came from but it certainly was a lot to do with that year and a half of Hillsborough. I came back with no confidence. Like [at a case conference]...just to introduce myself without contributing anything, that much was very difficult. Then trying to pull back from [wanting to] go out and do a visit and spend three hours there because you're picking up all these other issues... People came looking for me.

There was a widespread feeling that colleagues who had not been involved either did not understand or did not wish to hear about what disaster workers had been doing. This was communicated in a variety of ways, but the end result was generally that workers felt that did not have permission to talk about the disaster work. Not only did this make them feel isolated, but the isolation and the silence compounded feelings that the work had gone largely unacknowledged by colleagues at all levels.

There was little evidence from the research to support the often made assertion that involvement in disaster leads to eventual withdrawal from the profession. Though this obviously does happen from time to time, there is no evidence as yet that staff turnover is higher than might otherwise be expected. It should be said at this point that the Hillsborough research was being conducted at a relatively early stage after the disaster and that the situation with regard to loss of staff from the profession may change in years to come. Nevertheless, the picture two to three years after Hillsborough, whilst containing significant levels of resentment, anger and bitterness about the actions of employers, does not include the withdrawal or resignation of large numbers of workers. A number of workers have moved on, but only one of these linked this directly and unambiguously to disaster work. Although with the closure of their teams most workers have had no choice but to return to mainstream work, the few who have had to make a decision about whether to remain or return have also had their difficulties:

> [I] applied to return to a mainstream departmental post, but when I asked for time [two months] to terminate the [disaster] work professionally, in a good practice way, [I] was refused this and consequently turned the job down. I feel the senior management should have facilitated this and supported me.

Another perspective on this whole issue is provided by someone who was not a social worker but who was deeply involved in Hillsborough work over a long period of time. After spending time at a day conference that been organised in the North-West to discuss the issue of terminating the work, this worker commented:

> I felt jealous... of social workers who were able to 'walk away from it' in a way. I was still in the community.

Finally, in relation to the organisational context of the work, there were the difficulties faced by almost all the staff who were not in teams: the staff that took on Hillsborough work, but continued in their mainstream posts and with their day-to-day work. First, and in almost all cases, little or no provision was made by their departments for the extra work they were taking on (either in terms of the increase in workload, or for the nature of the new cases). Many of these workers took on a considerable amount of quite stressful Hillsborough-related work, and yet received little supervision, management or formal support.

> The main problem in my particular case was being isolated from the... main [group of Hillsborough workers] and the fact that the [Hillsborough] work that I did often took on less importance than my general work – the two were certainly not compatible.

The data from this study suggest that there are a variety of problems experienced by social workers working in the aftermath of disasters. These are related not only to the nature of the work and to the levels of distress that they encounter, but also to the organisational context in which the work takes place. One of the consequences of this is that any system that attempts to provide support for workers undertaking such work will have to confront both these sets of issues. The following chapter looks at the management, supervision and support of disaster staff in general, and at the operation of the staff counselling service set up after Hillsborough in particular.

Conclusion

- The maintenance of the response over an extended period of time is one of the most crucial objectives, yet one of the hardest to achieve. The good intentions expressed by senior managers caught up in the emotion of the tragedy, that are visible at the outset, either soon disappear, or are undermined by changes in the local political climate. Long-term strategic decisions need to be taken in the early weeks – for example, what sort of team will be set up and how long it will operate for – and these need to be adhered to. The stresses experienced by workers can easily be exacerbated by organisational problems affecting the work. Crucially, although some flexibility is necessary, workers need some indication of how long the service will be maintained and that the work is supported and valued by their department. Failure to provide a secure environment for the work is likely to undermine the extent to which staff feel they can work effectively.

- Long-term commitments need not only to be made but adhered to.

- Social services should be prepared to maintain a response for upwards of two years.

- The impact on the staff can be divided roughly into three categories: the nature of the work, the emotional and behavioural consequences of the work, and the organisational problems and role stresses experienced by social workers. Disaster work is highly stressful and staff therefore need to be closely and sympathetically managed, as well as having access to support outside their organisation.

- There was a widespread feeling amongst the disaster workers that the professional training that they had received had not prepared them for what they had encountered in the aftermath of the disaster. Consequently, the social workers felt they had benefited from the 'orientation' training that they received immediately after the Hillsborough disaster – training which gave them some idea of what to expect, and which carried the message that their basic social work skills were the ones they should rely on. Nevertheless, the majority of workers felt that further training would have been valuable, and there was agreement that it was counselling skills that should form the focus of this. These should be developed in the context of providing practical help and working with relationships.

- There is an urgent need to review the process by which workers are selected for disaster work.

Notes

1. It is important at this stage to remember a number of simple points, including: some of the social work staff attended the semi-final and were therefore 'survivors' or 'witnesses' of the disaster; some of those who didn't attend had relatives or friends who were there; many were Liverpool supporters and even larger numbers were football supporters; the vast majority lived in the communities that were directly affected by the disaster and most likely the majority were born and brought up in those communities.

2. Just as friends and relatives of 'primary' victims of disaster are affected and, on occasion, require support and/or help so, similarly, it should not be surprising to find that relatives of rescue and recovery personnel and relatives of carers may also require support. In this context see Dixon, P. (1991) and Weaver, K. (1990).

CHAPTER 7

Caring for the Carers

> In the training of several disaster teams over the years, it has become apparent that the great majority of professionals have never asked for professional help and are certain that they would never use their own agency. (Hodgkinson and Stewart 1991)

This chapter looks at the question of providing support for social work staff involved in the aftermath of disasters: in short, how agencies should care for the carers. Although it focuses on disaster work, the arguments that run through this chapter, as was the case in previous ones, are held to be applicable in many ways to so-called 'mainstream' social work. The chapter opens by examining the sources of support that were available to workers of which there were, essentially, two: first, the normal route of supervision from a line manager – a managerial relationship in social work which is generally held to be one that not only involves control and direction, but also guidance and support (Bamford 1982); second, the counselling service set up specifically for those involved in the disaster work by the authorities responsible for co-ordinating the social services response to Hillsborough, in conjunction with the British Association of Social Workers (BASW).

Having examined the main sources of support, the chapter moves on to look at the circumstances under which workers took advantage of the available services, any barriers that they felt impeded them from doing so or, alternatively, anything which they felt made it easier for them to look for support. It then examines their experience of, and the impact of, supervision and other forms of support. First, however, what was available to workers?

Sources of support

The most usual avenue through which social workers receive guidance and support is via the supervisory line-management structure of most social services departments. Basic grade social workers would expect to talk through their work, and any problems they might be experiencing, with their team leader; the team leader with some form of area manager, and so on depending on the size and structure of the department in question. Early on, however, it was recognised by the IAG that the impact of disaster work was likely to mean that the usual supervisory arrangements would be unlikely to meet all the staff care needs required. It was made clear from the beginning, however, that any staff care initiative that was taken would be an addition to rather than an alternative to the usual supervisory arrangements.

The bulk of the core authorities responding to the disaster organised their workers into teams although, as was described earlier, some staff took on disaster work alongside their normal caseload. The latter therefore presented a somewhat more tricky supervisory task. In addition to these standard arrangements, one of the core teams made its own provision for debriefing (Dyregrov 1989, MacLeod 1992) or counselling. They arranged for a number of psychologists from one of the local hospitals to offer a service to the team. This included a number of facilitated group sessions, at least one compulsory session of individual counselling, with follow-up counselling if thought appropriate and desirable by the worker. This arrangement came about largely as a result of an initiative by the team leader in question who felt it important to make provision for support for the team, and used personal and professional contacts to secure what he felt was necessary.

Aside from these arrangements, the major source of support for the disaster workers came in the form of a specific service known as 'Staffline'. Immediately after the disaster a huge number of offers of help were received from social services departments, individual social workers and a variety of other trained counsellors. At the beginning of the week following the disaster BASW offered to act as a co-ordinating body for all the agencies offering staff counselling and support – a presage of the more extensive role that it would soon occupy. BASW, who already had an office in Liverpool, decided that those premises would be the logical place from which to organise the co-ordination process, and they were able to make an adjoining room available for counselling purposes.

By Wednesday 26 April (11 days after the disaster) the BASW office was up and running, a telephone number – a helpline for staff – had been established, and arrangements were underway for the production of leaflets to publicise the service. It is worth reproducing the text of the first publicity document that was produced, for it gives some flavour of the scheme and its original aims and approach:

A personal message to staff currently working on or whose work has been affected by the Hillsborough Disaster

STAFFLINE 051 XXX XXXX

Since the Hillsborough Disaster on Saturday 15th April the work load for Social Workers and other professional colleagues has increased enormously. Many of you will have had direct or indirect experience of the trauma caused by this disaster and many of you will have counselled and will continue to counsel people who have been touched by this tragedy.

Both the British Association of Social Workers and your colleagues up and down the country became aware that this work is demanding of yourselves and you in turn may want the opportunity to talk to someone.

Consequently STAFFLINE has been set up which will provide a confidential service to yourselves by Social Workers trained in staff support from outside the immediate area. Initially it has been set up with the direction of Simon Cole CSS Dip.Coun. from the Royal School for the Blind, Leatherhead and assisting him will be seven Social Workers from Sandwell Social Services. The latter have been trained as members of a departmental support group.

STAFFLINE will initially be open weekdays from 11.00 a.m. – 7.00p.m. with an answering machine outside these hours. Arrangements can be made to see you by appointment at one of the counselling centres and there will also be an opportunity to meet STAFFLINE staff at the HELPLINE and ADVICE centres at the end of key shifts.

Please do not hesitate to use STAFFLINE if things get difficult; it is there to help you.

Although Staffline was managed by BASW and was outside of the control of any of the local authorities involved in the co-ordinated response to the disaster, the funds for the initiative were provided via the IAG, and representatives from BASW and Staffline continued to attend meetings of the group from time to time. Staff care always remained fairly high on the agenda for the IAG and in the final report or overview of their work the group noted that Staffline had been an item for discussion or consideration on 17 occasions during the period in which the IAG met. Furthermore, they concluded that one of their successes lay:

> ... in identifying particular periods of continuing stress for staff, eg., at anniversaries; during the inquest proceedings; during the transition period following the cessation of Hillsborough work and organising

preventive staff care policies via the BASW Staffline service, in the
forum of group meetings to debrief, individual counselling and con-
ferences to plan and share experiences. (Report of the Hillsborough
Inter-Agency Management Group, unpublished)

At the stage at which the offer to co-ordinate the offers of help was made,
the assumption within BASW was that this would be all that was
required. Longer term plans were being considered on Merseyside,
however, and with the prompting of one or two BASW members in the
region the Association was eventually approached with a view to providing a service. The work in the early weeks was undertaken by
volunteers from Sandwell and Somerset Social Services whilst a full-
time staff counsellor to run the Staffline initiative was sought. In the
event, the co-ordinator began work in early June 1989, but because she
had ongoing counselling and training commitments, the arrangement
was that she would work approximately 25 hours per week.

It was quickly evident to all those working on Staffline that the phone
line would not elicit much work and consequently the service almost
immediately became an outreach one. Towards the end of the project the
co-ordinator herself said 'if I'd just operated as a formal counselling
service I'd probably only have had about six clients'. Parallelling many
of the experiences workers had with their clients, the co-ordinator found
that many of her early visits to the teams and individual workers were
both informal and informational in character. Much of the early contact
was of a practical kind, with support or counselling work coming only
at a later date.

However, such a description of the work masks many of the difficulties that needed to be overcome before the service could be offered at
all. There was, according to the co-ordinator, for example, a 'considerable amount of hostility towards (the service) at the beginning'. Indeed,
she suggested that there was a very frosty reception in certain places
and much scepticism about what, if anything, she could offer. The first
task, therefore, involved not only going round and introducing herself,
but also describing what the initiative was about in a way that would
not be perceived as threatening or undermining. In the long-term, her
view was that she was largely successful in this regard, but that there
were still pockets of resistance that she had not been able to overcome,
on occasion simply because of lack of time and resources.

In the event, despite resistance in some quarters, the co-ordinator was
able to do some work with members of all of the teams set up after
Hillsborough with the exception of St. Helens whose members had
returned to their ordinary duties before she was properly in post. The
level of involvement with the other teams varied considerably. With
some of them she merely visited from time to time and, on occasion,

counselled or provided advice to individual workers. With others she did some rather more formal group work and with one team she acted as an external consultant, meeting with them regularly to 'air concerns, share experiences and look at different approaches to their work'.

In her own view, although there had been some initial difficulties and, indeed, some ongoing resistance, the co-ordinator felt that the work with the social services departments had been a success. She felt that it had been particularly gratifying to find that take-up of the service did increase over time, and that word-of-mouth had been behind most of the new calls she had received. Interestingly, one of the areas of resistance that was identified by the co-ordinator, was amongst men. Her experience of the Staffline initiative was that men were considerably less likely to come forward for help – they were much less likely than women to acknowledge that were not coping well – and that male users of the service tended to be 'in a much worse state than the women before they came for help'. Although this pattern held for most of the time the project was in existence, there was some change in the last few months, when several male members of staff came forward for support.

In addition to resistances within the Merseyside region, the co-ordinator had also been unable to do as much work with social workers outside the North-West as she would have liked. She had tried to engage team members from both Sheffield and Nottingham, but had less success than with some of the Merseyside workers. Her explanation for the lower success rate was the limited time that she had available for the work. She was employed via BASW by the Inter-Agency Group – a committee dominated by social services in general, and the Merseyside and neighbouring departments in particular. As a consequence, she felt that she was, at best, extending her remit by spending time outside the region working with other departments and consequently not being available to staff in the North-West.

Recognising 'need'

Whilst the issues that were outlined in Chapter 6 may be the *necessary* ingredient for making contact with a counsellor, rarely will they be *sufficient*, for as one respondent succinctly put it, 'it's quite hard for a helper to ask for help' – a view that was widely held:

> I remember when I first heard about [Staffline] and I remember thinking 'you won't catch me going to that'... I really feel I've been caught up in the thing, like so many people are, that if you're a helper, you have to be able to deal not only with everybody else's problems, but all your own. Otherwise you must be a lousy helper. And now I really feel that... to provide a good service it isn't necessary... not to have tried the service yourself. Having seen [the co-ordinator] I really feel I've

benefited from it. Not just for the particular problem, but in terms of my whole view of myself and, yes, it is OK to seek help.

Another worker said 'I was against using the BASW Staffline scheme that had been set up because I didn't feel in the early stages that it was necessary'. The widespread resistance to acknowledging the need for support is explored further below. It is important to note at this stage that it appeared that there had to be some other ingredient that would act as a catalyst to the process of contact between worker and counsellor.

As was suggested above, from very nearly the earliest days the Staffline initiative was less of a helpline than it was an outreach support service. It was clear to all those involved in the practical day-to-day operation of the initiative that it was going to be necessary to 'sell' the service to its potential clients. It was predictable, therefore, that when interviewed about their contact with the service, respondents would report that the process of making contact most frequently began at the instigation or prompting of the Staffline co-ordinator. Such prompting occurred in a variety of different ways – distinguishable by their explicitness. At its most explicit, this simply meant that the co-ordinator had said 'why don't you come and see me? I'm available', or on another occasion 'I'm aware that you're having difficulties, I'm there if you need me'. Other workers reported that they had taken the initiative, but that the co-ordinator had popped in to see them several times, either individually or as part of a team, to 'to introduce herself', 'to see how they were doing', or simply 'for a cup of coffee':

> If [the co-ordinator] had not contacted us, had not got in touch and said 'look I'm around' – a letter came – we would have had to cope with it all ourselves.

The outreach nature of the service served a variety of functions. Perhaps most obviously, it enabled the co-ordinator to get to know some of the workers and to let them know about the service. Having introduced herself, it allowed her to begin to do a few things for some of the teams or for groups of workers. Thus, although it was some time before any formal counselling work got off the ground, she was engaged in a number of other activities – giving advice about particular areas of work or ways of working, providing bits of literature and so on. This furthered the process of getting known, but more importantly it allowed the process of 'credibility testing' to take place. Just as the workers found that many of their clients were sceptical about what they could offer them – how they could help – so the workers themselves were sceptical of what this outsider could offer them. This was reinforced by the fact that they felt themselves to be in a specialised area of work, and one that outsiders would have little understanding or appreciation of. Her job at first was often one of convincing the workers that she had skills and expertise that could be of value to them. One worker, describing why he finally used the service, commented;

> [By that time] both the team and I had begun to get to know her...
> [Furthermore] she'd been the only person for this team at one stage...
> It was only [the co-ordinator's] head that was out of the sand... she had been seen to prove herself.

Having 'popped in', the co-ordinator let the staff know that they could see her privately and confidentially if they wished. What then seems to have been required is some other issue to prompt such contact:

> I think it was the feeling of being overwhelmed and being quite angry about not being relieved of a lot of the work.

> It all crept up on me and hit me... I would liken it to standing behind someone in a rounders... or baseball match and he... follows through and hits me... It was a bolt from the blue... I was doing the job. I was totally immersed in it... and then BANG!, like that, and I went down like a sack of spuds.

> I contacted [the co-ordinator] as a result of a general feeling of being depressed at what had gone on.

For some, however, it was seeing in their own behaviour reflections of things they had observed in their clients – 'mirroring' as some would call it (Stewart 1989) – that led them to seek some advice:

> What happened was that in opening my heart to [clients]... I began to recognise stuff in my own life that was unresolved... Just like them I was reacting to things in a way that I knew was over the top.

Even after all this, workers still reported difficulty in picking up the telephone to make the first appointment, and this reinforces the emerging message about the need for proactivity or outreach when providing a staff care service in the aftermath of disaster:

> The first time I phoned I felt like a grade A twit... Somebody had to be very proactive in engaging me... It was very difficult to take the first step.

Finally, there were those that did not recognise that they had been in receipt (in some formal sense) of support from the Staffline co-ordinator. The contact that there had been with the co-ordinator in these instances was viewed as having been simply informal and friendly, for the purposes of information-exchange or simply 'catching up with one another':

> I never actually used [Staffline]. I never felt that things had got that bad that I needed to do that. [The co-ordinator] came to visit me on at least one occasion just to see how things were going... and just before I left the team she visited us to see how we felt about it.

The point to be made here is that not only was much of the work that was done by the Staffline co-ordinator proactive in character, but a considerable amount went unrecognised as 'support' as such. There appears to have been a working assumption amongst some staff – despite what they were doing with their own clients – that staff support consisted either of one-to-one counselling or formal group work. From the co-ordinator's point of view, however, although the 'dropping in for coffee' was often a necessary precursor to more formal support or counselling work, it was itself, on many occasions, not dissimilar to what might be perceived to be formal support work – 'dropping in' often lasted several hours and, according to the co-ordinator, 'involved the unloading by staff of issues that were upsetting or unsettling them at the time'. They were also, on occasion, the forum for the airing of intra-team difficulties. What for some workers, therefore, appeared to be largely casual visits were, for the Staffline co-ordinator at least, a fairly fundamental part of the overall support work.

The legitimacy of seeking support

Quite a number of the workers that were interviewed made comments about the difficulties they experienced in asking for help. Like the one quoted in the previous section, a lot of these difficulties related to workers perceptions of professionalism and, more particularly, their desire not to be seen to have 'failed'. Such difficulties were in many ways anticipated in the setting up of Staffline, for it was both extra-departmental and intended to be private and confidential.

Seeking confidential help, however, is not quite as straightforward as it sounds, for visiting a counsellor requires time away from the office and 'off work'. If the worker is concerned that their colleagues should not know that they are using the service, then their visits will inevitably involve some element of deception. Under such circumstances the role and views of the team leader are crucial – a subject that will be returned to below. Nevertheless, it is fair to say that staff care was high on the agenda from the beginning of the disaster response and senior managers in most of the departments were supportive of the idea that it was legitimate for their staff to seek help and support.

Nonetheless, there remained a variety of barriers to 'owning up' to the need for support, some of which actually *stemmed* directly from the willingness of departments to recognise the possibility of such need. Almost all the social workers interviewed in this part of the study were agreed that staff care was low of the agenda (sometimes not on the agenda at all) in mainstream social work. Consequently, although departmental recognition of the need for formal staff care after Hillsborough may not always have been everything that the workers might have hoped for, the fact that it was on the agenda at all set Hillsborough apart from other work.

Amongst more than one of the core teams, the response to this was, ironically, to attempt to deny need. They did this for two reasons. First, they did not want to appear either 'elitist' or 'precious'. They did not want to be seen to be accepting things that were either not on offer or were actually denied to their colleagues in other areas of work:

> We were being offered things that as workers we never normally got... like 'essential car user'. Now that has got a long history in [our department]... the management punished us twelve years ago by taking [it] away... Then all of a sudden we [the Hillsborough team] could be essential car users.

Just as their colleagues were not given an essential car user allowance, so neither were they offered counselling or support for the stressful work they were engaged in. Under such circumstances – in which there was already jealousy – it is perhaps not surprising that workers did not always feel able to take up offers that were made. In addition to the perceived problem of elitism, there was the parallel difficulty of 'why this work?'. As one worker expressed it:

> I think as well I felt a bit naff... Like I'd done social work for ten years – all of us [in the team] had, we'd done child abuse work, we'd done sexual abuse work. Nobody came out and offered us counselling before... We've survived all this. [Hillsborough] is just more of the same.

These are, in some respects, the two sides of the coin of elitism. The disaster teams were often treated quite differently by their departments, certainly initially, and not only did the staff outside the special teams find the differential treatment difficult, but so did many on the 'inside'. Many of the disaster workers recognised and identified with the resentment that their erstwhile colleagues felt. Consequently taking up an offer of support – a service that was not available to their non-Hillsborough peers – was by no means unproblematic. Nevertheless, whilst take-up was slow, quite a number of Hillsborough workers did eventually use the Staffline service. How did those who did take up the opportunity view this activity, and how did their colleagues view it (if at all)?

Staff reported a variety of different experiences in relation to their take-up of the service. One or two of the teams in particular made a special point of being very open about staff care needs, and were openly supportive, even encouraging, of colleagues who wanted to avail themselves of any opportunities for support that were available. In these teams, it was not only more likely that staff would be aware of others among them who were using Staffline, but it was likely to be a source of explicit discussion and comparison:

> ... the time when I looked to staff support... There were other people [in the team] seeing [the co-ordinator] around that time and I can't remember whether it was someone suggesting or whether it was me deciding... so I picked up the phone.

In other teams, however, there was considerably less tolerance of the idea of looking for support outside the team. This intolerance was expressed in a number of ways. In some cases it was done by poking fun either at the idea, or at those who were foolhardy enough to express it, in others through open antagonism towards those seeking support. Finally, there was at least one team that presented itself collectively from the outset as being strong, mutually supportive and consequently not needing support. In such a culture it was therefore almost impossible for team members to later admit to wanting to use the Staffline service. Thus, despite the widespread impression amongst staff doing Hillsborough work that one team member expressed as 'in disaster there is permission "not to cope"', there was, at least for a time, quite general and on occasion long-lasting reticence about and resistance to the Staffline initiative, particularly by managers:

> It felt quite risky to own needing [support] within the team.

> Rightly or wrongly I picked up vibes that [Staffline] was a bit of a luxury, and that we shouldn't need it.

> It would have been very risky in our team [to admit to using the service] because it would have been quite hard to have said in that team 'I'm struggling'.

> [Team leader] made a big deal once about someone seeking help from another team... [He shouted] THAT IS NOT GOING TO HAPPEN IN THIS TEAM.

It is clear as a result of interviewing staff at all levels, and having talked to the co-ordinator in detail about her experiences, that it was the team leaders who were crucial in determining – at least in the early stages – whether or not staff felt able to look for support. As the comments of the workers above testify, more than one of the Hillsborough support teams appear to have had cultures in which it was difficult to ask for help. Their team leaders appear at certain times to have encouraged either a strong sense of individual self-sufficiency or, alternatively, a belief that the team should be able to deal with anything that might arise without help from others. Such explicit barriers to a service such as Staffline reinforce what is generally already a well developed resistance to seeking help that exists amongst social workers anyway. If initiatives like Staffline are to have any chance of success, they will need to be viewed by team leaders as a positive development.

The operation of the counselling service

The bulk of the work that was undertaken or facilitated by the Staffline co-ordinator can be placed within two major categories: individual counselling (and/or case supervision), and groupwork and networking. Despite the changing nature of the service, it was generally assumed – at least by those outside the day-to-day work of the initiative – that one-to-one counselling would still form the bulk of the co-ordinator's workload. Whilst to a degree this was true, that belief masks the time-consuming nature of the rest of the work that was undertaken. Nevertheless, much one-to-one work was done and although it is probably realistic to describe the majority of it as 'counselling', some workers described the service they had received as 'supervision'. These workers became involved in cases that they felt their line managers did not have either the skills or the specialist knowledge to help them with and, consequently, turned to the Staffline co-ordinator.

In addition to the outreach work and the individual counselling, there was also group work. Though only a limited amount of work with groups was undertaken by the co-ordinator, some of it appears to have been quite successful. The nature of such work varied from regular meetings with one of the support teams as an external counsellor, to one-off meetings with groups of staff from particular regions or organisations. What later turned out to be one of the most successful and most crucial areas of work undertaken by the Staffline co-ordinator began almost by chance. An attractive local residential adult education college had been offered to the IAG free for a period of five days, as a site at which disaster training could take place. The IAG representative who had responsibility for training initially turned down this offer and the Staffline co-ordinator, seeing an opportunity to get staff together, went ahead and, in her words, 'booked the college for a day and left it to the last moment to think about what to do'. In the event, this became the first of four very successful 'training days'.

In addition, a one-day workshop was held in the Midlands for workers from Nottinghamshire, Sheffield, Derbyshire and Leicestershire who had been involved in either Hillsborough work, or work after the Kegworth/M1 crash. This was successful in attracting workers from all those named regions except Sheffield. On the other hand, it did, the co-ordinator suggested 'uncover a number of workers who were obviously badly affected by their experiences' despite the fact that 'as the months have passed the interest in debriefing declines, and the possibility of reaching people who were adversely affected diminishes'.

Using the service

Perhaps not surprisingly, given what has just been said about the general level of resistance amongst social workers to the idea of counselling for themselves, there was very little of what might be called 'counselling' work in the first few months of the Staffline project. The first counselling appointment was almost a month after the main co-ordinator took over, and nearly two and half months after the disaster. There were a small number of counselling sessions each month during the rest of the year, but nothing that could be described as a regular flow of work until the following year. There was a lot of less formal work being done, visiting teams, giving advice, providing bits of training and setting up the first of the training days, but the general reluctance of social workers to seek help, and the resistance to and suspicion of Staffline meant that the number of counselling appointments generally remained low.

The level of counselling work picked up about eighteen months after the disaster. Whilst this might partly be explained by the increasing familiarity of the workers with the initiative and with the co-ordinator, it was also linked to the start of the full inquests and to the fact that several of the teams were either closing or planning to close. It was a particularly stressful time for workers and there were quite a number of new referrals to Staffline during the period. The workload remained fairly constant right up until the last days of the project, with new referrals coming in within the final two months.

Somewhere in the region of 25–30 social workers were seen for one-to-one counselling during the course of the project. Whilst this may seem a relatively low number, the vast majority of them were members of the core teams that had responded to the disaster, and the number therefore represents quite a high proportion (over a third) of the staff involved long-term with Hillsborough. Almost all those who received individual counselling were main grade workers or administrators, with only a couple being managers.

Because of the nature and set up of the service it was not possible, by and large, for long-term counselling to be considered. There were, in any case, only a small number of cases in which this might have been appropriate if it had been available, and for the most part it was only a small number of sessions that was necessary. Approximately two-thirds of the clients saw the co-ordinator on only one or two occasions, with the other third having between three and ten sessions. Exceptionally, there was one client who did establish a long-term counselling relationship that lasted over a year and involved more than 25 sessions.

As with the work that was undertaken by the social workers themselves, finishing was not entirely unproblematic. Although there was fair warning of when it was likely that Staffline would close, there were nevertheless still clients who felt that they continued to need to see the co-ordinator. That this proved difficult to arrange, particularly with regard to payment for the service, did not improve the way those who were seeking the support were feeling. Indeed, there were reports of especially insensitive handling of one worker who had suddenly to contend with a severe domestic crisis at the time Staffline was being closed.

Views of the service

What, then, were workers' perceptions of the counselling service and, more particularly, how helpful did they find it? The work undertaken by the co-ordinator that was described above as 'group support and counselling' was largely of two types: the informal – dropping in for coffee, attending team meetings, and so on – and the formal – group debriefings and structured group meetings. As was suggested above, the usual pattern was for the group work to precede any individual support work that was done. The informal group work in particular tended to precede, or perhaps more correctly even facilitate, later contact for individual counselling. The Staffline co-ordinator estimated that she had probably only been contacted on three occasions by people that she had not previously introduced herself to. There was negligible unsolicited contact and it was the group work that tended to, eventually, prompt individual contact:

> I spoke to [the co-ordinator] on the phone [after receiving a letter from her]... and she came out and did the two group sessions. Then I fixed up some time when I used [her] on a number of occasions, to go through some of the effects which were a direct result of my experiences of Hillsborough.

The numbers of people in the groups varied considerably, from the three or four who perhaps made up a team, to 25–35 people from one authority or department. The following quotes give some flavour of the issues and feelings that were raised at such meetings:

> We used [the co-ordinator] quite a lot to sound off about our anger, about fighting to keep the team going.

> There were a lot of tears in those sessions. Anxieties about lack of skills, about the possibility of not being able to cope and breaking down. Feeling inadequate to deal with the raw emotions and not being able to control them. There was a lot of camaraderie as well.

> It really provided us with group support. I don't think we would have got that from our team leader or other colleagues. We wanted to share some of the things we were coming across. We wanted to learn.

> We were looking for some sort of supervision as a group.

Such support for the group or team was often presented as having been in direct contrast to the efforts made by some of the senior managers who, it was suggested, either did not attempt to provide support, or if they did try to put something in motion, often failed to provide the amount or the type of support that was needed:

> When the team closed we had a meeting with the Assistant Director – just a normal kind of debriefing. My experience has been of not a great deal of support from management.

> There were support meetings set up throughout the inquests and we had a debriefing afterwards. They were OK in terms of following issues up... I wouldn't be able to say that they provided staff support.

> [The department] didn't take the initiative. I think the onus was put on us and that was unfair.

The activities that are subsumed under the heading 'individual coun-selling' are also many and varied. Nevertheless, the core activity was the seeking of advice from an independent support service. Those who had had only the one session with the co-ordinator tended to describe it using such terms as 'information', 'advice or 'consultation'. Those who had several meetings described what occurred in them as something akin to 'counselling':

> We went through a process of beginning to deal with some of the things around Hillsborough that had been getting to me... [helping] me to see more clearly, to work through why I was feeling like that, why I was feeling powerless. There are things which you are not responsible for, which you feel responsible for, and in the absence of a staff care system, people don't really have the time to sit down and talk.

and the one worker who saw the co-ordinator for a year said:

> I would say it's been a therapeutic relationship, and that I have had therapy.

Some of the workers reported having approached Staffline primarily for advice or information about particular cases or issues that they were having difficulty with. Suicide risk was perhaps the most common source of difficulty, with workers often having little or no experience of how to deal with clients who either threatening to, or in some cases had tried to, kill themselves. In one case, a disaster worker was in regular contact with someone who had tried to kill themselves on several occasions, and the co-ordinator had made a variety of suggestions about how the case could be handled with such things as contracts. Things reached a real crisis for the worker when it was time for an annual holiday and the client seemed particularly unstable. The solution, with the client's consent, was for the Staffline co-ordinator to take the worker's place for the duration of the holiday, making several visits to

the evident satisfaction of all concerned. Such a close level of co-operation was, of course, unusual, but it illustrates quite vividly just what can
be involved under the rather bland rubric of 'staff support'.

'Supervision' is how some of the workers described what they had
received – 'case-consultation' the phrase used by the co-ordinator.
Clearly, most of the cases that came under this category were not as
complicated as the one described above, but many workers found that
not only did they feel inadequate or impotent in the face of some of the
problems they were confronting, but that they did not feel that the
solution to their difficulties was to be found within their team or their
department. This also was the cause of some difficulties, for a few
workers reported awkwardness from team leaders who weren't keen on
their staff going elsewhere for what appeared to be case supervision.
The workers themselves appear to have responded to this in two ways.
Some, understandably, were reluctant to seek help outside the team for
fear of the response it might bring. Others became almost belligerent in
defence of their 'rights':

> I didn't consult anybody, tell anybody or ask permission. By that stage
> I felt it was my right.

> It felt quite risky... I thought if people can't handle the fact then that's
> their problem not mine.

In the event relatively few workers used the service without any of their
colleagues knowing about it. Such a situation reflected the extent to
which the service had become accepted by staff, and perceived by them
as being safe, legitimate and, generally speaking, non-threatening.
There are two main reasons for this. The major reason for the eventual
acceptance of the service was undoubtedly the fact that many of those
who used it found it helpful, so much so that they passed on their
experiences and encouraged colleagues to use it. The other reason, and
one that is somewhat more difficult to determine, is related to the nature
and structure of the service. Although the initiative has been referred to
throughout this report as Staffline, and reference has been made to the
work of its co-ordinator, the reality was that the service *was* the co-ordinator. Although there was also an administrator who played a most
important role in the running of the initiative, it was the co-ordinator
who provided the service to staff, and with whom they identified. That
this was the case is illustrated by the fact that the service ceased after a
while to be referred to as Staffline, and rather was known by the name
of the co-ordinator. Through a considerable amount of outreach work
and networking, large numbers of Hillsborough workers came to know
the Staffline co-ordinator, to trust her, to use her services and, if and
when they found it successful, to tell their colleagues about it. On such
occasions, because of the way Staffline operated and was staffed it was

not some impersonal service that was being recommended to colleagues, therefore, but an individual that was already likely to be known to them.

The final major area of work undertaken as part of the Staffline initiative was the loose-knit collection of activities which can be subsumed under the general rubric of 'networking'. The bulk of this work centred around the four training days and the study day that was arranged in the Midlands. These were primarily opportunities for workers to get together, to meet each other, to discuss their work, to share ideas, worries and problems and to focus on and think about a number of distinct issues. For some workers they were the first point of contact with the co-ordinator and led more or less directly into counselling. For workers outside the region this could be a lifeline:

> It was actually going to the conference in the Wirral, which was the August [1989], I'd held it until then... and that triggered off other things for me... I was having difficulty enough at that point helping myself without having to help others.

All the workers interviewed had been to at least one of the training days, and over a third had been to at least three. Without exception the days were reported as having been a useful and valuable experience, and it is interesting to note what it was that was found to be valuable. Each of the days was organised around a specific issue, such as long-term work, inquests, terminating the work and so on, and presentations were given by the co-ordinator and by a variety of other speakers, frequently disaster workers themselves. The days were thus presented as fairly standard training exercises. Although some of the workers did report finding some of the presentations and the information given useful, and as being the major *purpose* of the occasion, it was the other aspect of the days – being brought into contact with other Hillsborough staff – that had the greatest impact:

> They were great. I think like everybody said at the time there wasn't a lot of structure to [them], but the most important thing out of it was that it wasn't until then that we met other [workers]. It was meeting them... and not feeling so isolated.

Isolation appears to have been quite a common feeling among the staff doing disaster work. Not surprisingly, this was particularly the case for workers in Sheffield and Nottingham and others outside Merseyside who felt cut off from what was happening in the North-West, and even more so for those workers who were in the region, but were not organised in teams and were operating with little or no support or contact:

> ... very useful. I found it isolated here. It was good to talk to others doing the work... to feel part of the core... Within that setting I felt more

valued than I did here... I came away feeling rejuvenated, and wanting to get on with the work.

Just meeting with the other workers who were working in the same field... sharing the same anxieties... [the co-ordinator] was a facilitator for that.

The overall impression of the days is well summed up by the following worker:

The main thing was just meeting up with other people. Hearing them say what you're thinking. Because when you're on your own it is easy to think 'I'm the only one doing this' or 'if anyone heard me say this'... I think the... days were quite low key... not too structured... [they] gave you a chance to talk to people, to make allies. It was like one long debriefing session.

However, there is a certain irony at the heart of these training days. As has been suggested, the workers, pretty much unanimously, found them useful. What they valued them for was the opportunity to meet their colleagues, and they recognised, again almost to a person, that the days were only very peripherally about training. Most days involved perhaps a couple of sessions where the standard accoutrements of social work training – small groups, flip charts – would be in evidence. Yet the major function was mutual support and debriefing.

The days were, however, officially presented as if they were training days. There was a good reason for this: the days had to be financially supported and workers had, by and large, to get permission from their employers to attend. Not surprisingly, both of these were easier to achieve if the activities for the days were perceived as 'training'. Had they been set up and presented as 'debriefing days' or an opportunity simply for the disaster workers to get together, funding and participation would have been altogether more problematic. Indeed, participation may well have been problematic for another reason as well. High commitment to the job, with a consequent problem of a tendency to overwork, was evident amongst the majority of workers. Many found it difficult to take time away from the work, and 'good reasons' had to be found for absence. It is likely that presenting the days as 'training exercises' was, at least in the first instance, important in attracting social workers to the event. As it was, they often felt guilty leaving their clients unattended for a whole day, and attendance at days that were *just* a 'get together' would probably have been poor.

The results of such presentations were twofold. First, and positively, the turn-out to the days was high and the workers were given an opportunity to mix in a way that they otherwise might not have had. The second and unintended consequence, however, was that it enabled senior managers to continue in the belief that training needs were being met. The lessons from this seem fairly clear. Disaster workers appear to need – they certainly appreciate – the opportunity to meet each other and to share their experiences, their problems and their worries. Whilst such an activity can take place alongside some formal training, it is important that it is not itself described as training. In this particular case it easy to see why this was done, but it is important for the future of disaster work that senior managers are persuaded of the value of mutual support for workers as something in its own right. Those who organise such events should not have to disguise them as training exercises in order to justify their existence.

The impact of Staffline

How did those who used the service feel about what they had been offered and had received? Whilst some expressed slight reservations about the limitations of the service, none expressed doubts about its value, and the vast majority were very positive in their overall evaluation. The impact that the work that was done under the banner of Staffline had is clearly illustrated by the words of the following four workers:

> Somewhere to offload a lot of emotion. An opportunity to begin to stand back and to look in a more objective detached way at the issues that were affecting me. Something that challenged me to face up to some realities, some of which were about Hillsborough, and some of which were about things that had been triggered by Hillsborough. A lot of growth and a lot of personal development, and a more realistic expectation of myself.

> It gave me a clearer perspective about my role in that situation [Hillsborough support], also about my role more generally, and about me. If counselling is about helping you to see, to grow and develop, and to come to terms and a greater acceptance, then in success terms, the time I spent with (the co-ordinator) was very successful. That is unequivocal. She enabled me to move a tremendous distance in a relatively short period of time... There's still a long way for me to go and it has helped me to see that... A total success. There was nothing that didn't live up to expectations. A very, very traumatic experience though.

> I would be overstating it to say I'm around today because of [the co-ordinator]... although certainly I'm working today because of [her].

> I think my organisation has done well out of Staffline. I think I function better as a manager than I would have done had I not had the opportunity to spend that time with [the co-ordinator] working through the issues.

The only reservations expressed by workers concerned either the geographical location of the service or the limitations of only having one counsellor. For workers based in Sheffield, Nottingham, or even in Lancashire or Cheshire, it was some distance from their offices to those of Staffline. For those a long way away, it meant that opportunities to see the co-ordinator were few, and the only times they were able to justify going to Merseyside were for the training days. Many disaster workers located outside Merseyside were unaware that the service existed. Thus, for example, for the social workers who staffed the helpline and the drop-in centre in Nottingham, using Staffline was not an issue. The following comments illustrate the problem:

> I did not know the service existed.

> I do believe that everyone involved in the disaster work should have had some professional support. I had none.

> I have never heard of [Staffline].

> I did not realise that the staff line [sic] was available, perhaps because I live and work in Nottingham.

> If I had known about Staffline I would probably have used and appreciated it.

For workers closer at hand, visiting the Staffline office for counselling might nevertheless still necessitate half a day off work – something that workers who were suffering at least partly from overwork found difficult to do, or to justify. Furthermore, many were aware that the co-ordinator was very busy and was only employed on a part-time basis anyway.

Although there was little in the way of explicit criticism of the length of time someone had to wait for an appointment, there was an underlying assumption in much of what the other workers said that they needed to think carefully about how many demands they made upon the service. They felt they needed to use it sparingly and couldn't 'just pop in when they liked'. The major criticism of the service then, if it could be called a criticism, was that there wasn't enough of it. Staffline was widely valued and the workers interviewed who had used the service were unanimous in their support of it. Indeed, as one of the Support Team members commenting on the general issue of staff care said:

> The only things that I can think of that have been useful are [Staffline], and meeting and sharing with some of the other workers.

As a consequence of the reluctance of social workers to ask for help or to admit to needing support from an outside agency, one of the important latent functions of such a service is as a vehicle for breaking down resistances to staff counselling and myths about staff support. Shame and stigma about needing help are by no means confined to the more macho professions. Social workers appear to be just as reluctant to admit that they cannot or will not be able to cope with everything that confronts them in their jobs, as are policemen or firemen, if not more so. One of the greatest successes of the Staffline initiative, even though it was focused on a small number of workers, was that it encouraged a healthier view of what carers are able to do. By implication it also forced some of them to reflect rather more critically on their views of their clients and what they were providing for them. As one worker most perceptively commented:

> ... being a person who won't seek help easily, I've learnt a lot about the need to seek help. I'm now prepared to take the medicine I dish out.

The Hillsborough workers themselves – both those interviewed and those who responded to the survey – were in no doubt about the lessons that should be drawn from the Staffline initiative. In essence the lessons all boiled down to making the service more widely available: they felt it should have had a greater number of staff, that the staff should be full-time, that the service should be available permanently, and that it should not be confined to disaster workers. The reasons given for extending such a service were essentially twofold. First, other areas of social work and other social workers were viewed as being just as 'needy' as disaster workers, and just of deserving of care.

> [The service] should be available to all social workers – not just disaster workers. Many social workers suffer stress and work with very distressed clients... [they] should have use of the service.

Secondly, several workers expressed the view that extending such a provision would affect the culture of social work more generally:

> Social work is a stressful occupation and a situation in which the helpers can be helped would be a healthier way of working.

> One of the most important lessons I have from the work is how crucial staff care is in all aspects of social work. We ask colleagues to become involved in situations which can have significant personal consequences for them, but often fail to acknowledge this, let alone provide readily available support, or even acknowledge this is necessary. Help such as Staffline should be readily available and accepted as *normal* for staff in such work.

Management and supervision

At team level, the supervisor is expected to fulfil a multiplicity of roles – to allocate work, to organise the work of the team, to set and maintain good standards of practice, to ensure that statutory requirements are fulfilled, to act as a consultant, to advise senior management of the needs of the team and the area, and to communicate and explain management decisions. (Bamford 1982 p.53)

The role of the first line manager in social work is a multi-faceted one. The job carries a wide variety of responsibilities, some of which do not always appear to be mutually compatible. Most obviously, it is the supervisor's 'marginal position' (Smale and Tuson 1988, Smale *et al.* 1988) as the conduit between workers and management that carries with it the greatest potential for difficulty or conflict. As Bamford implies, the supervisor not only needs to be sufficiently in tune with the everyday needs and priorities of main grade workers to communicate these to management, but also be able to maintain sufficient distance from staff not to compromise the standard-setting and more obviously managerial aspects of the role.

In the type of situation that exists in the aftermath of a disaster these very specific skills are all the more important. In the early stages, not only does the social services department have to respond to a crisis, it is more than likely that it will itself be in crisis: it is faced with a variety of difficulties that it is inadequately prepared for, has little knowledge about and yet which demands quick and decisive action. Generally speaking, such action involves the setting up of a team of social workers which will not only respond to the immediate needs of the stricken community, but is also likely to have to provide a service over an extended period of perhaps two years or more.

Someone has to have responsibility for the everyday management of this team and not only does this person face the usual pressures that confront the team leader but, as has been illustrated in the preceding chapters, there are also a number of other significant difficulties: there is, for example, no easily definable population of potential users of the service; relatively small numbers of those affected by the tragedy are likely to come forward and seek professional help; many of those who are approached proactively by social workers will be very resistant to offers of support; many workers, at least at first, will feel that they do not have the skills to take on the work; once involved, workers will often tend to overwork and put themselves at risk; the impact of the first few days after the disaster is likely to place extraordinary emotional demands upon workers; and, in the longer term, workers face a variety of stresses which may themselves necessitate some form of counselling or other support. Whilst the disaster work will be highly valued by departments at the beginning, as 'things return to normal', disaster teams are likely to become isolated from the everyday activities of social services departments – indeed the team leader may well have to make strenuous efforts to ensure that proper communication is maintained between the team and senior management. This is by no means a full list, but it does give some indication of the difficulties faced by first line managers in the disaster situation and illustrates not only why there is a significant amount of support work that they need to undertake on behalf of their staff, but why they too may require a significant amount of support. How then did the workers and team leaders experience this management and supervisory role?

Without wanting to overstate the case, the general impression given by both groups was an unsatisfactory one. Both main grade workers and team leaders complained of lack of support from their line managers. There was strong criticism from workers in several teams about the lack of adequate supervision from their team leaders. The criticism was directed at both the major aspects of the supervisory role, i.e. the managerial (including the educational) and the support aspects (Kadushin 1976, Pettes 1979, Payne and Scott 1982). Thus, with regard to the managerial aspects of the job, some workers complained that they received little guidance in their work and that supervision did not really appear to involve an evaluation of their practice:

> I want to be challenged... I don't feel as if in supervision I've been challenged... Because I've been around social work a long time, I think people make assumptions that... I know more than I do... To not question my judgment, actions, decisions because I've been around a long time, it's not good enough.

There was a feeling that some managers shied away from some aspects of supervision because of the nature of the work. In particular, the fact that what was being done was perceived as not having been done before meant that the normal rules were not applied and that workers were trusted to simply get on with it. Such an attitude was all the more explicit in those authorities in which workers took on disaster work alongside their normal caseload and were not brought together as a disaster team. In some of these cases the complaint from workers was not that supervision was inadequate, but that it was non-existent:

> My team manager, in supervision, a couple of times... he'd say 'of course we won't talk about the Hillsborough work because that's sort of different'... I think he found it difficult. I remember him saying he couldn't do it, which doesn't exactly fill you with confidence.

Under these circumstances the responsibility for supervising what was acknowledged to be potentially difficult and traumatic work was completely abdicated. It would appear that the decision not to adopt a supervisory role was based on the belief that disaster work is 'different'. Even if this were true – and it has already been argued here that at the most fundamental level the work is *not* different – it is hard to see under what circumstances a manager feels that the correct course of action is to assume that the worker will act appropriately and responsibly at all times in relation to the disaster work without any supervision, when this assumption would not be made about any other area of work they might be involved in. One can only speculate on what underpinned such an attitude: perhaps a similar fear of lack of skills that beset many of the workers, or simply the view that the disaster work was not important?

> My own line-management were either totally unskilled in the whole area of bereavement or thought that the Hillsborough response was a total over-reaction and didn't really want to know... I was totally left with really no support and feeling very inadequate, very unable to tackle such a task.

As the above quotation suggests, workers were also critical of the lack of support that they received from line managers. With some exceptions, there was a widespread feeling that one could not turn to one's team leader for help or support with *significant* difficulties. The emphasis on 'significant' is important here for workers distinguished between everyday difficulties – fairly straightforward things that they felt it would be useful to get another opinion about and more intractable problems that were associated by them with the notion of 'not coping'. Team leaders were not perceived as a likely or realistic source of support in the latter areas. Part of the reason for this was that many workers believed that their team leaders did not have the skills that were necessary to help them work through the difficulties they were experiencing. What truth there was in this is, of course, open to question, but the fact that many workers felt this to be the case is in itself an indictment of the line-management system. More significantly, perhaps, for the question of staff care arrangements, the majority of workers were absolutely clear that they would not admit to not coping to a line manager:

> It was useful to have [the Staffline co-ordinator] so that we could talk about the personal things. It felt as if you could talk about things that were going on within the department that were very difficult, and know that it wasn't going to go to management.

This was confirmed by several of the team leaders who recognised that because of their position in the management structure their workers were unlikely to feel that they – or anyone in a managerial position – could be trusted with personal information:

> Social workers... were very suspicious of relating to somebody within the authority. What's going to go down on paper? What would happen in the future? They'd apply for another job... it would've been difficult for social workers to use anyone appointed [by the authority]

Furthermore, there was more than one occasion on which the social workers felt that the team leader was part of the problem. This tended to be the case when it was organisational factors that were at the root of

the problem that the worker(s) needed to deal with. Under these circumstances, being part of the management structure and therefore party to
unpopular decisions effectively undermined any possibility of the team
leader being used as a source of support:

> I certainly didn't use [team leader] in the supervisory way I maybe
> would have liked to use somebody. I couldn't go to him about team
> closure as he was one of the people who seemed to want to close us
> down.

Not only did the workers feel that they were insufficiently supported
by their line managers, but many suggested that they felt that this was
partly the result of the inadequate support and supervision available to
the team leaders. There was widespread recognition, confirmed by some
of the team leaders, that supervision of the teams and their managers
was inadequate. The end result was the potential for a greater number
of personal and professional problems than would otherwise have been
the case. Many social workers carried out their duties with less than full
supervision from line managers who, in some cases, also felt that they
were struggling to keep things going without adequate support from
their senior managers. Poor supervision meant that the onus tended to
be on the workers (and the team leaders) to set their own boundaries,
to control their own work, and to judge when they were failing to
maintain professional standards or to cope physically, emotionally or
psychologically with the work. As one of the social workers from a core
team commented:

> There was a great danger that someone could've come unstuck in it.
> That would be the only thing I would say, you need somebody over-
> seeing it. We didn't really have that. We were set up and left to get on
> with it, and there were a lot of risks in it. I remember [team leader]
> saying to me towards the end 'I feel I've let you down, because people
> are saying to me you look dreadful, that you're not right. I'm just
> missing it, I've not offered you the support I should be offering. There's
> no supervision or anything like that'... I said 'I know you well enough.
> If I need it I demand it. That's not a problem'... I was actually physically
> ill at the time.

In summary then, there appear to have been a number of problems in
relation to the supervision of staff at most levels in relation to disaster
work.[1] Staff do not tend to feel able to talk to their line managers about
any severe difficulties they might have experienced, either because they
thought that it was possible that it might be used against them in the
future, or because they didn't feel that their line manager had the skills
or expertise to provide the necessary advice or support. In addition there
is a widespread assumption that the work being undertaken in the
aftermath of disaster is sufficiently 'different' to mean that the usual

rules about supervision and management no longer apply. Consequently, line managers tended to allow social workers (and team leaders) a degree of autonomy and self-management that would tend not to exist in day-to-day social work.

There appears to be a danger in disaster social work that, as a result of the pressure of work both in terms of numbers and emotion, that managers and workers will simply immerse themselves in the work without taking the time to stand back and examine exactly what is being done. Indeed, such is the degree of autonomy available that general procedures are often held not to apply to the work at all.

One example of this is to be found in the area of recording. Practices varied considerably between the teams and at least one continued with its department's usual procedures. However, at the other end of the spectrum, more than one team took the view that the keeping of full records was inappropriate in such circumstances and consequently did not do so. Such a position was based on the view that 'normal social work assumptions' did not apply to disaster work and that the people they were working with should not become *clients* of the social services department. More specifically, the justifications for not keeping full records included the following: the people being worked with were not the 'usual social work clients'; that they were difficult to engage, that some objected to records being kept and would have nothing to do with social services if records were kept; that the work was not statutory and that therefore record-keeping was largely unnecessary.

To an extent some of this is true. Many of the people that the social work teams were working with were indeed articulate, professional people and therefore atypical of many who come into contact with social services. However, none of the teams that did maintain full records felt that their work had been more difficult or less successful because of that. One team leader commented:

> I cannot remember any incident when somebody said they weren't going to work with us any more because of our policy on files. It was more on the general level of people's reluctance to come to us because we were Social Services and kept files. I don't think that once we started to engage with somebody it caused a problem... You made it understood that it was the way in which we work, the tools of our trade. You did it in order to provide a better service.

Without records, not only is the relationship with the service user changed, but one of the keys to effective supervision of staff is removed, for recording is both a means whereby supervisors acquire knowledge about clients and an aid to the process of assessing the work of their staff (Bamford 1982). Without records, the likelihood that the supervisor will be an effective manager, both in terms of oversight and support, are reduced.

Because of its focus on the impact of the work, on the stresses and strains that are part and parcel of offering a social work service in the aftermath of a disaster, this chapter has, of necessity, been somewhat negative in its tone. It is important, however, that such problems should be kept in perspective for the vast majority of workers involved in such work describe it as having been exhilarating, satisfying and a source of fulfilment and growth. This is not to deny any of the above discussion about stress, or about the frustrations and occasionally the turmoil that workers found themselves experiencing. It is simply that, for the most part, workers were able to recognise that both elements appeared to have been an integral part of the work:

> The work was very draining, but I was still able to enjoy it, if enjoy is the right word. The work seemed to make a difference to people – obviously I don't know if it did – but it made it a very worthwhile job to do. Looking back now, it was an incredible experience and one I wouldn't have missed for anything. It had its costs but then everything does.

> I know how much it cost me… I wouldn't change it for the world. It's been the best job I've had. It's certainly been the most rewarding job. It's been the most stressful job as well.

So strong was this sense that they had experienced something special that this increased anxieties about what work after the disaster would feel like, and whether they would be able to readjust to work back in the mainstream:

> It'll never be the same challenge. Never be the same high as it was after that. Professionally, nothing will ever meet, I'm sure, the disaster, the work after the disaster. Those things are hard to come to terms with. Nobody else will understand that either, except for people that had experienced it.

In a broader sense than the personal experience of the work, there was also a widespread feeling that the disaster response had been positive professionally (Chamberlain 1987, Lunn 1989). Many felt that they had rediscovered their desire to be social workers and, for the first time in a long time, were actually offering the type of service that had prompted them to enter the profession in the first place. More particularly, the rewards were greater because, as one of the workers quoted above said, there was a sense that what they were doing was actually appreciated by the users of the service. The following social worker was expressing the experience of many when he said:

> This is the first time I've ever heard anybody say social workers have done a good job.

Finally, the work undertaken in the aftermath of the disaster was perceived by many as having provided an opportunity to challenge the widely-held negative image of social work in Britain. As one of the managers involved in the Inter-Agency Group on Merseyside commented (*Insight* 1989):

> I am proud to be associated with social work following Hillsborough. The effort, commitment and skill shown is quite exceptional. Social workers have given hours of their time. No-one has refused to do anything. It has shown social work in its true light, a positive light.

Conclusion

- The role of the team leader as manager, professional supervisor and major source of support for workers needs to be radically rethought.

- Social workers view looking for support for themselves as evidence of 'failure'.

- Disaster work is highly stressful and staff therefore need to be closely and sympathetically managed within their organisation, as well as having access to support outside of it. Social workers appear to be just as reluctant as anyone else to admit that they need help, especially if their employers are involved.
  Consequently, services need to be:

  Proactive – The 'helpline' model is not one that is appropriate for a staff care system. It places the onus on the caller to recognise that they might benefit from support at any given time, and requires them to make the first contact. The outreach model that is employed by social workers for use with their clients is the one that needs to be utilised by those attempting to care for professional staff.

  Extra-departmental – Social workers are unlikely to trust any counselling service that is linked to their own organisation and particularly to line-management structures. Because of the association of looking for support with the idea of having 'failed' in some way, workers assume that if it were known within their organisation that they had sought help, this would be likely to affect their future career prospects. As a consequence, unless there is some radical cultural change within social services departments, supervision from a line manager is unlikely to be able to fulfil this function.

  Available – Again, directly mirroring any service that is provided for bereaved families and survivors of a disaster, a staff care service needs to be accessible both geographically and in terms of the length of time that it remains available. It needs to be local and available for at least as long as the disaster social work service continues to operate. Similarly, there needs to be some agreement amongst all the involved parties as to how long this should be, with the ending of the service being negotiated long in advance of closure.

As a direct consequence of their negative experiences of disaster work, many social workers said that without a written contract they would not consider, and they would advise any colleagues not to consider, taking on work of this sort in the future. Indeed, 40 per cent of those involved in providing support over an extended period of time after the disaster said that they would not want to become involved in support work if another disaster occurred in their locality.

Compulsory – Whilst any service will be dependent on potential users recognising 'need', early on after the disaster it is important that some form of compulsory debriefing is agreed to in the initial contact between workers and their managers, and that senior managers ensure that both sides keep to the agreement. At this stage – at the height of the crisis after the disaster – staff are most likely to overwork. Unless all workers are 'compelled' to talk to a counsellor, the majority will simply avoid doing so. This initial debriefing meeting will help break down some of the barriers that exist, and may facilitate later work.

Notes

1. The availability of support for the Staffline co-ordinator was one of the subjects explored in interview. In the event, the co-ordinator made private arrangements for formal support, and received more informal support from individual members of the Steering Group, from some of the senior managers in the region, and, in particular, from the Staffline administrator. Looking back, she felt that this had by and large worked but it is easy to see how it might not have. It seems strange when people involved in disaster work have been at considerable pains to point out that the work needs to be proactive and not rely on people recognising their 'needs' and then making the decision to ask for help, that the person who had sole extra-Departmental responsibility for staff care should not have been provided with a formal, structured source of support herself. That is not to underestimate the supportiveness of many of those in contact with the co-ordinator, merely to reinforce the point that other sources *should* be made available. If it is accepted that there is sufficient need to set up an independent counselling service, some formal procedure for ensuring that the staff of the service also have support should be set in train at the same time. As with all the other services, this needs to be done without delay.

CHAPTER 8

Conclusion
Some Lessons from Hillsborough

The Hillsborough research reported here looked in considerable detail at the nuts and bolts of the social services response to one disaster. The primary purpose of the research was to attempt to learn further lessons about the practicalities of providing social and psychological support in the aftermath of such a tragedy. The key lessons – in relation to the organisation of the response, the nature of the disaster service itself, the voluntary sector, and staff care – are described below.

The consequences of disaster

The disaster impacted on people's lives in a variety of different ways. Thus, although it is the emotional consequences of these terrible tragedies that most frequently elicits greatest attention, Hillsborough, like other disasters, also had an effect on people's behaviour, on their relationships, on their work, as well as affecting them in a variety of practical ways. One of the consequences of this catalogue of problems that faces those affected by disaster is that considerable strain is often placed upon relationships. Family and personal relationships frequently came under enormous stress after Hillsborough and, perhaps not surprisingly, there were some that simply did not survive – another loss to add to those suffered more immediately as a result of the disaster.

- It is not only those directly involved in disasters who need support, but also their relatives and partners. Just as professional carers require supervision and support, so too do non-professionals. They are 'victims' in their own right.

- Social services, when planning their responses to civil emergencies, need to think about how they can intervene in ways that support relationships as well as individuals.

The organisational response

Perhaps the only thing that is predictable about disasters is that they are unpredictable. Some, for example, are quite localised in their impact, others more widespread. Hillsborough affected quite a dispersed population and, consequently, there were many social services departments involved in the organisational response. The model that was adopted – a 'federal' response from a region, with individual teams placed in each of the authorities – worked well in many ways, though as time passed cracks in the structure started to show. Whilst all the authorities pulled together during the 'honeymoon' period just after the disaster, it was not long before some started to go their own ways. The consequence was that services were not kept in place for comparable periods across the region, and whilst there might have been a logic in slowly closing down teams as demand decreased whilst directing any future referrals to those teams that remained, this was not the basis upon which decisions were actually taken. Rather, individual authorities, managers and teams decided their own futures largely without reference to what was happening in other authorities. Regional inter-agency co-operation may be hard to organise, but it is even harder to maintain. Despite the difficulties, this must continue to be the aim of any senior managers involved in disaster response work.

- For a disaster of the scale of Hillsborough, a period of two years would appear to be the minimum period that services should realistically be kept in place.

Although maintaining the social work response over an extended period of time is one of the most crucial objectives, it is also one of the hardest to achieve. Often the good intentions expressed at the outset disappear. Many long-term strategic decisions have to be taken in the early weeks – for example, what sort of team will be set up and how long it will operate for – and these need to be adhered to. Crucially, although some flexibility is necessary, workers need some indication of how long the service will be maintained and that the work is supported and valued by their department. Failure to provide a secure environment for the work is likely to undermine the extent to which staff feel they can work effectively. The stresses experienced by workers can easily be exacerbated by organisational problems affecting the work.

Generally speaking, under the federal structure, the North-West, together with Sheffield and Nottingham (the regions deemed to be primarily affected) were served well after Hillsborough. Unintentionally, however, this structure served to reinforce the view that they were the only regions affected. Many Liverpool supporters living outside these regions, unless they chose to travel considerable distances – and many did – were not offered a service. As was the case after Hillsborough, and no doubt other disasters, local authorities that have few bereaved or *only* survivors in their area will tend to perceive themselves to be largely unaffected and will do little in response.

- Unless specific measures are taken to set up an 'away' team as was done after Piper Alpha and the Herald disasters, it is likely that large numbers of those affected but who live outside the main areas will fall through the net.

- Authorities that are not located near the epicentre of a disaster also need to consider how best they can provide a service for those affected in their locality.

As was described in Chapter 3 the majority of authorities chose to set up dedicated disaster support teams under the supervision of a team leader. Unfortunately, many workers reported feeling both inadequately managed and poorly supported by their team leaders. Many felt unable to talk to their line managers about any severe difficulties they were experiencing, either because they thought that it was possible that it might count against them in the future, or because they felt that their team leader lacked the requisite skills to provide the necessary advice or support.

For those workers that stayed in post and took on disaster work alongside their normal caseload there were, if anything, greater problems in relation to management and supervision. Indeed, some workers were simply not managed at all. The solution to this problem is not necessarily to be found in the search for an alternative model but, rather, in rethinking the nature of the supervisor's role. It is unreasonable to expect a team leader to provide the degree of managerial oversight, administrative control and professional supervision and support that social workers require in post-disaster work.

- The research suggests that the role of the team leader as manager, professional supervisor and major source of support for workers needs to be radically rethought.

- In addition, it should not be assumed that setting up dedicated teams is necessarily the most effective or efficient way to respond to a disaster. Whilst this model may help avoid certain problems, it is not the only model that could be successfully employed.

The voluntary sector

There is no local authority, or even group of authorities, that is likely to be sufficiently well resourced to take on complete responsibility for the 'care' response to a disaster. Consequently, close co-operative links need to be established with the voluntary sector, and where appropriate, voluntary groups should be involved in the response as quickly and thoroughly as possible. The Hillsborough Helpline, for example, was run very effectively for a period of eighteen months by the voluntary sector in Liverpool.

- It is vital that social services and voluntary groups establish and maintain good relationships and lines of communication prior to a disaster, if they are to work together well in the aftermath.

The nature of the disaster service

The work undertaken after Hillsborough is not accurately or fully described by using the term 'counselling', and in many cases very little counselling actually took place. Practical support tends to dominate in the early stages, and the research found that the practical support provided early on by social workers was of crucial significance. Not only was it often of great value to families and survivors at this most difficult of times, but it also enabled workers to establish credibility and trust. It was then, in many cases, followed by a strong element of 'personal support': accompanying people to a wide variety of public and private events and adopting a befriending role – essentially 'being there' for people, not just in early days, but later on when other sources of support had disappeared or when particularly stressful occasions arose. Counselling – individually or in groups – did of course take place, often a considerable time after the disaster. The published records of the disaster – newspaper and television coverage – were also put to positive use, and they were vital in helping people to piece together what happened to them, and as a means of encouraging them to talk about their experiences.

A variety of skills and qualities of social workers were mentioned by users. Those most frequently referred to were: *friendliness, honesty* and being *supportive, patient, reliable, flexible,* and able to *listen*. Friendliness, honesty and supportiveness related to the extent to which disaster workers frequently worked outside 'normal' professional-client relationships, patience to the extended period of time the work often took, reliability to the extended period of time that the service needed to be in place, and flexibility to the non-directive role often perceived by user's as being of greatest value.

The skill that was most often referred to by both users and workers was *listening*. This lay at the heart of the bulk of significant work undertaken by social workers after the disaster. It is a skill that is frequently underestimated despite the fact that it forms the core of most counselling work. Sadly, the majority of workers felt that their professional training had not prepared them sufficiently for the disaster work, and there was a considerable feeling that further counselling training would have been valuable. Although social workers benefited from the 'orientation' training that they received after Hillsborough, training which gave them some idea of what to expect, and which carried the message that their basic social work skills were the ones they should rely on, they continued to feel underprepared. It would be quite impractical in the aftermath of disaster to provide anything more than the 'orientation' or 'awareness' – type training that was set up after Hillsborough. Providing further training in the basic counselling skills that workers feel they need has to happen at an earlier stage and, given that such skills are potentially central to most social work situations, the most appropriate stage would appear to be as part of the initial qualifying training. Indeed, this general view is supported by the Disasters Working Party (1991 p.46) which commented:

> Many of the skills required for work in disaster areas have wide applicability in the caring professions, e.g. crisis intervention, stress management, debriefing and bereavement counselling. These should be included in the basic training of the professions concerned.

Hillsborough is an ongoing tragedy for many of its victims. The social work task continued for months, indeed years after the disaster, and this leads to what is perhaps the key message in the research, and one that bears repetition:

- Crucially, social workers involved in post-disaster work need good listening skills. There would appear to be insufficient emphasis on these and other related skills in professional social work education and training.

- Disasters are not simply isolated or one-off events which recede into the background as the years pass. They are followed by a series of events – official inquiries, inquests and other legal proceedings, which are not only vivid reminders of the tragedy but, because they are not geared to the needs of 'victims', often exacerbate rather than mitigate suffering.

- Consequently, there needs to be provision made for training for social work staff to help them support families through the arduous and often extensive legal proceedings following disaster.

- The media coverage of a disaster – the newspaper and television reports and any other similar material – can often be used in a very positive way as a method of encouraging or facilitating discussion of the events.

As would be expected, not everybody sought or accepted professional help in the aftermath of the disaster. Equally it was clear that some of those that did not come to the attention of social services or other welfare organisations might well have benefited from the services that were available. A number of barriers to accepting or requesting help were identified, each of which has important implications for the organisation and running of a post-disaster service. Consequently, services need to reach out to those affected by the disaster. It is clear that the majority will not seek help without being prompted. These services need to be provided by staff who feel confident about what it is they are offering. Services need to be available over an extended period of time, and it needs to be clear at the outset to all concerned – staff and potential users – that this will be the case.

The research identified two factors as having been crucial in determining whether the first approach by a social worker would be likely to lead to further contact and to some form of relationship being established. The first was the extent to which and the manner in which social workers made clear why they were calling. The ability to present a straightforward and positive reason for calling was central in overcoming resistances to social workers. Second, the time at which first contacts were made also seemed to be important – though in different ways to different people. There is conflicting advice about this, with some arguing that it is crucial to make approaches early, others that this is intrusive and unlikely to yield satisfactory results. The data from this research are far from unequivocal – there is some evidence to support both arguments – but the overall impression from users was that early approaches tended to have at least symbolic importance, even if their practical utility was limited at that stage.

- Some form of early contact by workers is often important in facilitating more substantial contact later on.

- Social workers must be clear about what they can offer to people affected by disasters and how they will communicate this to potential 'clients'.

- Social workers involved in providing support in the aftermath of disaster will often have to overcome considerable resistance to the services they are offering. It is vital that the services are 'proactive'; i.e., that they are offered rather than waiting for people to come forward and ask for help.

Staff care

There is now mounting evidence that providing psychosocial care in the aftermath of disasters places a very heavy burden on social workers (Harrison 1988, Stewart 1989). The departments in and around Merseyside and in Sheffield and Nottingham are, quite rightly, proud of the effort that was put in response to Hillsborough. Because of what they have been through in the past four years and more it might be tempting for them to believe – and it is quite likely that some do – that they are in a good position to respond to any future emergencies that might occur in their locality, i.e., to assume that having had support teams in their region that they continue to be well-equipped to deal with disaster. Whilst this may be the case, the assumption begs a number of questions.

First, the assumption is based on the notion that all disasters are the same and that workers trained to deal with a crisis such as Hillsborough will consequently be able to turn their hand to other emergency situations. There is increasing evidence which does not support such a simplistic view of disasters (Taylor 1991). Second, the assumption fails to consider the views of those workers who have 'been through' a disaster. Do they wish to become involved in future disaster work? Do they feel able to become involved in future disaster work? Is it appropriate for them to become involved in future emergency responses? Departments have not necessarily asked such questions. If they are placed once again in the position of having to respond to a major emergency, they might well find that considerable numbers of ex-support team members decline to become involved. The organisational problems and role stresses described in this book will be by no means unimportant in influencing such decisions.

The evidence from this study points to a number of important lessons about providing a staff care service. Most obviously, trying to provide such a service for staff is prey to many of the same difficulties that staff themselves have to confront with their own clients: they have to go out and introduce themselves and their service – the work will tend not to come to them; having done that, they will have to sell their service – there will be considerable scepticism about what they have to offer; once 'through the door' they may well have to begin by concentrating on everyday practical matters until such time as they have established sufficient trust and credibility to allow for personal interaction. Second, however skilled the 'counsellor' not everyone will be persuaded to accept help and support, although some resistances may be broken when others report positive experiences.

There may be greater difficulties, however, when resistance comes from someone in a position of power, for example a senior manager or team leader, as they are often in a position to act as a kind of unofficial gatekeeper between the counsellor and their staff. The crucial 'gatekeeping' role of team leaders needs to be understood. This position is perhaps one of, if not the most, difficult to occupy in a social services department. The major problem revolves around role and identity, for the occupier of such a position is neither properly a member of the managerial hierarchy nor 'one of the workers'. As such, they occupy a 'buffer' role, caught between the proverbial rock and hard place. The power they do have is to set the general tone of, and the agenda for their team. In the case of the disaster teams, the attitude that each took toward the issue of staff care – especially in the early days – was seemingly crucially influenced by the views of the individual team leaders. As such, therefore, they are a vital constituency that any staff counsellor needs to 'win over'. Without their support, however tacit that may be, a service along the lines of Staffline will struggle.

As has been described in some detail, there was, at least at first, considerable mistrust amongst some of the social work staff of the initiative. In general this took two forms. First, mistrust of its primary employee: the co-ordinator. What could she offer? What did she know about disasters/bereavement/social work etc.? Could she be trusted? Second, and perhaps more surprisingly, there also seems to have been quite widespread mistrust of 'counselling' and support for staff. There were widespread and deeply-held views about the need for social workers to remain 'strong', to 'be able to cope' or, rather more extremely, to avoid being seen as 'someone who is likely to crack up'. Part of the work of the co-ordinator of Staffline – indeed a large part – centred around a variety of activities aimed at establishing credibility, not only personally, but crucially, for the idea that it is reasonable for helpers to ask for help.

The term 'credibility' in this context means several things and is tested in a number of ways. Most obviously, as has been suggested, the 'counsellor' will not, at first, be trusted by many of the staff. They will doubt the worth of the service and, more particularly, they will doubt the abilities of the counsellor. At the heart of this lies the highly stigmatised notion of 'client', which is a label that workers will go a long way to avoid themselves. In order to overcome scepticism and even hostility the counsellor has to engage in a variety of more or less practical tasks. The manner in which these are addressed and dealt with the determine to some extent how *credible* the counsellor becomes in the eyes of the workers – the potential 'clientele'.

With disaster work at least – although there is no reason to suppose that this cannot be applied more generally to 'specialised work' – there is another aspect to the question of credibility. This can be summed up as 'knowing but not knowing'. It is important for the counsellor to be trusted, to be viewed as someone who understands what the work entails and involves, but who is yet in some fundamental way outside the everyday structures and concerns of the work. This can, understandably, become something of a precarious balancing act. Personal and professional credibility is difficult to achieve at first, but it is essential to the success of the enterprise.

Any services that are set up must take account of the likely geographical impact of the disaster. Thus, in the aftermaths of disasters such as Hillsborough, Piper Alpha and the M1 aircrash, where those affected (and therefore those who care for them) are likely to be widely dispersed, staff care provision should be broad-based and flexible. Additionally, there may be areas (such as Nottinghamshire after Hillsborough) where little long-term work is undertaken and the bulk of the support work is done in the weeks immediately following the disaster. In such cases, support systems for staff need to be up and running immediately.

- At the same time that helplines are set up for the 'primary victims' of the disaster, and that workers are called upon to staff the lines and join support teams, so staff care plans should be put into action. The credibility of any staff care system will only be undermined by a delay in its introduction.

Two further elements of the initiative – the fact that it was extra-departmental and that a considerable amount of outreach work was undertaken – were also central to any successes it achieved. It seems clear from the evidence presented here that the workers would have been most unlikely to seek help or support from a counsellor who was located *within* their own organisation. Although, as was suggested above, few workers used the Staffline service without their line-manager knowing that they were doing so, most expressed doubts about whether such a service would be used if it were not 'independent'. In the main they feared that intra-departmental services would, in reality, not be truly confidential, and that using them would adversely affect future career opportunities. Furthermore, many of the workers who did eventually use the extra-departmental service that was provided after Hillsborough were only engaged because the Staffline counsellor had, in effect, gone out and recruited them. As they themselves admitted, she had to do this not because they weren't in need of support, but that they would not admit that this was the case.

- Establishing 'credibility' is the key to the success of a staff care service. Once the person or people providing the service are trusted, what they are offering will appear less threatening.

One of the major successes of Staffline was the initiative that led to the four one-day 'training days'. Just as the social workers themselves used support groups as one method of encouraging self-help and mutual support among their clients, so the 'training days' facilitated similar processes amongst the workers. They allowed the workers to spend time together, to share their experiences, worries and problems, and to offer each other support and encouragement. Because they were both enjoyable and successful, they were also an important part of establishing the credibility of the Staffline co-ordinator, and several occasions led directly to appointments for one-to-one counselling. These activities illustrate the importance of bringing disaster support workers together, not just for the purpose of formal debriefing, but to engage in the much less structured activity of mutual support.

In summary, and as a minimum, services for staff need to take into account the following points:

Because of the general reluctance of social workers to seek support, it is vital that support is offered, i.e., that it is *proactive*.

- The Helpline model is not one that is appropriate for a staff care system. It places too much emphasis on the worker making the first move.

Because at least some staff will be reluctant to talk about how they are feeling about what they have seen and heard, and about the work they have done, there needs to be some element of *compulsion* in the debriefing process. There is a reluctance to look for support within the organisation. Consequently, supervision from line-managers is unable to meet the support needs of all workers and some form of *extra-departmental* service is required.

- Some of the support for staff should come from an independent source. It should not only be outside the line- management structure but, preferably, outside the department itself.

It hardly needs saying that services need to be accessible if they are to be used. This means accessible both geographically and in terms of the length of time that it remains available. Services should be local and should remain in operation at least as long as the more general social work service continues to run. Indeed, an argument can probably be made for keeping support services going for some period after the main service has closed.

- In general terms, staff care services should mirror the general disaster social work service in terms of their length of operation and methods of work.

References

Aries, P. (1981) *The Hour of Our Death*. London: Allen Lane.

Bagshaw, H. (1991) 'The Hillsborough Disaster – Interprofessional relationships between clergy and social workers: The clergy viewpoint'. *Research, Policy and Planning* vol.9 no.2.

Bamford, T. (1982) *Managing Social Work*. London: Tavistock.

Barclay Report (1982) *Social Workers: Their Role and Tasks*. London: National Institute for Social Work/Bedford Square Press.

Bishop's Council (1990) *The Diocese of Liverpool and the Hillsborough Disaster*. A Report for the Bishop's Council. London: The Children's Society and the Board for Social Responsibility.

Bolin, R.C. (1982) *Long-Term Family Recovery from Disaster*. Monograph No.36 Institute of Behavioural Science. Boulder, Colorado.

Bowlby, J. (1980) *Loss, Sadness and Depression* (Attachment and Loss. vol.3) London: Hogarth Press.

British Psychological Society (1990) *Psychological Aspects of Disaster*. Leicester: British Psychological Society.

Brook, R. (1990) *An Introduction to Disaster Theory for Social Workers*. University of East Anglia Social Work Monographs No.85.

Brown, L., Christie, R. and Morris, D. (1990) Families of Murder Victims Project: Final Report. London: Victim Support.

Burningham, S. (1988) 'Planning to deal with disasters.' *Social Work Today* 11 August.

Chamberlain, L. (1987) 'Basic skills applied in very difficult circumstances'. *Community Care* 21 May.

Cohen, D. (1991) *Aftershock: The Psychological and Political Consequences of Disaster*. London: Paladin.

Cohen, R.E. and Ahearn, F.L. (1980) *Handbook for Mental Health Care of Disaster Victims*. Baltimore, M.D.: Johns Hopkins University Press.

Coleman, S., Jemphrey, A., Scraton, P. and Skidmore, P. (1990) *Hillsborough and After: The Liverpool Experience*. Ormskirk: Edge Hill College of Higher Education.

Cranwell, Rev. B. (1989) 'Helping disaster victims and their families'. *Bereavement Care* vol.8(3) Winter.

Davie, G. (1992) 'You'll never walk alone: The Anfield pilgrimage'. In I. Reader and A.J. Walter (eds) *Pilgrimage in Popular Culture*. London: MacMillan.

The Diagnostic and Statistical Manual of Mental Disorders 3rd edition (DSM III) (1980) Washington DC: American Psychiatric Association.

Disasters Working Party (1991) *Disasters: Planning for a Caring Response*. London: HMSO.

Dixon, P. (1991) Vicarious victims of a maritime disaster. *British Journal of Guidance and Counselling* Vol.19 No. 1, 8–12;

Drabek, T.E., Key, W.H., Erickson, P.E. and Crowe, J.L. (1975) The impact of disaster on kin relationships. *Journal of Marriage and the Family* 37, 481–96.

Dudasik, S.W. (1980) Victimisation in natural disaster. *Disasters* 4, 329–338.

Dumfries and Galloway Regional Council (1989) *Lockerbie: A Local Authority Response to the Disaster.*

Dyregrov, A. (1989) 'Caring for helpers in disaster situations: Psychological debriefing'. *Disaster Management* 2, 25–30.

Eitinger, L. and Askevold, F. (1968) 'Psychiatric aspects'. In. Strom, A. (ed) *Concentration Camp Survivors.* New York: Humanities Press.

Erickson, P.E., Drabek, T.E., Key, W.H. and Crowe, J.L. (1976) Families in disaster: Patterns of recovery. *Mass Emergencies* 1, 302–4.

Erikson, K.T. (1979) *In the Wake of the Flood.* London: George Allen and Unwin.

Fairbank, J.A. and Nicholson, R.A. (1987) Theoretical and empirical issues in the treatment of PTSD in Vietnam veterans. *Journal of Clinical Psychology* 43, 44–55.

Fawcett, J. (1987) Diary of a disaster. *Nursing Times* October 28 vol.83 no.43.

Gibson, M. (1991) *Order from Chaos: Responding to Traumatic Events.* Birmingham: Venture Press.

Glaser, B. and Strauss, A. (1967) *The Discovery of Grounded Theory.* Chicago: Aldine Publishing Co.

Gorer, G. (1965) *Death, Grief and Mourning in Contemporary Britain.* London: Cressett.

Green, S. (1991) The development of personal and professional responses to man made public disasters, with reference to the Hillsborough Disaster. Unpublished M.A. dissertation. University College of North Wales, Bangor.

Harrison, W. (1987a) *The Bradford City Fire Disaster: Social Services Response Information Pack.* City of Bradford Metropolitan Council.

Harrison, W. (1987b) After the Bradford fire: Steps towards recovery. *Bereavement Care* vol.6 pp.6–8

Hart, N. and James, P. (1990a) After Hillsborough. *Social Work Today* 17 May.

Hart, N. and James, P. (1990b) In the wake of disaster. *Social Work Today* 24 May.

Haynes, R. (1991) Just a phonecall away. *Co-ordinate* November.

Hillsborough Interlink nos.1–9.

Hill, D. (1989) *Out of his Skin: The John Barnes Phenomenon.* London: Faber and Faber.

Hodgkinson, P. (1988) Outreach to a nation. *Community Care* September.

Hodgkinson, P. and Stewart, M. (1991) *Coping with Catastrophe: A Handbook of Disaster Management.* London: Routledge.

Hodgkinson, P.E. (1990) 'The Zeebrugge disaster III: Psychosocial care in the UK'. *Disaster Management* 2, 123–127.

Horowitz, M.J., Wilner, M., Kaltreider, N. and Alvarez, W. (1980) Signs and symptoms of Post-Traumatic Stress Disorder. *Archives of General Psychiatry.* 37, 85–92.

Home Office (1989) The Hillsborough Stadium Disaster. 15 April 1989. Inquiry by The Rt Hon Lord Justice Taylor Interim Report Cmnd 765.

Home Office (1990) The Hillsborough Stadium Disaster. 15 April 1989. Inquiry by The Rt Hon Lord Justice Taylor Final Report Cmnd 962.

Insight (1989) Hillsborough: 'Showing social work in its true light'. May.

Janis, I.L. (1951) *Air War and Emotional Stress: Psychological Studies of Bombing and Civilian Defense*. Westport, Connecticut: Greenwood Press.

Johnston, J. (1990) Haunted by memories. *Bereavement Care* Vol.9 No.1 Spring.

Jordan, B. (1979) *Helping in Social Work*. London: Routledge and Kegan Paul.

Kadushin, A. (1976) *Supervision in Social Work*. New York: Columbia University Press.

Keane, T.M., Fairbank, J.A., Caddell, J.M., Zimering, R.T. and Bender, M.E. (1985) 'A behavioural approach to assessing and treating Post-Traumatic Stress Disorder in Vietnam veterans'. In C.R. Figley, (ed) *Trauma and its Wake*. New York: Brunner Mazel.

King, J. (1991) 'Taking the strain'. *Community Care* 24 October.

Kubler-Ross, E. (1970) *On Death and Dying*. London: Tavistock.

Lifton, R.J. (1967) *Death in Life: Survivors of Hiroshima*. New York: Random House.

Lindemann, E. (1944) 'Symptomatology and management of acute grief'. *American Journal of Psychiatry*. 101: 141–48.

Lindy, J.D. and Green, B.L. (1981) 'Survivors: Outreach to a reluctant population'. *American Journal of Orthopsychiatry* 51, 468–78.

Lowe, The Ven. S. (1989) The Hillsborough Disaster – Lessons for the Churches. Unpublished paper.

Lunn, T. (1988) You bring the sadness with you. *Community Care* 18 February.

Lunn, T. (1989) Recognition – but at what price? *Community Care* 27 April: 8–9.

MacLeod, D. (1992) Psychological debriefing: Rationale and application. *Practice* vol.5 no.2.

McFarlane, A.C. (1988) The longitudinal course of post-traumatic morbidity: the range of outcome and their predictors. *British Journal of Psychiatry, 152*, 116–121.

McFarlane, A.C. and Raphael, B. (1984) 'Ash Wednesday: The effects of a fire'. *Australian and New Zealand Journal of Psychiatry* 18: 341–53.

Murray Parkes, C. (1975) *Bereavement: Studies of Grief in Adult Life*. Harmondsworth: Penguin.

Newburn, T. (1991) Organisational pressures and role stresses in the 'lives' of the Hillsborough social work teams. *Disaster Management* vol.3 no.4.

Newburn, T. (1992) *Caring for the carers?: The BASW Staffline initiative after Hillsborough*. Unpublished report to the British Association of Social Workers.

Payne, C. and Scott, T. (1982) *Developing Supervision of Teams in Field and Residential Social Work*. London: National Institute for Social Work.

Pettes, D. (1979) *Staff and Student Supervision: A Task Centred Approach*. London: Allen and Unwin.

Powell, J.W. (1975) An introduction to the natural history of disaster. In R.L. Wettenhall, *Bushfire Disaster: An Australian Community in Crisis*. Sydney: Angus and Robertson.

Quintyn, L., De Winne, J. and Hodgkinson, P.E. (1990) The Zeebrugge disaster iii: The disaster victim identification team – procedures and psychological support. *Disaster Management* 2, 128–30.

Raphael, B. (1977) The Granville train disaster: Psychological needs and their management. *Medical Journal of Australia, 1*, 303–5.

Raphael, B. (1983) *The Anatomy of Bereavement*. New York: Basic Books.

Raphael, B. (1986) *When Disaster Strikes: A Handbook for the Caring Professions*. London: Unwin Hyman.

Raphael, B., Singh, B., Bradbury, L. and Lambert, F. (1984) Who helps the helpers?: The effects of a disaster on the rescue workers. *Omega* 14, 1, 9–20.

Reeves, H. (1984) Victim Support Schemes – The United Kingdom Model. Unpublished paper.

Segal, L. (1990) *Slow Motion: Changing Masculinities, Changing Men*. London: Virago.

Seidler, V. (1991) *Recreating Sexual Politics: Men, Feminism and Politics*. London: Routledge.

Shapland, J., Willmore, J. and Duff, P. (1985) *Victims in the Criminal Justice System*. Aldershot: Gower.

Shearer, A. (1991) *Survivors and the Media*. John Libbey and Co. Ltd/Broadcasting Standards Council.

Shepherd, M. The Impact of Disaster Support Work on Helpers Offering Psychological Support to Primary Victims of Disasters. Unpublished paper. Bexley Hospital.

Shepherd, M. and Hodgkinson, P. (1990) The hidden victims of sisaster: Helper stress. *Stress Medicine* 6, 29–35.

Smale, G.G. and Tuson, G. (1988) *Learning for Change: Developing Staff and Practice in Social Work Teams*. London: National Institute for Social Work.

Smale, G.G., Tuson, G., Cooper, M., Wardle, M. and Crosbie, D. (1988) *Community Social Work: A Paradigm for Change*. London: National Institute for Social Work.

Small, S. (1991) Racialised relations in Liverpool: A contemporary anomaly. *New Community* 17(4): 511–537.

Stewart, M. (1989a) Mirrors of pain. *Community Care* 2 February.

Stewart, M. (1989b) Surviving the horror. *Community Care*, 9 February.

Stewart, M. (1989c) Selling social work. *Community Care* 16 February.

Taylor, A.J.W. and Frazer, A.G. (1981) Psychological Sequelae of Operation Overdue following the DC10 Aircrash in Antarctica. Victoria University: Wellington Publications in Psychology No.27.

Taylor, A.J.W. and Frazer, A.G. (1982) The stress of post-disaster body handling and victim identification work. *Journal of Human Stress* 8:4–12.

Taylor, A.J.W. and Frazer, A.G. (1987) A taxonomy of disasters and their victims. *Journal of Psychosomatic Research* vol.31 no.4 pp.535–44.

Taylor, A.J.W. and Frazer, A.G. (1990) The field of disasters and disaster stress. *British Journal of Guidance and Counselling* vol.19, pp.1–7.

Taylor, I. (1989) Hillsborough, 15 April 1989: Some personal contemplations. *New Left Review*.

Taylor, I. (1991) English football in the 1990s: Taking Hillsborough seriously? In J. Williams and S. Wagg (eds) *British Football and Social Change: Getting into Europe*. Leicester: Leicester University Press.

Thomason, J. and Hodgkinson, P. (1987) Zeebrugge – applying the lessons of tragedy. *Community Care* 21 May.

Titchener, J.L., Capp, F.T. and Winget, C. (1976) The Buffalo Creek Syndrome: Symptoms and character change after a major disaster. In *Emergency and Disaster Management: A Mental Health Sourcebook*. H.J., Parad, L.P. Resnick and L.P. Parad (eds) Charles Press: Maryland.

Tumelty, D. (1990) *Social Work in the Wake of Disaster*. London: Jessica Kingsley Publishers.

Verity, B. (1989) A day at the football match: the Bradford City Football Club fire, 1985. In M. Walsh (ed) *Disasters: Current Planning and Recent Experience*. London: Edward Arnold.

Walker-Smith, A. (1990) *The Kings Cross Disaster Report: Assessing Two Years of Co-ordinated Support*. London Borough of Camden.

Walter, T. (1991) The mourning after Hillsborough. *Sociological Review* vol.39 no.3 August 599–625.

Weaver, K. (1990) Painful lessons. *Social Work Today*. August.

Weisaeth, L. (1984) *Stress Reactions to an Industrial Disaster*. Unpublished paper. Oslo.

Whitham, D. and Newburn, T. (1991) *Coping with Tragedy: Managing the Responses to Two Disasters*. Nottinghamshire County Council.

Worden, J.W. (1983) *Grief Counselling and Grief Therapy*. London: Tavistock.

Subject Index

Name Index